About the Author

Jacques B. Gélinas is a writer and lecturer on Third World issues and globalization. He trained originally as a sociologist at the Universities of Ottawa and Laval in Canada, and subsequently at the University of Chile. He spent some time as a researcher with FLACSO, the Facultad Latinoamericana de Ciencias Sociales. For over a decade (1959–71) he worked in popular education and community development in the Bolivian Andes, during which time he collaborated with Paulo Freire and Ivan Illich. He became a university teacher during the 1970s at the University of Ottawa's Institute for International Cooperation, where he taught the Sociology of Development, and at the Université Nationale du Benin. Jacques Gélinas moved on in the 1980s to work for the Quebec government's Ministry of International Affairs, covering at different times Latin America, the Caribbean and Africa. In 1992 he helped found, and became the first managing director of, a new publishing house, Les Éditions Écosociété, which is dedicated to publishing on the political and social issues of a sustainable society.

He is the author of:

Freedom from Debt: The Reappropriation of Development through Financial Self-Reliance (Zed Books).

He is also the co-author of a number of other books, including:

Pour un pays sans armée (Éditions Écosociété)
Développement agricole dependant et mouvements paysans en Amérique Latine (University of Ottawa Press)
La Educación en América Latina (Editora Limusa, Mexico)
Dependent Agricultural Development and Agrarian Reform in Latin America (co-editor with Lawrence Alschuler) (University of Ottawa Press)

What the critics said about
Jacques B. Gélinas's *Freedom from Debt*:

'This book provides development NGOs, students and advocates of renewed practices of genuine cooperation - North and South - with a coherent critique of the Bretton-Woods-oriented development system on the one hand, and a feasible alternative illuminated by successful experiences of self-conceived, self-financed and self-managed development on the other. It is a highly accessible message of common sense and hope that is beginning to shake the old developmentalist ideology and which refutes with hard facts dogmas of globalization.'

Forests, Trees and People

'An essential tool for anyone seeking an introduction to the problem of development aid.'

L'Agora

'Lively and insightful, this book presents an excellent discussion and should be the bible of those involved in development.'

SAPEM

'Thought-provoking, clearly written, and free of jargon.'
Development Policy Review

'This is a good introductory work on a topic of much current debate.'

Choice

Juggernaut Politics

Understanding Predatory Globalization

JACQUES B. GÉLINAS

Translated by Raymond Robitaille

ZED BOOKS
London & New York

FERNWOOD
Nova Scotia

Juggernaut Politics: Understanding Predatory Globalization
was first published in 2000 by Les Éditions Écosociété,
CP 32 052, succ. Les Atriums, Montreal (Quebec), Canada H2L 4Y5

First published in English in 2003 by
Zed Books Ltd, 7 Cynthia Street, London N1 9JF, UK,
and Room 400, 175 Fifth Avenue, New York, NY 10010, USA

www.zedbooks.demon.co.uk

First published in English in Canada in 2003 by Fernwood,
8422 St Margaret's Bay Road (Hwy 3), Site 2A, Box 5,
Black Point, Nova Scotia B0J 1B0

Designed and typeset in Monotype Bembo by Illuminati, Grosmont
Cover designed by Andrew Corbett
Printed and bound in Malta by Gutenberg Press

Distributed in the USA exclusively by Palgrave, a division of
St Martin's Press, LLC, 175 Fifth Avenue, New York, NY 10010

A catalogue record for this book is available from the British Library

Library of Congress Cataloging-in-Publication Data available

National Library of Canada cataloguing in publication data available

ISBN 1 84277 168 X (Hb)
ISBN 1 84277 169 8 (Pb)
Canada ISBN 1 55266 116 4 (Pb)

Contents

List of Tables and Boxes

Translator's Note

I wish to thank warmly Lesley Kelley Régnier, Peter Feldstein, Tony Kwan and the author for revising the translation drafts. Their numerous suggestions greatly improved the translation. However, I remain entirely responsible for any errors or omissions. I also wish to thank my wife, Flor Angela, and our daughter, Maya, for their invaluable support and patience.

Please note that a large number of quotations in the original French version of this book were taken from works in English. The author and I did our best to trace these original quotations instead of retranslating them from French to English. As a rule, if an endnote refers to a text in English, the quotation was taken from the said text. All other quotations were translated from French to English.

Raymond Robitaille

Glossary of Acronyms

ABF	Americas Business Forum
BIS	Bank for International Settlements
CEO	Chief executive officer (of a major corporation)
CSO	Civil society organization
DSB	Dispute Settlement Body of the WTO
ECOSOC	United Nations Economic and Social Council
FAO	Food and Agriculture Organization
FTAA	Free Trade Area of the Americas
GATT	General Agreement on Tariffs and Trade
GCP	Gross criminal product
GDP	Gross domestic product
GHG	Greenhouse gas
GNP	Gross national product
ICC	International Chamber of Commerce
IMF	International Monetary Fund
IOC	International Organization of Commerce
IPCC	Intergovernmental Panel on Climate Change
ITC	International Trade Center (headed by the WTO and answerable to ECOSOC)
ITO	International Trade Organization (stillborn in 1946)
MAI	Multilateral Agreement on Investment (stopped in 1998)
NAFTA	North American Free Trade Agreement (Canada, United States and Mexico)
NATO	North Atlantic Treaty Organization
NGO	Non-governmental organization

OECD	Organization for Economic Co-operation and Development
SAP	Structural adjustment programme
TCO	Transnational criminal organization
TNC	Transnational corporation
TRIPs	Trade-Related Intellectual Property Rights
UN	United Nations
UNCTAD	United Nations Conference on Trade and Development
UNDP	United Nations Development Programme
UNEP	United Nations Environment Programme
UNICEF	United Nations Children's Fund
WHO	World Health Organization
WTO	World Trade Organization

Preface

According to British psychiatrist R.D. Laing, what Ken Kesey describes in his 1962 novel *One Flew Over the Cuckoo's Nest* is a universe in which a kind of 'politics of madness' reigns supreme. If that book, and the film it inspired, met with so much success throughout the world, it is no doubt because they bore a prescient warning that subsequent events have only confirmed. The blindness and greed of the global players border on madness. These voracious monopolists now seek to claim for themselves the entire planet's resources, including humanity's very gene pool. This is at the expense of the rest of humanity struggling to get its fair share of life's bounty, and also at the expense of those who demand that the commons be protected and shared fairly.

The present book takes as its subject this predatory madness devastating our spaceship Earth, newly baptised 'the global village' by the plunderers themselves. The book aims to describe not only the globalization of the economy but also the globalized world itself. In a bird's-eye view, it presents the agents and mechanisms of this global system so that the reader may understand its workings and architecture. A glance at the table of contents should suffice to grasp the book's flight plan.

Part I starts with a historical detour, an essential step in understanding how and why globalization emerged at the beginning of the 1980s. This is followed by an overview of the system's main institution: the deregulated market. Globalization's cast of characters is then presented: the masters of the globalized world, their overseers, their ideologues and the extras from the United Nations system. Finally, the most perverse effects of globalization are analysed: the destruction of the environment and growing inequalities, both between countries and within each society.

In Part II, gliding under the radar screens of conventional media coverage, we shall examine the outline of an alternative model that is taking shape at the grassroots level, in the belly of the old system. This exercise does not aim to present a theory or a practical guide for action, but rather display, in their proper light, the challenges facing communities struggling to create an alternative and to reclaim the processes of social and economic life.

This book was written for informed readers who are not necessarily specialists. In particular, I hope it may prove useful to young people who are concerned about the future of society and our planet, and wish to understand the world they live in... in order to change it.

PART I

Understanding the Globalized World

CHAPTER I

From Worldwide Colonial Mercantilism to Globalization

I would define globalization as the freedom for my group to invest where and as long as it wishes, to produce what it wishes, by buying and selling wherever it wishes, and all the while putting up with as little labour laws and social convention constraints as possible.

Percy Barnevik, President of ABB, a transnational corporation

Globalization – the word and the phenomenon it represents – is a creation of our age. However, this new system of concentration of wealth and power is rooted in the distant past, going back some five hundred years. But, unlike previous worldwide economic systems, which had always operated under the aegis of political powers, globalization has the contours of an ambitious project designed by powerful trans-national private interests to rule the world above the state and through the market. While international trade is nothing new, the global con-centration of economic power prevailing over state and public interest does represent a world–historical change.

Globalization includes something old and something new. This is why, before embarking on our flight over the globalized world, wrongly called the global village, we need to take a quick look at the last five hundred years of economic and political life to grasp how globalization is unprecedented. This historical detour is essential if we are to under-stand how the international economic system has developed since the end of the fifteenth century in four successive stages: the first three under systems where states ruled supreme, and the fourth under the rule of a handful of transnational conglomerates and financial institutions.

The Age of Mercantilism, 1498–1763

The first wave of internationalization started at the end of the fifteenth century when European merchants sailed the seas to conquer the other continents. With the circumnavigation of Africa by Bartholomeu Dias (1488), the 'discovery' of America by Christopher Columbus (1492)[1] and the opening of a sea route to the East Indies by Vasco da Gama (1498), Europe's commercial empire extended around the globe. It would gradually expand and develop in the following years and centuries.

Overseas trade played a key role in opening up the planet. This movement took off rapidly in the Iberian peninsula, which had been converted into a vast commercial and financial centre by Genoese, Venetian and Dutch merchants. Spain and Portugal were at the epicentre of this mercantilist internationalization.[2] Curiously, it was poor and threatened Europe that imposed its will, at the expense of China's all powerful Middle Kingdom. This expansion was also carried out to the detriment of the Islamic world, which for centuries had maintained a monopoly over the circulation of gold from Africa and trade between Asia and Europe. The European conquest also crushed and plundered the Inca and Aztec civilizations, who, together with the other first nations of the Americas, had discovered, explored and developed this hemisphere separated from the rest of the human race during some 15,000 years.

The thirst for conquest of Europe's monarchs, together with the daring and avarice of the explorer-merchants, stoked the explosive expansion of transoceanic trade and gave an international dimension to the economy by the middle of the sixteenth century. Very soon, gold and silver, gemstones and ivory, spices and corn were flowing to European markets. As early as 1550, one could find in Potosí, a mushrooming city built in the heart of the Andes to exploit the Incas' mountain of silver, 'mirrors from Venice and porcelain from Saxony, velvet from Florence and silk from Grenada, steel from Toledo and musical instruments from Nuremberg, books printed in Antwerp or Lyon'.[3] Following their passage across the Atlantic, gold and silver ingots went on to Asia, reaching India and China via Manila. Thanks to the influx of precious metals, the volume of the European money supply increased tenfold in less than a hundred years, and Europe's economy, formerly dominated by barter, became a monetized system.

Merchants, then, were the spearhead of this economic internationalization. However, they needed the protection and financial support of monarchs who took advantage of the situation to commandeer the entire operation. In effect, the state claimed the lion's share of profits by levying high taxes on shipments. These profits were invested in new expeditions and the upkeep of fortresses protecting colonial administrations and trading posts. State policy and the interests of the merchant class converged in this worldwide expansion of the market.

In other respects, the European monarchies fiercely competed among themselves to secure control of the seas and peripheral regions. There ensued a long series of conflicts between colonial powers which ended with the Treaty of Paris in 1763, in which Great Britain's supremacy was enshrined.

Violence, plunder, piracy and often genocide were the key features of this first internationalization. In fifty years, Spanish and Portuguese conquistadors exterminated between 12 and 15 million Native Americans. Within a few decades, densely populated areas such as the island of Hispaniola (today the Dominican Republic and Haiti), Cuba, Nicaragua and the coast of Venezuela were completely depopulated. Slaves brought in from Africa replaced native populations. The slave trade was one of the most lucrative components of this period. Linking the old world with the new – that is, Africa, Europe and the Americas – the very Christian monarchs of the time encouraged the development of 'triangular trade'. Let us remember that Queen Elizabeth I bankrolled the construction of *Jesus*, the first English slave ship! The Crown found the slave trade so profitable that it honoured its leading practitioner, Captain John Hawkins, with its most prestigious medals. It also decorated Francis Drake, who became a national hero for having brought vast resources to England through the expedient practice of piracy. The English monarchy's shares in Golden Hynd, the famous privateer's company, provided Elizabeth I sufficient means to liquidate the Crown's debts and become the first creditor of Europe.

This period of so-called 'primitive accumulation' through agriculture, overseas trade, colonization, piracy and enslaved labour lasted almost three centuries. Near the end of this process, signs appeared in Great Britain which augured major economic transformations:

1. Newly rich overseas merchants became manufacturers and created the first large factories employing hundreds of salaried workers.

2. Increased productivity in agriculture, thanks to technological improvements and new high-yield crops imported from the Americas – corn, potatoes, beans, squash and tomatoes – freed up the labour required to man factories of the nascent capitalist system.
3. A tenfold increase in the money supply contributed to the creation of embryonic national markets that would gradually destroy the existing city-based economic and social protection systems.

The Age of Capitalist Expansionism, 1763–1883

In the second half of the eighteenth century, the emergence of the capitalist production system gave a new thrust and form to the internationalization process. At the centre of the phenomenon, England became the heart of the world economy. This is where the Industrial Revolution first took shape, establishing a new mechanized production system based on an abundance of capital, technical progress, wage-labour and a new organization of labour. This system, which would later be called capitalism, played a key role in the second stage of development of the world economy. In contrast to mercantilism, which had always depended on external resources, capitalist development was driven by its own limitless internal dynamics.[4]

With the advent of large-scale industrial production, economic and commercial relations between so-called mother countries and their colonies changed. The exporting of mass-produced products became a necessity for the colonial powers, since overproduction had already become a feature of the system. In a word, colonies were forced to buy surplus goods whether they needed them or not. Once simple purveyors of raw materials or precious metals, colonial possessions became markets. Also, the continuously expanding European production apparatus developed an insatiable need for raw materials from the colonies. As a result, each colonial power gradually created production and exchange networks composed of a clear international division of labour between the centre and its periphery: the colonies provided cheap basic products to the mother country, which then transformed and resold them at a high price to the former. Under this 'colonial pact', colonies could export and import products only to and from their respective mother countries, and could only produce articles that did not compete with home products. As a result, capitalism imposed its law of unequal exchange everywhere on Earth, to the advantage of the metropolitan countries.

The story of the English textile industry is a case in point. At the outset of the nineteenth century, when it was a major importer of textile fabrics, England decided to provide for its own textile needs. At the same time, it set itself an even more ambitious target: to displace India and China, the two countries which had been the main worldwide providers of textile products for centuries, and even millennia. This paradox is worth noting: at the outset, the textile industry, which would later become the flagship of the Industrial Revolution in England, was not a strong sector of that country's economy. As late as 1815, India continued to hold a great advantage over Great Britain. The latter imported from India cotton fabrics worth £1.3 million sterling, while it exported only £26,000 of similar products to that country. At the time, Asian fabrics cost 50 to 60 per cent less than their English equivalents.[5] Given this situation, British products could not be sold without an airtight protectionist policy backed up, when necessary, with gunboat diplomacy. Some merchants even practised an extreme form of protectionism: they eliminated competition at the root by cutting off the fingers of skilful Bengali weavers.

In the end, the situation was reversed: India, whose level of development was comparable to that of Europe before the Industrial Revolution, was deindustrialized to help England become industrialized. In the 1830s, it started exporting raw cotton to England and importing large quantities of cotton fabric from it. By 1850, India alone purchased 25 per cent of all the production from Lancashire, then the most important industrial region of Great Britain.

And the tragedy did not end there. India, the granary of Asia until the beginning of the nineteenth century, would gradually be forced to give up food crops in order to supply the English textile industry with cotton, jute and indigo. Since then, famines and undernourishment have constantly tortured the subcontinent. Economist Daniel Cohen keenly notes that the same methods produced the same results throughout the world:

A thousand other examples litter the ongoing chronicle of the comparative advantage theory. From Ceylon [Sri Lanka], compelled to abandon all crops other than tea, to the Ottoman Empire or Latin America, which lost its industrial base during the nineteenth century, most of the countries that are today part of the Third World were subjected to the deindustrializing effects of trade with the first industrial country of that age, England.[6]

Another keen observer, economic historian Emmanuel Todd, concludes that 'founding capitalism [that of the mother countries] is naturally protectionist'.[7] As we have seen, British industry took off under the state's strict protection. Countless measures helped fuel this take-off. The Navigation Acts of 1651 gave English vessels the exclusive right to ship merchandise beyond the limits of England's colonial possessions. Enacted in 1660, the Corn Laws prohibited English merchants from importing cereals; strengthened several times, they would be lifted only in 1846.

By the middle of the nineteenth century, its industry having gained dominance on the world market, Britain now was in a position to advocate, and even impose, trade liberalization throughout the world. Showing a large trade surplus with its colonies, it became the sole champion of free trade. The United States, whose industrialization remained hampered by the slave system and the Civil War, continued to apply strict protectionism throughout this initial phase of American capitalism.

During this period, not only Great Britain, but all colonial powers, including France, practised unequal trade, which is not always a product of protectionism as such; it often derives from the clash of two civilizations with different degrees of technological development. Fur traders mocked the supposed naivety of Canadian Natives who sold five beaver pelts in exchange for a single knife. The Natives were unaware of the relatively small effort required to produce this metal tool compared with the amount of work needed to capture five beavers and prepare their pelts. In overseas trade, explains historian Fernand Braudel, the home merchant has three decisive advantages over his trade partners from the colonies: superior information, capital and political support. He alone 'knows the market conditions at both ends of the line. He alone has the capital required to stock and transport the merchandise. Finally, the supreme advantage, he is an ally of the Prince.'[8]

As a result, this period of capitalist internationalization under the aegis of colonial monarchies saw the development of two trade patterns:

• competitive and transparent trade between the merchants within each European country undergoing industrialization;

• unequal, protected and unethical trade between metropolitan countries and their colonies or former colonies.

The latter type of trade contained the seeds of underdevelopment. In order to avoid falling into this trap, the thirteen British American colonies closed the port of Boston to English products in 1774. Led by George Washington, they rose up in arms against the mother country to create an independent centre of capitalist accumulation. Despite losing this important group of colonies, which, ironically, separated from the British Empire only to develop stronger economic ties with it during the ensuing century, Great Britain would remain the centre of a global empire upon which the sun never set. At the height of its power, throughout the nineteenth century, it reigned supreme over the internationalization of the capitalist economy.

As with the first internationalization, this second internationalization took place under the authority of sovereign states, and was simultaneously carried out by colonial empires yearning to expand and nascent capitalists in search of foreign markets and raw materials. It established the basis of the international division of labour which was to be institutionalized during the subsequent phase.

The Age of Multinational Corporations, 1883–1980

In 1883, after having ruined or bought out all of his rivals, oil baron John D. Rockefeller created Standard Oil Trust, the first major multinational corporation. From then on, the internationalization of the economy entered a third phase, the age of the multinationals, with the emergence of American big business. This second industrial revolution was powered by petroleum and electricity, on which machines and the economy ran with unprecedented efficiency. The steel and chemical industry boom added to this revolution, which featured the ceaseless search for innovation and the scientific organization of labour aimed at augmenting to the utmost the productivity of the capital–labour combination. The birthplace of this innovative mass production and consumption model was the United States. As early as the end of the nineteenth century, America became the most important industrial power, while Great Britain remained the main trading power.

A true monopoly, the Standard Oil Trust acquired the means to operate on a continental and worldwide scale. Holding the shares of each of its companies, the new trust controlled the entire petroleum industry, from the wellhead to the pump. It monopolized 90 per cent of all refining and oil pipeline transportation. With its army of lawyers, it succeeded in circumventing the antitrust laws passed, from 1890 on, by the federal government and by the various state governments with jurisdiction in those areas to which it had extended its tentacles.[9] Rockefeller later proudly noted: 'This movement was at the origin of the whole system of modern economic administration. It has revolutionized the way of doing business all over the world.'[10]

The era of the titans

Indeed, this revolutionary method of eliminating competition by friendly or hostile takeovers,[11] mergers, vertical and horizontal alliances and, in general, by the amalgamation of companies under a single management, did not fail to inspire other empire builders of an era called the age of the Titans. These titans were, first and foremost, John D. Rockefeller; followed by Andrew Carnegie, the steel baron; J. Pierpont Morgan, alias Jupiter, the finance baron; Du Pont de Nemours, the knight of the chemical industry; and Henry Ford, the automobile pioneer. From 1890 to 1929, American economic and social life was dominated by these industrial conquerors who, having cannibalized their adversaries, founded the first multinational corporations and accumulated huge fortunes.[12]

The development of transportation and communications (steam boat, railroad, cable, telegraph and telephone) furthered the multinationalization process. In 1914, over 40 American companies had established production subsidiaries abroad. Enjoying the support of colonial administrations, European firms were not left behind. They founded subsidiaries in their colonies or in quasi colonies where raw materials and cheap labour were plentiful. They also invested in the United States. French tyre firm Michelin opened its first US factory in 1907.

In this period, the economy was marked by industrial and financial concentration through different types of monopolies, oligopolies, conglomerates, holdings and cartels, and so on – despite anti-trust laws, which always proved to be insufficient to the task. The Titans reigned supreme over every economic sector. Morgan took upon himself the role of America's central banker, until the creation in 1913 of the Federal Reserve System. Carnegie made his employees work 12 hours a day, seven days a week, calling upon the police and troops to crush sporadic worker revolts, when necessary. The state intervened as little as possible and only when the exasperated public and wronged small entrepreneurs rose up in anger against the abuses of the robber barons, as the general public called them.

The Great Depression

The business class's optimism had reached its peak when, on 24 October 1929, the collapse of the New York Stock Exchange suddenly signalled the end of the euphoria. In three weeks, the shares index fell from 469 to 220. The financial crisis spread throughout the world and gradually stalled the entire economic system. The Great Depression would last ten years. The capitalist system, which for 150 years had claimed to be self-regulating, came to a standstill. The decline in the price of industrial products was supposed to revive demand, and thus production, but nothing of the sort happened. It was expected that the collapse in wages would lead to new hiring, but unemployment never ceased to rise. From 1929 to 1933, world industrial production fell by 40 per cent and world trade by 30 per cent. In the United States, unemployment peaked at 24 per cent in 1933; in three years, the country's national income fell from $85 billion to $42 billion. Observing the drastic fall in food prices, farmers had no other choice but to fall back on subsistence farming. Instead of reviving the economy, deflation worsened the situation.

Contrary to what has often been said, the 1929 stock-market crash did not cause this crisis. It was simply the trigger. Serious imbalances had already appeared as early as 1926, but everybody chose to ignore them. The basic cause of the Depression is to be found in the general collapse of demand, a fact hidden from view by the exuberance of financial markets corroded by speculation and corruption. An even more fundamental cause was the uncontrolled concentration of income in the hands of the wealthy, resulting from competition skewed in favour of the monopolies. During several years, profits rose at a far higher rate than wages, while stock prices rose faster than profits. The stock-market crash further weakened the purchasing power of the general population, which only further weakened demand.

Among the aggravating causes of the crisis, it is also worth noting the double failure, national and international, of an economic order ill-equipped to manage the multinationalization of the economy. The lack of financial and monetary regulation, in an increasingly internationalized economy, helped bring the capitalist system to a grinding halt.

Facing this failure, the big bosses, only yesterday zealous advocates of laissez-faire economics and state non-intervention, pleaded for government action to break the deadlock by pump-priming the production apparatus. In Germany and Italy, where totalitarian states had taken over the economy, grateful bosses threw themselves body and soul into the arms of fascism.[13] In the United States, a visionary politician, Franklin Delano Roosevelt, tackled the problem head-on. Prisoner of no preconceived theories, he decided to fight the recession with the New Deal, which was, in essence, a social contract involving the state, big business and civil society. Under the New Deal, government did not shy away from taking innovative measures to create a certain balance between capital and labour. Defying the recommendations of his country's most prestigious economists, defying the conservative establishment and, occasionally, even defying the ultraconservative Supreme Court,[14] FDR had Congress pass laws designed to increase the purchasing power of workers, farmers and the middle class. Laws supporting the unionization of workers and protecting the unemployed and destitute were adopted. *Social Security* was established in 1935. All industrialized countries soon followed suit.

The emergence of the social state in the capitalist world – today pejoratively called the welfare state with the clear objective of discrediting it – while undoubtedly a solution to a very serious specific crisis, was really the outcome of 150 years of social struggles.[15] It showed that solidarity is a basic ingredient of any efficient and smooth-running economy and society. All things considered, the social state civilized capitalism, thus ensuring its survival, by allowing a fairer redistribution of the wealth produced with the resources and work of the entire national community. It corrected the natural myopia of a system whose horizon is the short term.

The world shifts towards America

From 1939 to 1945, a trail of fire marked history: the Second World War signalled the end of a world. The American elite was convinced that this war and the crisis that preceded it were caused by the 'failure of the international economy', as Cordell Hull, the American Secretary of State of the time, liked to repeat. This elite reproved protective tariffs, unfair competition and the colonial powers' private domains or reserved areas and called for an end to all restrictions in access to raw materials and areas for investment.[16] They clearly sensed that the old imperial powers, once again engaged in a frenzy of mutual destruction, would emerge from the conflict weakened and disheartened, unable to maintain control over their overseas colonies; and, especially, unable to rebuild a stable world order in which the American economy, anticipating continuous growth in the post-war years, might expand freely all over the globe.

In short, America's leaders were convinced that the world needed a new leadership that only the United States of America could provide. This is why they planned nothing less than the creation of a new economic and geopolitical world order. A task force, entrusted with this historic mission and passionately versed in economics as well as geopolitics, developed a genuine strategy to create a new world order. As soon as the war broke out in Europe, this select group was formed around the Council on Foreign Relations (CFR), a private organization that put a premium on the participation of high ranking politicians. This task force comprised about a hundred persons from political, financial, industrial and academic circles. Cordell Hull in person and his undersecretary, Sumner Wells, were members. They were the liaison between the group and President Roosevelt, who closely followed its work.[17]

Starting with a simple slogan – 'America first, Business first'[18] – the CFR focused on three imperatives considered vital to US national interests:

1. *Free access to all raw materials* worldwide to ensure their sure sources of supply to the formidable American production apparatus, which was growing ever stronger thanks to the war.
2. *Free access to foreign markets*, for the unrestricted sale of the American economy's abundant products and services.
3. *Free movement for the country's excess capital*, in order to open up the entire planet to direct foreign investment.

In plain language, this meant first of all the dissolution of the European and Japanese empires – no more private domains for the colonial powers.

The three above-mentioned imperatives required that all countries accept the principles of free trade and free movement of capital. In other respects, it was understood that, with the end of the colonial empires, the liberated colonies would become, following the term coined by CFR strategists, 'underdeveloped areas',[19] destined to enter the world markets in accordance with the international division of labour. It was also understood that, as soon as the war ended, the economic and financial heart of the world would be officially moved from London to Washington/New York.

Creation of the three pillars of the new economic order

The transfer of power was enshrined in July 1944 at Bretton Woods, a small New Hampshire vacation resort. The delegates from the forty-four allied countries invited by President Roosevelt signed the terms and conditions of a new world economic order based on free trade, free competition and free enterprise. Despite the opposition of Great Britain, represented by renowned economist John Maynard Keynes, the dollar was recognized as the key currency of the new international monetary system, by virtue of its status as the only currency convertible to gold at a fixed rate. As a result, the American Federal Reserve System became, in effect, the world's central bank.

The Bretton Woods International Monetary and Financial Conference gave birth to three transnational institutions in charge of implementing the new economic order: the International Monetary Fund (IMF), whose duty would be to preserve the stability of the international monetary system henceforth pegged to the dollar; the World Bank, which would initially focus on financing the reconstruction of a war-devastated Europe before adopting its present mission of promoting development and foreign investments in underdeveloped countries; and the GATT (General Agreement on Tariffs and Trade), created in 1947 after painstaking negotiations. The GATT would later become the World Trade Organization (WTO) in 1995. In the 1980s, the IMF and World Bank broadened their original mandate to become the bankruptcy trustees of overindebted Third World countries and took advantage of their disarray to 'adjust' them, one after the other, to the global market.

After the war, the multinationalization process proceeded at an accelerated pace. In 1970, there were 7,000 multinationals with almost 50,000 subsidiaries established throughout the world.[20] American for the most part, these multinationals made almost all foreign investments during this era. However, they remained focused on their country of origin, clung to their national government and were dependent on their respective domestic markets. Indeed, during this third internationalization, there was an almost organic link between multinational corporations and their countries of origin. Captains of industry, often torn between patriotism and the interests of their company, maintained loyalty towards both. Who could ever forget the famous saying of Charles Wilson, a former CEO of General Motors who later became Secretary of Defence: 'What's good for the country is good for General Motors.' The opposite was also true.

First harbinger of globalization

In the early 1970s, the American gold reserves were under threat of depletion. Bogged down in the Vietnam War, the United States printed too many dollars and could no longer guarantee the gold convertibility of the greenback, as required under the Bretton Woods system. The Europeans pressed the American administration to cease creating artificial currency. Instead, President Nixon engineered a power grab. On 15 August 1971, he unilaterally announced, without any prior consultation, the demonetization of gold – that is, the end of the dollar's gold convertibility at a fixed rate. This policy – which allowed the United States to export its financial imbalances and thus dodge the structural adjustments inflicted upon other large debtors, such as the Third World countries – led to an unprecedented period of financial instability. It provoked a complete disarticulation of the international monetary system, producing runaway inflation throughout the world. With gold having ceased to be a stable reference value for currencies, they started 'floating', and as such were at the tender mercies of speculators. In 1976, floating currencies having become a worldwide fact, the member states of the IMF officially confirmed this de facto regime in the Jamaica Agreements.

This first major deregulation of the financial system represented the early harbinger of globalization. But its cornerstone had been laid thirty years earlier, in the midst of the war, when a new world economic order was designed based on the absolute imperatives of free trade and the free flow of capital.

The Age of Globalization, 1980 Onwards

At the beginning of the 1980s, the best-funded and best-positioned multinationals became transnational corporations (TNC). As their name indicates, in addition to extending into several countries, these mega-enterprises stand beyond or above the nation-state. Their financial and technological capacity defies borders and transcends state powers. With increasingly numerous mergers, takeovers and alliances, the concentration of wealth at the top reached such a degree that, for the first time in history, economic power succeeded in liberating itself from the national legal framework and from governmental control, which henceforth has been reduced simply to voicing apologies for its impotence. 'There is no alternative' has become the favourite mantra of all kinds of politicians who deliberately let big economic lobby groups impose their corporate agenda on local and national governments.

Roosevelt's New Deal had imposed a social pact of sorts, establishing a balance between public power, big business, trade unions and civil society. As they became transnationals, the giant corporations felt hamstrung by what they denounced as constraints hindering freedom of enterprise and economic progress. There followed a huge campaign to reconquer areas occupied by the invading state which had the impudence to claim for itself the duties of divine providence by providing for the needs of one and all. Today, the TNCs call for an end to this welfare state as well as the elimination of all legislation regulating prices, wages, investments and the environment. They call for the privatization of state enterprises and a host of public services such as transportation, water, health care and education, and demand the total liberalization of foreign trade and investment. They attack the rigidity of the labour market and the power of the unions, which, according to them, limits competitiveness and the exercise of free competition. They demand 'labour flexibility'.

The information revolution of the 1980s, marked by an extraordinary influx of new telecommunications, computerization and automation tools, played an important role in transforming multinationals into transnationals. These tools allowed them to go beyond the former limits of time, space, borders, languages, cultures and courtesy.

This transnationalization of a growing number of corporations, together with the political class's abdication of public-sector responsibilities, are reshaping the fabric of the world economy. As a result, the nature of internationalization has changed... and so must the name by which it is called. Hence, 'globalization', a term connoting a process with both totalitarian and worldwide designs. Transnational corporations prefer calling themselves 'global'. The two adjectives are practically synonymous, but 'global' has the advantage of doing away with any references to such obsolete notions as the nation, the state and borders. The term reveals the new economic system's claim to the entire globe, all of its resources and all human activities. The objective is no longer simply to integrate the world through trade – 'shallow integration' – as multinationals had been doing for decades, but rather to integrate it through production networks – 'deep integration'. Transnational corporations are no longer satisfied with exporting their products the world over; they now multi-localize their production throughout the world with subsidiaries, mergers and strategic alliances. Wal-Mart, the world's largest corporation by sales, is only a retailer, but nevertheless it plays an important role in production because it can move its sources of supply, at will, to regions offering lower wages.

What is the difference between a global, or transnational, corporation and an ordinary multinational? There is no standard model. Atop the economic Mount Olympus, the homes of the gods are many and come in many shapes and colours. It hardly matters what they sell. Exxon Mobil provides fuel without which the entire system would literally break down, while Coca-Cola only produces sweetened water seasoned with a secret formula. Both of them rank among the largest global corporations. More generally, the following are common features of these so-called global corporations:

- a huge direct foreign investment capacity of over $4 billion embodied in a network of subsidiaries and subcontractors everywhere around the world;
- a financial and strategic potential for carrying out mergers and forging alliances capable of concentrating supply and demand in order to neutralize and, ideally, eliminate competition;
- an unlimited capacity to 'delocate' and relocate production units anywhere in the world – that is, to those benighted places where labour is cheapest and environmental and social laws and regulations are least restrictive;

Box 1.1   A providential 9/11

The intellectual authors of the bloody September 11 attacks have shown themselves to be very poor strategists. 'The golden rule in war is to not do what your enemy most wishes you to do', advised a Chinese general of antiquity. In light of the events subsequent to the attacks, it seems that the strategists behind 9/11 ignored this lesson. US leaders and transnational corporations were quick to see this terrible tragedy as an opportunity to reposition themselves on the geopolitical map and thus reinforce their hegemony. In concrete terms, the USA–TNC tandem is taking advantage of this new, sufficiently dangerous and menacing, global enemy to satisfy seven of its strategic needs:

1. The need for the United States and its major oil companies to carve out a permanent position of predominance in Central Asia, an energy-rich region, at the crossroads of the Middle East, China, Russia and Europe.

2. The need to legitimize US military interventions in the Third World, interventions that have become necessary to protect the interests of the TNCs against the frustration of impoverished masses, who grow increasingly 'envious' of the unfair distribution of wealth throughout the world.

3. The need to stem migratory flows from poor countries whose people are starved by the globalizing policies of the IMF and betrayed by their own elites. These people are forcing the doors of the rich countries in the hopes of joining the banquet.

4. The need to reinforce, through billion-dollar contracts, the military–industrial complex, which had been somewhat deflated since the collapse of the Communist bloc brought an end to the Cold War.

5. The need to justify renewed government aid for the TNCs, which are theoretically opposed to any state intervention, but constantly ask for state financial support in order to remain competitive in the jungle of globalization.

6. The need to suppress dissent in and tame civil society, through so-called anti-terrorist, law-and-order legislation, as said civil society has become too turbulent with the heightened consciousness of the adverse effects of globalization on the environment, democracy and social rights.

7. The need to fill the credibility gap and boost the failing authority of George W. Bush, who only took office in January 2001 thanks to the fabulous electoral contributions of the TNCs and help from the Supreme Court.

- global marketing supported by its own culture, capable of fitting in all specific cultures;
- leaders with a global and supranational vision, combined with a total lack of any sense of social, moral and environmental responsibilities; these leaders form the 'global power elite'.

The Communist regimes, which still reigned over half of the world in the mid-1980s, were a geographic barrier and at the same time a social antidote against the transnational corporations' ambitions. The socialist threat, whether explicit or implicit, forced the TNCs to tolerate social policies as a safeguard against political shifts to the left. Paradoxically, the USSR and its anticapitalist satellites helped humanize the system. The downfall of these regimes, symbolized by the fall of the Berlin Wall in 1989, eliminated this barrier and antidote. The markets' horizon really became worldwide and all-encompassing. In 1990, a great neoliberal offensive was launched, designed to reshape the world into one single global market and reduce to a bare minimum the role of public authorities in governing states and the world as a whole.

Following this logic, President Clinton declared, in his State of the Union address of January 1996, that the age of big government had ended, implying that the time had come to make more space for big business. In October of the same year, he signed, in the middle of an election campaign, a bill to cut back social security. This represented an about-turn for the Democratic Party – the heirs to the legacies of Roosevelt and Kennedy and, ostensibly, the representatives of the progressive wing of the American political establishment. This only goes to show that politicians, even so-called social democrats, are soluble in the ideology of globalization.

At the dawn of the twenty-first century, as a vast worldwide social movement is protesting against globalization, an ultra-neoliberal president has taken over the government of the only remaining world superpower. George W. Bush's entourage is stacked with people closely tied to the petroleum industry, high finance and transnational corporations. The 11 September 2001 terrorist attack has converted this president elected under dubious circumstances into the commander-in-chief of a country at war and leader of a new global crusade. His war cry, 'Either you're with us or with the terrorists' won the adhesion of the world's political leaders in their entirety, with a few exceptions. The attack against the World Trade Center and the Pentagon has given the White House the opportunity to militarize globalization and to give it a repressive legal arm.

What is Globalization?

Is it a system? A process? An ideology? A modern mythology? An alibi? Globalization may well be all these things, depending on one's point of view. It is an often misused word, as are all of its derivatives: *global market, global economy, global business, global players, global power elite,* and so on. Nevertheless, the term means something very specific and hides a reality that has such an impact on our lives that it is worth dwelling on its different aspects.

A system

As a system, *globalization is the total control of the world by powerful supranational economic interests* through a global deregulated market. It is economic power tending to exert its hegemony over the entire planet and all aspects of the material, social and cultural lives of women and men.

The market is the mechanism by which said economic interests – that is, transnational corporations – exert and justify their influence. Their ambition is to convert the entire world into one vast market – one single global market – which would encompass literally everything: water, the air, the soil, the subsurface, culture, health, education, information, money, work, the planet's gene pool and even the human genome. From this perspective, globalization is defined by its most direct effect: the *commodification* of the planet *in toto.* Everything becomes a commodity, and the law of the market, as perverted by its appropriation by global monopolies and oligopolies, is imposed everywhere and transcends all institutions.

The globalized system is converting the entire planet, and its adjacent suburb in space, into its object of rationality and management. It is far more than simply a system with a higher degree of global communications and trade internationalization. It constitutes the in-depth integration of production networks, and consequently technological, ethical and cultural usurpation through direct foreign investment. This deep integration not only changes relations between states but also impacts on national economic spaces and social relations.

In contrast to earlier stages in the development of the world economy, which had always taken place in a context where the state represented the final point of reference, politically, socially and economically, globalization is being constructed over and above nation-states. What makes globalization unprecedented is that transnational corporations want to remove the state from the economic sphere and, as much as possible, from the social and cultural spheres. The few remaining tasks of the state would be protecting private property, maintaining social order and ensuring the provision of certain infrastructures. This is a managerial view of government, which is called upon to work as a private enterprise, free from any social interference. It represents a qualitative jump in the economy's management and in its relationship with the political, social, cultural and environmental spheres.

We have already encountered this bold definition of globalization offered by a distinguished member of the global elite, the president of ABB, an electronics and electrical transnational:

> I would define globalization as the freedom for my group to invest where and as long as it wishes, to produce what it wishes, by buying and selling wherever it wishes, and all the while putting up with as little labour laws and social convention constraints as possible.[21]

As explained by a *Business Week* editorialist, 'Globalization is the most powerful manifestation of capitalism yet seen.'[22] Globalization is in fact a variant of the capitalist system that has become somewhat schizophrenic, and as such is unable to relate its thoughts and deeds to what is happening in the real world. 'There comes a point where greed and madness can no longer be told apart', keenly notes British novelist Jonathan Coe.[23] The billionaire who likes to play philosopher George Soros likes to quote Hegel, who had observed a disturbing historical pattern in his *Philosophy of History*: 'The crack and fall of civilizations owing to a morbid intensification of their own first principle.'[24]

A process

Globalization is also a process, a series of actions carried out in order to achieve a particular result. A totalitarian worldwide integration process. And an ongoing process, since in this monumental project there will always remain laggard sectors, areas and countries which must be rounded up and brought into line.

At the centre of the system, while industrialized countries have no doubt gone very far in commodifying the Earth's resources, there still remain insufficiently integrated sectors, such as agriculture, culture, services in general and life itself. In other respects, the imperatives of competition are pushing global corporations constantly to restructure, rationalize and re-engineer themselves, as financial and technological resources become increasingly concentrated. As long as there are competitors to eliminate, mergers, alliances and takeovers will remain on the agenda.

At the periphery, Third World economies are being subjected to drastic regimes in order to structurally adjust them to the global market, under the leadership of the IMF and the World Bank. As for the so-called emerging countries, who are struggling to free themselves from the problems of underdevelopment by embarking wholeheartedly on deregulation, they are periodically shaken by unpredictable and uncontrollable financial upheavals which submerge them anew in the murky waters of underdevelopment.

In fact, globalization is an ongoing insidious revolution whose true objectives have never been clearly stated by its champions. They hide behind seemingly blind market mechanisms to engage in the boundless appropriation of both the Earth's resources and the wealth produced by humankind.

Consequently, the globalization of the world proceeds unabated. Experts have estimated that if mergers and takeovers continued at the present rate, in 2030 there would be only one conglomerate left in the world, controlled by an extremely efficient mega-holding, benefiting, in effect, from freedom from the shackles of competition. This is black humour, of course, but undoubtedly, if nothing is done to check such excesses, much sooner than 2030, each major sector of the economy will be controlled by a monopoly or an oligopoly.

An ideology

Globalization is also a discourse, a semantic system aimed at rationalizing and explaining the world according to the world-view of those who hold power. In this sense it is an ideology: that is, a coherent set of

Box 1.2   And what of Marshall McLuhan's 'global village?'

In 1968, Marshall McLuhan, a Canadian cutting-edge thinker with a gift for aphorisms, published an essay entitled 'War and Peace in the Global Village'. In this book and in countless lectures, he coined and popularized the expression 'global village'. He was the first to see the world as a vast expanse wired by the new electronic media, namely radio, television and computers. He perceived that humanity was undergoing vast transformations induced by electronics. Pessimistic about the future of mass media, he warned his contemporaries against the perverse effects of this mutation: 'We shape the tools and thereafter the tools are shaping us.' The observation is crystallized in the title of another book: *The Medium Is the Massage* (1967).

McLuhan died in 1980 as another global phenomenon added itself to the preceding one: the worldwide deregulation of trade and financial flows. This voluntarist policy gave rise to the globalization of the economy – that is, a new form of capitalism ruled by transnational corporations. As a result, the world has become an unregulated marketplace that the global movers and shakers, by a crude distortion of meaning, like to call the 'global village'. It is in fact a fake village dominated by voracious monopolists and irresponsible polluters such as Enron, WorldCom, Exxon Mobil, Nike, Wal-Mart, Merck and Monsanto. These plunderers have converted McLuhan's vision into a cuckoo's nest.

Those who, like Professor Majid Rahnema, have seen the devastating effects of globalization on the actual villages of the Third World denounce in no uncertain terms this linguistic perversion: 'As to the notion of global village, it uses a vernacular concept only to destroy it. For it aims at wiping out the thousands of villages whose great diversity has actually made the world's singularity and richness. The proposed 'one world' seeks to substitute the thousands of real and living worlds with a single non-world, a totally acultural and amoral economic corporation whose only purpose is to serve the interests of its shareholders.'[25]

beliefs, views and ideas determining the nature of truth in a given society. Its role is to justify the established political and economic system and make people accept it as the only one that is legitimate, respectable and possible.

The ideology of globalization is roughly the neoliberal creed pushed to its extreme limits. The creed can be summed up in three articles of faith:

1. *I believe in private property* and in the benefits of the unlimited appropriation of wealth by transnationals and their leaders.
2. *I believe in market laws* as a superior mechanism of optimal resource, wealth and income distribution.
3. *I believe in free enterprise and free trade* as the best mechanisms for ensuring the prosperity and enrichment of all peoples and individuals.

Neoliberalism is a very cunning ideology because it manipulates the concept of liberty or freedom which has always been recognized as a primordial good that facilitates all other worthwhile pursuits and values. The trap lies in the fact that, in the final analysis, the free market provides freedom to the biggest, the strongest, the slyest and the most aggressive. Naturally, all these qualities are considered cardinal virtues by the ideologues of globalization.

A modern mythology

Told as a fabulous epic, globalization stars the titans of triumphant capitalism at the zenith of its power. Having subdued the evil forces of history – communism, underdevelopment and the welfare state – these titans are now tackling the colossal task of harnessing the Earth's technologies and resources in their entirety in the pursuit of infinite economic growth. Flattered by the business press and the media in general, these modern-day Atlases enjoy giving the impression that the Earth and the destiny of all of humankind are resting on their shoulders.

An alibi

Globalization is also a tremendous alibi. Presented as a natural, inevitable and irresistible phenomenon, it lets the major economic and political decision-makers off the hook; in short, it frees them of any social, environmental or moral responsibilities, the mantra being 'There is no alternative.'

A New Word for a New Reality

American business schools were the first to perceive the importance of this new phenomenon in the economic world, one concurrent with the emergence of the transnational corporation. The first to speak of global business, global markets and global liberalization, Theodore Levitt, a Harvard professor, coined the term in a 1983 *Harvard Business Review* article. 'The Globalization of Markets' was a timely description of a novel way of managing an economy in which the sovereignty of nation-states had been transcended and for which the entire world had become the sphere of economic rationality.[26] *Globalization*: the object is new; so is the word. Ever practical, the Americans invented a new concept and word to identify a new reality.

Apparently most British and American dictionaries still shun this neologism although it has become commonplace. In an interview with *Finance & Development*, an IMF publication, J.K. Galbraith made a surprising statement: 'I am an advisor to the *American Heritage Dictionary* on language use and I will not allow the word globalization. It is a very ugly term.'[27] It is as though the venerable economist, who has spent his life trying to humanize capitalism, preferred to turn his gaze away from this global capitalism that has become very ugly indeed. One is tempted to quote him Victor Hugo's mocking remark: 'If the word shocks you, how much more must the reality it describes!'

Shocking indeed! It is the first time in history that such a concentration of material wealth has found itself in the hands of such a small group of individuals bent on claiming, through the market mechanism and in the name of globalization, the right to control all aspects of human life, all of the planet's resources and, in so doing, the very destiny of humankind.

CHAPTER 2

The Hidden Face
of the Global Market

Whosoever commands the trade of the world commands the riches of the
world and hence the world itself.

Sir Walter Raleigh

The market is the supreme institution of the new global transnational
economic order. In the global power elite's 'village', the market takes up
all the space. It encompasses everything and tends to dominate all other
institutions, particularly governments and the United Nations. For the
advocates of globalization, it represents the final and supreme stage of
economic and social organization. It is the brilliant and irreversible
victory of the infallible market law logic over ethics, politics and social
responsibility.

Yet, several questions need to be addressed. Is this ubiquitous global
market really a market? What are its origins? How does it work? What
is the secret of its so-called self-regulating power? What are its main
agents and what interests lie hidden behind the market's façade?

Two Kinds of Market

The creation of the market goes far back in time. It appeared with the
first agricultural revolution – some 10,000 years ago – which gradually
produced the first durable food surpluses. From then on, part of the
community, freed from the toil of daily sustenance, could take on other
tasks. The development of specialized skills – such as spinning, weaving,

pottery, basketry, blacksmithing and cosmogony – contributed to the emergence of trade-based cities. At the heart of the city, the market, the bazaar or the souk was set up as an area for trading products.

The market is an essential mechanism linking production and consumption, where suppliers and buyers meet on a regular basis to exchange products and objects required for sustaining and developing life.

From the outset, town authorities intervened to organize and regulate the market. They wanted to ensure that producers, artisans, merchants and other citizens be satisfied. Experience showed them that a smooth-running market is key to prosperity and strengthening the city's social fabric. Tradesmen and merchants developed customary rights in order to share the marketplace as efficiently as possible.

In eighteenth-century Europe, the emergence of capitalism together with the nation-state shattered the old market concept. A national market appeared which was no longer a building or an actual physical area for commercial barter and trade, but rather a nationwide mechanism for coordinating the supply of and demand for products and services. The prices agreed on in the market conveyed useful information for decision-makers regarding the quality and quantity of goods to be produced and services to be offered. Dominated by industrialists and merchants, the state created laws, regulations and infrastructures to ensure the proper operation of the market. Such state intervention was based on the time-proven postulate that a well-oiled and efficient market requires true free competition, which is always under the threat of being distorted or eliminated by monopolies.

However, on the fringes of this publicly regulated market, there has always been a counter-market where faithless and lawless private trades of all kinds are commonplace.[1] This is why British economic chroniclers of yore would usually distinguish two main types of market:

1. *The public market* operates under government supervision designed to foster equal market access and gives it a legal framework to protect it against monopolistic tendencies.
2. *The private or underground market* develops without any controls; its agents use numerous stratagems to bypass public-market rules and even control them.

Type 2 includes, among other players, the unscrupulous merchant who seeks credit-hungry farmers and buys future crops at rock-bottom prices.

Mexican peasants call him a coyote.[2] Enjoying means of transportation
and access to credit, the coyote can easily monopolize the foodstuffs
market in a given region. His monopoly becomes absolute if he secures
the complicity of local and regional authorities.

For example, coyotes have almost completely cornered the Mexican
coffee market after the Mexican government totally privatized and
deregulated this sector in the wake of globalization.[3] Coyotes canvass
the countryside offering credit to coffee farmers on the condition they
sell them their 'harvest in the tree' at a price unilaterally determined in
advance. From the small coyotes to the big coyotes, coffee beans make
their way to export brokers in Mexico City and end up being sold on
the New York and London commodity markets. In this final stage, the
four coffee supercoyotes, namely Nestlé, Philip Morris, Procter &
Gamble and Sara Lee, use their ultramodern organizations and information networks to speculate profitably in these markets and even fix
coffee prices from the coffee plantation all the way to the supermarket.

From the Local Market to the Global Market

Let's examine the workings of the trade and commerce system at the
three market levels: local, national and global.

The local market

Quebec City's Vieux-Port Market, as well as Ottawa's venerable Bytown
Market, are both regulated, type 1, public markets. These are local
markets, similar to those that still exist in most of the world's large cities
and that abound everywhere in the Third World on the broad fringes of
the global market.[4]

This type of market is competitive, transparent and monopoly-free
because it is duly regulated by customary and municipal laws. The buyer,
no matter whether he is a minister or a receptionist, goes from stall to
stall, feeling the produce on display, comparing, enquiring about its
price, even haggling if need be. After making up his or her mind, the
transaction is carried out, 'eye to eye, hand in hand'.

The modern urban public market is a heritage of the markets and
fairs that made up the market economy before the advent of the

Industrial Revolution. It is worth noting in passing that this is the prototype that conventional economists have used, and are still using, when defining market laws, forgetting that public law and customary law frame the relatively healthy competition found in the local market. The idea of pure and perfect competition without a legal framework is found only in economics textbooks (see Box 2.1 below).

The national market

As we have seen above, capitalism did not invent the market economy; it only used and generalized it. With help from the state, it destroyed feudal and city barriers to create a national market. As the Industrial

---

Box 2.1 Market law according to conventional macroeconomic textbooks

The market is a place where the sellers' supply and the buyers' demand meet to be traded.

This meeting of a host of free suppliers and free buyers determines the *equilibrium price* establishing quantities and methods of production, product quality and an optimal allocation of resources and revenues. The equilibrium price evens supply and demand so that the market is in equilibrium.

This is the *law of the market*, also called the *law of supply and demand*, which, to operate properly, requires pure and perfect competition. Conventional economists detail this requirement in five points:

- *atomicity* – that is, a market made up of a large number of buyers and sellers, all of a relatively small size (like atoms), and without any one predominant;
- *transparency* – that is, all economic agents are perfectly and simultaneously informed, particularly regarding product quality;
- *free entry* into the market for sellers and buyers, and particularly no obstruction to the entry of new companies;
- *product homogeneity* – that is, a guarantee that goods offered are not affected by factors other than their own intrinsic value (such as packaging or disinformation);
- *mobility* of the production factors: labour and capital must be able to move freely to secure the jobs, goods and services likely to produce the greatest earnings.

Revolution spread, the state–private enterprise partnership converted the entire nation into a single production, trade and consumption area. The national market pioneers realized that the market would be efficient only if the state protected it. In its start-up phase, which can last a long time, the capitalist economy needs borders to create centres of capital` accumulation sheltered from foreign coyotes. More importantly, it needs a legal framework to protect it from domestic coyotes and their suicidal instincts. Having reached maturity, capitalism still needs to protect itself from the natural monopolizing tendency of large enterprises. For every major corporation dreams of eliminating the competition either by converting itself into a monopoly or by creating an oligopoly with its former competitors. This is why all developed countries have created, since the beginning of the twentieth century, a set of antitrust laws and institutions designed to preserve the free-competition system.

We can therefore conclude that the national market is a public market. It is of the first category, at least as long as political leaders don't completely give in to the onslaught of globalization.

The global market

In contrast, the global market, which is totally dominated by transnational corporations, is a new kind of market that is more of the second type, that of the private market, which tries to bypass or dominate the public regulated market. Not only do its advocates insist that it be self-regulating; they also aim at disallowing any state control, which is said to be harmful. The global market's distinctive feature is not its planetary scope but rather its totalitarian globality, embodied in the following features:

- Effective predominance of the market over all other social or political, national or international, institutions; society is seen as nothing more than a mass of individual consumers.
- Ambition to convert everything into commodities, including currencies, culture, information, education, health, water and air.
- Integration of all countries into a single homogenized model of development and trade.

The global market's triumph over the political, social and cultural realms is not the result of a natural and spontaneous historical process, as is claimed by the champions of globalization. It is the result of a hard-won battle against governments that little by little gave up portions of their power to global corporations and transnational financial institutions. Aggressive strategies and policies have presided and still preside over market globalization, politicians becoming allies, if not instruments, of economic movers and shakers they are supposed to control.

The state's withdrawal process in favour of the market happened in five big waves that fed into each other:

- *Deregulation of the Bretton Woods international monetary system*, starting in 1971. The ensuing generalized currency fluctuation transformed all of the world's currency assets into speculative capital. This was the beginning of financial globalization.
- *Systematic and gradual deregulation of Third World economies* – starting in the early 1980s – through structural adjustment programmes, under the stewardship of the IMF and the World Bank, aimed at integrating underdeveloped countries into the global market.
- *Deregulation of the stock markets* inaugurated in 1986 with the 'City's big bang',[5] setting a deregulation trend for all of the world's stock markets, from New York to Tokyo.
- *Deregulation of agricultural production* and commercialization of services resulting from international agreements such as the Marrakesh Agreement (1994), establishing the World Trade Organization, or regional agreements, such as the Maastricht Treaty (1993) and the North American Free Trade Agreement (NAFTA, 1994).
- *Proliferation of tax and banking havens*, since the mid-1990s. Today, about half of the world's financial flows pass through these offshore havens, free from practically any legal constraint because public powers have followed a policy of benign neglect.

NAFTA, the Prototype of All Future Free Trade Agreements

The year 1994 represents a decisive turning point in the globalization process, when governments implemented, signed or prepared agreements stripping them of their power to legislate and regulate investments, the environment and services.

Here are three key dates:

- *1 January*   The NAFTA Agreement signed by the United States, Canada and Mexico comes into force.
- *15 April*   Signing of the agreement creating the WTO which replaces the GATT, with a far broader mandate allowing it to impose decisions superseding national policies. This intergovernmental treaty contains no environmental, social or cultural clause.
- *14 December*   First Summit of the Americas, bringing together all the heads of state and government of the Americas, except for Cuba. This meeting convened by the president of the United States approved an agenda to create a Free Trade Area of the Americas based on the NAFTA model by 2005.

Compared with other free-trade and common-market agreements signed previously, NAFTA is a masterpiece of American economic diplomacy that introduces major innovations. It not only facilitates the circulation of commodities but also converts the environment and services – health, education, culture – into objects of free trade and guarantees national treatment for foreign investors, as well as iron-clad protection against any profitability loss. The broadest interpretation is given to the anti-expropriation clause: any law, regulation or standard causing a loss in profit compared with the expected ideal setting is considered to be equivalent to an expropriation decree.

Facing two weak and dependent partners, the US negotiators took advantage of their strong bargaining position to impose conditions giving transnational and multinational corporations absolute priority over state economic, cultural, social and environmental policies. In a way, the agreement is an investors' charter of rights and freedoms.

NAFTA's main innovations are hidden in two chapters that have been largely ignored by the media and the general public. Chapters 10 and 11 give foreign multinationals the same rights as local companies, big or small, and allow them to sue governments should their rights to profitability be violated. The chapters' provisions prohibit public authorities from enacting laws or regulations which might adversely affect the free deployment of foreign investments in their territory. By virtue of these provisions the government of Canada lost two major cases against S.D. Myers and Ethyl Corp., two US companies. The latter manufactures a gasoline additive that Canada prohibited because it was considered a health risk. Reacting to this 'harmful ban for investments and trade', Ethyl Corp. sued the Canadian government under NAFTA Chapter 11 provisions and won. Canada was not only forced to lift the ban, but also to pay the company 13 million dollars in damages for losses incurred before the trial. As for S.D. Myers, it won a major case involving the banning of polychlorinated biphenyls (PCBs) exports.

These two chapters pave the way for the liberalization of services under the 'negative principle' which states that all services fall under the free-trade law, except those that are specified in an appendix to the agreement. These exceptions are basically temporary, since they are the topic of permanent negotiations. Major manoeuvres regarding these exceptions are currently being conducted by secretive public officials. Who in Canada, the USA or Mexico knows about these negotiations and their content? Who knows that the aborted Multilateral Agreement on Investment (MAI) is already included in NAFTA's Chapters 10 and 11? The MAI is a draft agreement negotiated in secret by senior public servants and international technocrats within the Organization for Economic Cooperation and Development (OECD), designed to strengthen and extend the power of transnational corporations to the detriment of governments. A worldwide civil society mobilization triggered by a leak on the Internet stirred the politicians and forced them to take on their responsibilities. Several of them admitted that they weren't even aware of the MAI's content. The project was withdrawn in October 1998, but the manoeuvring has since resumed behind closed doors at the WTO.

NAFTA's greatest innovation is the creation of a three-judge tribunal whose decisions, with no right of appeal, transcend the powers of the member countries' local judicial systems. This *sui generis* court has precedence over national supreme courts by virtue of the unprecedented powers relinquished by the agreement's signatories. It hears company complaints against public powers accused of enacting laws or regulations hindering their profitability. This was the case of the above-mentioned Ethyl Corp. In another case, *Metalclad v. Mexico*, the tribunal reinterpreted the Mexican constitution. The state government of San Luís Potosí had refused to grant Metalclad a permit to set up a toxic-waste dump on a site located near a water source supplying the local population. The tribunal ruled that the state had acted *ultra vires* according to the national constitution and that, consequently, it had to pay the company $16.7 million in damages. Even conservative *Business Week* magazine is starting to find that this tribunal has been given too much power. In a report entitled 'The Highest Court You've Never Heard Of', the writer wonders: 'Do NAFTA judges have too much authority?'[6] One would believe so, but the magazine notes that this is not the opinion of the TNC lobby. 'Business groups want to include NAFTA's strongest investor-protection provisions in all future free-trade agreements.'

Indeed, the main purpose of US business and political circles is to create a Free Trade Area of the Americas (FTAA) that would extend NAFTA's provisions throughout the continent. The ongoing APEC (Asia–Pacific Economic Cooperation) negotiations are also based on NAFTA, which was designed as the prototype for all trade, investment and services deregulation treaties. The Marrakesh Agreement creating the WTO also reflects NAFTA's general thrust.

The deregulation offensive is also advancing on other fronts. In 1996, the American Congress voted in quick succession three policy packages aimed at abolishing or weakening antitrust laws passed since the beginning of the century in three key sectors: aviation, communications and finance. This systematic deregulation allows previously dismantled monopolies to re-form into even more powerful trusts.

The government of the United States not only tolerates but also openly encourages this monopolistic tendency. In a speech entitled 'The New Wealth of Nations', former Treasury Secretary Lawrence Summers stated that, in the new economy, 'the only incentive to produce anything is the possession of temporary monopoly power'.[7] And he went on to explain that if such power is exercised intelligently, it leads to growth and, consequently, prosperity. Big is beautiful! In order to remain competitive with the United States, other governments are implementing the same policy. The Canadian Bureau of Competition still barks from time to time but does not bite any more.

The recent charge by the US Secretary of Justice against Microsoft, formally accused of being a monopoly in May 1998, seems to contradict the suggestion made by Summers. But the genius of liberal ideology consists precisely in allowing these apparent contradictions that give credibility to the system. While judges, lawyers and politicians bickered and the case dragged out in court, Microsoft continued to reinforce its monopolistic stranglehold. And, a godsend for Bill Gates, George W. Bush took office and moderated the fervour of the Department of Justice, which announced on 6 September 2001, that it would not insist

Box 2.2 The Free Trade Area of the Americas

The architects of the Free Trade Agreement of the Americas (FTAA) designed it to be the most far-reaching trade agreement in history. Closely modelled on the North American Free Trade Agreement (NAFTA), the FTAA goes far beyond the latter in scope and power in its embodying of sweeping authority over states and all aspects of citizens' lives. Integrating 34 countries, 800 million people and a combined GDP of $11 trillion, the FTAA will be the largest free-trade area in the world. This project is both openly ambitious and obviously incongruous in that it integrates economies whose sizes and levels of development are in no way comparable. On its own, the United States represents 79 per cent of the continent's GDP — that is, four times more than that of all the other countries combined. Nicaragua and Haiti together account for only 1/2000th of the total. Despite these obvious disparities, the USA has clearly indicated in a document on 'subsidies, anti-dumping and countervailing duties' that they are not contemplating 'the establishment of any exceptions or special rules for certain economies'.

In 1990, President Bush Sr., at the urgings of US big business interests, launched the so-called 'Bush Initiative' for a large free-trade area comprising the three Americas, from Alaska to Tierra del Fuego. Consensus reigned among both major political parties and economic decision-makers on the need to consolidate the United States' economic and political dominion over its immediate area of influence. In December 1994, President Clinton convened all the heads of state and government of the Americas (except for Cuba's *lider maximo*) in Miami to define a negotiations agenda which would culminate in the signing of a free-trade agreement by 2005.

Two other summits — in Santiago in 1998 and Quebec City in 2001 — established standing negotiating bodies. Nine working groups were created to deal with the project's major issues: services, investments, government procurement, market access, agriculture, intellectual property rights, subsidies, competition policy and dispute settlement. These groups, which bring together hundreds of senior officials and experts, are working behind the scenes. Nobody has access to their documents, except for the Americas Business Forum (ABF) which has been an integral part of the process from the outset.

However, some documents were made public in July 2001, thanks to the insistence of civil society. These draft papers clearly show that the principles upheld by President George W. Bush at the Quebec City Summit have prevailed throughout. Now converted into objectives, these principles can be summed up as follows: (1) elimination of barriers to foreign investments and a legal framework to grant 'national treatment' to foreign investors; (2) inclusion of services, including health, education, culture and water, in the sphere of trade; (3) liberalization of agricultural products; and (4) elimination of tariff and non-tariff barriers to trade.

These documents also reveal that the FTAA project includes provisions on investments similar to those found in the defunct MAI and in NAFTA's Chapter 11 – under which corporations may sue governments directly for lost profits resulting from laws, decrees or provisions designed to protect public health and safety or social and environmental rights.

on having the monopoly dismantled. It should be added that Bill Gates greatly helped George W., who received $3,686,781 in campaign contributions from Microsoft.[8] The case ended in November 2002 with a judgement in favour of Microsoft. *Business Week* commented: 'Antitrust law itself was on trial – and it has clearly been weakened by the outcome.'

A Market of Coyotes and Monopolists

With no public power capable of controlling the giant corporations' ferocious appetite, transnational coyotes are roaming freely the global market's lawless space. Competitiveness makes them aggressive and even cruel, if necessary. In all the management schools and universities, future managers are shown that, in order to survive, they must not give any chance to their competitors, their employees, or their fellow citizens. Business students learn that the key is completely to prevent the adversary from breathing. A young entrepreneur from California faithfully repeats the lesson: 'I learned that you can't leave your opponent with even a breath because they may be able to revive. You have to take them out entirely. I've left a few dead bodies behind me', she crows.[9] The global system has totally perverted market mechanisms. It is estimated that when four or five corporations control over half of a sector's world market, they hold a de facto monopoly over its world prices. Some twenty strategic sectors are in that situation today, including oil, aviation, aerospace, electronic components and steel. Microsoft corporation alone controls 90 per cent of all desktop computer systems. In the automobile industry, General Motors, Ford, Toyota, Volkswagen and Daimler–Chrysler together control 54 per cent of the market share. Philip Morris, Nestlé, Procter & Gamble and Sara Lee share 70 per cent of the coffee bonanza. In the agro-industry, five companies control 96 per cent of the processed-food market. This has prompted American economist J.K. Galbraith to conclude:

> It follows that if the economic system is taken over by large corporations, you no longer have an impersonal, competitive market. The individual firm has an important share of the total output. And its acceptance of the need to conform gives the industry an oligopolistic market in which there is power to set prices and for the group to regulate itself in its own interest.[10]

Mergers, acquisitions, takeovers, alliances, the objective is always the same: to become big enough to dominate alone (monopoly) or with a handful of corporations (oligopoly) entire sectors of the economy. The champions of unregulated markets claim that a gifted player always has a chance of winning against the strongest. This is to ignore that the strongest also can be gifted and that, not being so, he has the means to hire gifted technicians, administrators and lawyers.

Intra-group trade represents another way of distorting market laws. This captive trade between different units of the same multinational today makes up one-third of world trade. As a result, prices are determined outside the market and governed by global strategies defined by corporate headquarters.

Big manoeuvres to regroup companies are certainly not a new phenomenon. They have been going on since the first multinationals were created. But the wave of giant mergers and acquisitions that has been surging on the global market for some ten years is unprecedented. The total value of all mergers and acquisitions carried out in 1990 reached about $500 billion. A record at the time! In 2000, it reached US$2.7 trillion (2,700,000,000,000). As for cross-border mergers and acquisitions, they rose from $400 billion in 1992 to $1.5 trillion in 2000. It is worth noting that 60 per cent of international mergers and acquisitions benefited US corporations, a clear indication that the United States is profiting the most from the renewed concentration of economic power.

Three factors are behind this merger mania:

1. the desire to eliminate competition;
2. the falling rate of profit;
3. the greed of investment banks.

The first factor is nothing new. It stems from the desire of the strongest to ensure market stability – that is, to control prices and increase market share at the same time. To put it plainly, mergers and acquisitions are carried out to create monopolies. The presence of competitors always represents an unpredictable turbulence factor that reduces price stability and consequently the company's effectiveness. After all, to control turbulence, and therefore forecasts, is also a natural market law, or at least a natural instinct among senior managers. So they do their best to eliminate competition, if not their competitors, often with success for the simple reason that without regulations they have the power to do so. This is what Bill Gates explained one day to one of his competitors: 'I can buy 20 per cent of your company, buy you out or crush you.'[11]

The second factor, the falling rate of profit, stems from the over-abundance of capital invested in production. To be more precise, the overconcentration of capital at the top, in the hands of the global entrepreneurs – a few thousand global players – leaves insufficient cash for consumption. In other words, there are too many producer-suppliers on the global market and not enough creditworthy consumers. The overconcentration of invested capital leads to production overcapacity; overproduction leads to a decline in prices and, as a result, in a decline in profits. And since global corporations will not make do with modest profits, the easiest solution is to reduce costs through economies of scale. How? By concentrating capital even more, by multiplying mergers and acquisitions. For example, as of 31 May 2000, the 1,000 largest TNCs made $708 billion in annual profits, an 18 per cent increase compared with the previous year.[12] These profits were for the most part reinvested. This caused production overcapacity, product overabundance, price drops, falling profits, mergers, layoffs, falling consumer spending, even greater product overabundance, more price drops, mergers. And this spiral continues!

The December 1998 Exxon and Mobil mega-merger is a good example of this merciless logic. The price of oil having fallen 50 per cent since 1977, the two giants needed to make economies of scale. The merger allowed them to save $2.8 billion per year. These savings were made mainly on the backs of the 90,000 employees laid off following this operation. Most of the laid-off employees either became unemployed or found low-paying jobs with no security. As a result, they consume less, while Exxon Mobil and all the other merging companies produce more, thanks to capital accumulation and new technologies.

And this applies to every economic sector. In 1998, the world automotive industry had a 20 per cent production overcapacity. Giant car corporations were building five million too many cars every year. A decline in profits was expected. What could be done? Mergers and alliances in order to lay off workers who would inevitably buy less. Here again, the merger festival will continue.

The situation has become so absurd that even major business magazines have started sounding alarm bells. *The Economist* talks of a global glut due to 'unprecedentedly high global excess supply'. 'The global glut is pushing prices relentlessly lower…. In the past two years, *The Economist's* index of industrial-commodity prices has fallen by 30%. In real terms, commodity prices are at their lowest since this index was first published a century and a half ago.'[13]

The third factor behind mergers and acquisitions is the greed of the investment banks,[14] which conduct and finance these gargantuan operations. The highly specialized and well-paid trade of brokering mergers and alliances has been taken by storm by 'golden boys' seeking to become instantly rich. To succeed in their merger and acquisition projects, global corporations need these dearly paid financial geniuses. For example, the financial go-betweens in the 1998 Daimler–Chrysler merger earned $105 million. For its valiant services in the Sandoz and Ciba–Geigy merger, Morgan Stanley cashed the fabulous amount of $500 million. But no one has surpassed Goldman Sachs, which conducted mergers and acquisitions worth $909 billion in 1998 (compared with $343 billion the previous year), pocketing a couple of billion dollars in commissions in the process.[15]

A dozen major banks share most of the lucrative merger and acquisition business. By order of size, the best known are Goldman Sachs, Merrill Lynch, Salomon Smith Barney, Morgan Stanley and Crédit Suisse–First Boston. This trade is so profitable that the strategists of these mega-corporations go out to the big bosses to suggest to them fabulous raids. They often succeed in convincing CEOs to become number one in their sector and automatically to increase their own remuneration. And this brings us to a fourth factor behind the mergers, the one that is least talked about: the super-managers' greed and thirst for power.

From Competition to Collusion

The other method of countering competition involves the different kinds of formal and informal, visible or invisible, alliances established every day between mega-corporations. There has always been some degree of collusion between large capitalists, but today it has become an unprecedented form of cronyism. 'A New Chumminess' headlines *The Economist*. The British magazine estimates that 32,000 alliances were 'created throughout the world over the last three years, three-quarters of which are multinational'.[16] They exist in all shapes and sizes: joint ventures, co-marketing, co-production, cross-shareholdings, research agreements, company families. The magazine's analysts believe that all these agreements and alliances are 'the best way to ensure faster growth at lower costs'. Indeed, it is estimated that, in 1999, these alliances accounted for approximately 20 per cent of the transnational corporations' sales figure. In 1980, this figure was barely over 1 per cent.

Each year, *Fortune* magazine probes the hearts of Americans in order to determine the companies they admire most.[17] This survey reveals a surprising fact: the ten most admired corporations are highly promiscuous with one another. This is normal, note the survey's authors: 'The most beautiful girls go out with the most beautiful boys.' Thus, there is an unsuspected complicity between the software giants. As for Disney, it is in bed with practically everybody, although it has an exclusive relationship with Coca-Cola. Two pharmaceutical giants, Merck and Johnson & Johnson have undertaken over-the-counter joint ventures – that is, jointly financed ventures that are not regulated by any stock exchange. The major airlines have innovated by all officially joining four global alliances: Star Alliance, Oneworld, Wings Alliance and SkyTeam.

Given these facts, of which there are countless examples, many economists have concluded that, in a globalized economy, 'co-ordination between large firms is as important as market adjustments and planned co-ordination has largely replaced market co-ordination'.[18] In short, to reach their cost reduction objectives and increase profits, global corporations use one of two strategies: either war, with its often high cost, or the buddy–buddy formula, which is becoming more and more popular.

A keen observer of the petroleum giants, fighting to destroy each other one minute, plotting to create cartels the next, once summed up this behaviour with the following witty remark: 'Oilmen are like cats; you can never tell from the sound of them whether they are fighting or making love.'[19] On the global market, this ambiguous racket has been extended to every economic sector.

The Supremacy of the Financial Markets

In the global market, financial capital dominates all other sectors of the economy. This is the result of the predominant influence of banks, insurance companies, institutional investors, and hedge funds on the distribution of capital, mergers and acquisitions, competition, public debt, and finally on the behaviour of corporations and governments. As *The Economist* notes: 'Financial markets have become the judge and jury of all economic policies.'[20]

Four factors explain this remarkable situation:

1. *The broad autonomy enjoyed by financial markets* with respect to governments which, since the establishment of currency flotation, in 1971, and the Jamaica Agreement, in 1976, are making every effort to deregulate the financial sector and eliminate all restrictions against the integration of banks, brokerage firms and insurance companies.
2. *The interconnection of all financial institutions* – banks, stock exchanges, investment funds, pension funds, insurance companies, tax havens – thanks to electronic networks, which give financial markets the capacity to control capital flows completely at all times all over the world.
3. *The speed of the financial operators*, who, assisted by computers, make the rounds everywhere in the world twenty-four hours a day to swoop down on the best profit opportunities and just as rapidly withdraw their positions, as soon as their electronic program senses a drop.

4. *Massive speculation*, not only on currencies but also on countless financial derivatives, which renders the financial sector completely uncontrollable by governments and other economic sectors.

This last factor needs to be examined more closely since speculation has now become the quintessence of financial markets. The very concept of financial market has become sufficiently vague and abstract to include this casino economy. Money is no longer used mainly to finance industrial development and commercial transactions, but rather to speculate – that is, to bet on the markets' future performance. The economy's health now depends on the unpredictable movements of speculative capital.

To understand the effects of speculation, one must recall that, in a globalized and deregulated financial system, market laws undergo a permanent perversion. In an ideal market with healthy competition, prices are determined by supply and demand. For this to happen, economic agents need to be sufficiently informed to make decisions based on a certain degree of 'economic rationality'. However, in a speculative market, decisions depend not on some rationality, but rather on the agents' anticipations, which are far more sheep-like than rational: to determine their prices, these agents must anticipate the anticipations of others. The usual scenario is as follows: anticipating a rise in the price of a product, rich speculators buy it massively; this does in fact cause the price to rise; the rise attracts new buyers, therefore extending the price rise; the self-realizing forecasts, amplified by the legendary sheepish behaviour of speculators, cause trend followers to become euphoric in what Galbraith calls a 'collective flight out of reality'. This is how speculative bubbles begin, whose natural fate is to burst without warning, leaving small investors helpless, not to mention the serious damage they cause to the productive economy.

Stock-market speculation has always existed; globalization simply developed and extended it to all risks taken in capital markets. This is how 'derivatives' emerged, products that can be defined as insurance, for a premium, against market volatility. This system was copied from the grain futures markets created by American traders at the beginning of the twentieth century. Wheat producers, for example, wishing to protect themselves against a possible price drop, sold their harvest six months in advance, at an agreed-upon price that could not be changed.

The broker who accepted the contract wanted to protect himself against a possible price rise. As such, the idea is sound, for it can help stabilize markets. However, now overused to perversion and extended to currencies, interest rates and stock indexes, this same mechanism is no longer a tool that protects the market against price fluctuations. It no longer helps stabilize markets; it destabilizes them so the speculator may make a profit. As market makers, the commercial and investment banks make huge profits by creating volatility and then selling insurance against this volatility. Consequently, originally an insurance system, the futures markets have become purely speculative.

Wagers are made on a large number of financial products whose value 'derives' from underlying assets, such as currencies or interest rates. The financial market's creativity seems to be limitless. New, ever more sophisticated and complex products appear daily: derivative derivatives. The more complex it gets, the more lucrative it is for large speculators and banks, their privileged intermediaries. These mountains of wagers – US$55 trillion in 2000 – made by private agreement, are not subjected to any control, a factor that worsens the situation. Moreover, these operations don't appear in company financial results, since they are not included in the assets or in the liabilities.

Starting in 1980, a new kind of company emerged, designed exclusively to speculate in the financial markets: the famous hedge, or speculative, funds. These funds and the capital they handle have grown exponentially. In 1990, there were 200 hedge funds, a huge number at the time. Today, there are over 4,000 such funds managing an estimated US$4 trillion with a leveraged exposure of over $100 trillion – a virtual economy three times larger than the actual world economy.

The global financial market also includes the fabulous currency market. Originally a trade instrument used to facilitate transactions and hoarding, currency has become an ordinary commodity, a consumable and speculative item like any other. Each minute, computers make thousands of transactions, transferring huge sums from one hand to another, with no other purpose than speculation. According to the Bank for International Settlements (BIS), the daily volume of currencies traded this way was on average $1.21 trillion in 2001, or 75 per cent of all the monetary reserves of all the countries in the world.[21] Only 1 to 2 per cent of all these transactions are related to actual international trade and tourism activities. All the major banks now have 'arbitrage' departments, a euphemism for high-stakes gambling. The world's ten largest banks control over half of all speculative monetary transactions. With the surge in speculation as a legal source of enrichment, the job of arbitrageur has gained credibility. An army of young speculation geniuses now hold choice positions in financial institutions (see Box 2.3 below).

To these highly complex and opaque markets, one must add the champions of opacity, the tax or offshore havens where laundered money from corruption, drugs and organized crime is recycled (see Chapter 3 below).

The System's Strokes

Crises are inevitable in a global financial market that no government can or wants to control. There is no way to hide this plight which, since 1994, has repeatedly hit the world economy, leaving a number of underdeveloped or developing countries helpless. Just like strokes, global financial crises happen suddenly, causing convulsions that shake the entire organism.

This apoplectic syndrome afflicting the global financial system first appeared in Mexico. A signatory of NAFTA and a newly admitted member of the OECD (May 1994), Mexico started enjoying respectability in financial markets. In exchange for his country's admission into the club of rich countries, former president Carlos Salinas de Gortari (today self-exiled and prosecuted for swindling and misappropriation of public funds) accepted all the global market's demands spelled out by the IMF. Speculators and short-term capital investors rushed to Mexico.

It turns out that, at the end of 1994, speculative attacks against the peso forced the Mexican government to devalue its currency by 15 per cent. After the announcement, foreign investors/speculators sold their stake and rapidly converted them into dollars – just as the local 'insiders' had done a few days earlier. This incipient panic accelerated the spiralling fall of the peso. On 12 January 1995, warning lights went on in all the world's major financial centres: Danger of Contagion! Some twelve South American and Eastern European currencies might catch the Mexican peso's disease. On 30 January, the finance minister announced that he had no more reserves and that the country's financial system was

Box 2.3   Portrait of a cyber-trader

German journalist Hans-Peter Martin visited the cyberspeculation sanctuary of Barclays Bank. He saw 400 young wolves hunting down quick profits. Patrick Slough, 29 years old, was one of them. He managed trades made on Swiss francs, commonly called 'Swiss' in the language of the global currency market.

His workstation is a modest-looking console three metres wide, surrounded by a babble of voices and bellowed orders in the dimly lit hall. Three screens and two speakers are mounted behind the small work-surface, constantly supplying him with new optical and acoustic data. At the top right, the four-colour screen produced by Reuters connects Slough to 20,000 finance houses and all the major stock exchanges around the world.

The screen simultaneously displays the last three offers or supplies of 'Swiss', the highest and lowest rates of the last few hours for all currencies, and the latest news from the currency world. At the same time, Slough can contact any other user by keying in a code and immediately conclude a deal. But he is not allowed to rely only on that; he must also keep track of the prices that his two independent brokers communicate to him through the speaker. Every couple of minutes he himself makes a bid, either by telephone or from his key-board. If another broker–client accepts, a call soon follows....

In 'real time' and 'online', then, Slough can always find out from the EBS screen to his left what is the highest bid and the lowest offer for francs into dollars or marks that have been made within this system.... If Slough taps his 'buy' key, the computer displays the bidder's identity and automatically makes the connection....

After half an hour, Slough tests the market by buying '70 marks' for 'Swiss 575' at the Swiss UBS bank. Using an electronic pen, he enters the deal at high speed into the house system through the dots on the console: 70 million marks for francs at 0.81575 francs per mark. Not long after, a loud 'Fuck!' escapes him: the price has fallen by a hundredth of a centime; he has lost 7,000 francs, for the time being. But the 'Buba' – as the Bundesbank is known among professionals – is on his side. German interest rates remain unchanged. The mark is rising, and his loss changes in seconds into a gain twice as large. Slough plays safe by immediately selling and relaxes for a minute.

Source: Hans-Peter Martin and Harald Schumann, *The Global Trap: Globalization and the Assault on Democracy and Prosperity*, London: Zed Books, 1997, pp. 50–51.

going to collapse, unless he received immediate help in the form of a $50 billion loan to plug the holes. The IMF came to the rescue. It found in its emergency fund and at the US Treasury the sums required for the rescue, which for the most part would be used to cover the speculators' losses. (It is worth noting that these loans were guaranteed with Mexican oil reserves.) Relieved after having brought back the patient with a massive injection of public funds, Michel Camdessus, the ineffable former director of the IMF, summed up the situation with a confession of sorts: 'That was the first major crisis of our new world, that of the global markets',[22] implying that it would not be the last.

A second, far more serious, crisis erupted in Asia in July 1997. One after the other, it overcame the four Southeast Asian 'Tigers': Thailand, Indonesia, South Korea and Malaysia, four so-called emerging economies that, since the 1980s, were recognized for their vitality and hailed as models of economic development. These models started crashing when the region's governments were put under pressure by the IMF and the US Treasury to accelerate financial market deregulation and liberalization. This is how they lost control over capital flows and how speculative markets took over. Then panic set in, and the world witnessed a repetition of the Mexican scenario: capital flight, breakdown of the productive apparatus, massive lay-offs, devaluation, widespread impoverishment.

In July 1998, the same epileptic spasms attacked Russia. In this country in transition towards laissez-faire capitalism, the debacle was complete and caused the implosion of the banking system. In November 1998, it was the turn of Brazil, whose GNP is the eighth in the world, a giant thought to be immunized against such convulsions. This is when the so-called international community started worrying about a collapse of the world financial system.

Bolstered by its new role as fireman of the global financial system, the IMF came running again to the rescue with massive injections of public funds. Overall, $231 billion were directly or indirectly handed to the speculators. 'A present from the taxpayers to rich speculators', commented a J.P. Morgan economist. It is worth noting that in each rescue operation, the IMF seized the opportunity to impose its 'conditionalities': deregulation, privatizations, liberalization, currency devaluations, interest rate increases, social spending cuts. As if these crises were part and parcel of a plan for integrating Third World economies into the global market...

What consequences do these upheavals have? Any serious financial crisis involves a redistribution of power and wealth between the financial services sector, corporations, the state and the people. And this reorganization always includes winners and losers. In these cases, the losers are wage earners, small and medium entrepreneurs, small investors, women, and the poor in general. The final results are disastrous: bankruptcy of small and medium businesses, rising unemployment, worsening poverty, dropping school enrolment rates. According to the World Bank, the Asian crisis sent 60 million people under the poverty line. In Mexico, the peso devaluation caused a 30 per cent drop in wage-earner income. This is a permanent drop, because in 1999 the average wage was still 26 per cent lower than that of 1994.[23]

'The impact on women and girls is just catastrophic', noted an American Asian Development Bank consultant. 'Because of the financial crisis, women are disproportionately losing their jobs and families are pulling their daughters out of school. And once these girls have dropped out of school, they'll never go back.'[24] In Thailand, 80 per cent of the 2 million people laid off due to the crisis were women.

The big winners are the European and American transnational corporations. One year after the crisis broke out, the *International Herald Tribune* headlined triumphantly: 'West Snaps up Asian Businesses'. The assessment made under this headline is unequivocal:

> Since the financial crisis in East Asia began almost a year ago, western firms – led by US and European Corporations – have spent ten of billions of dollars to snap up Asian assets forced onto the market and made much cheaper by the economic slowdown and the plunge in local currency values.[25]

Quoting financial experts, the reporter added that this aggressive manoeuvre in Japan's backyard might very well place that country at a decided disadvantage for years to come. It has become obvious today that the Asian crisis did indeed break the rising economic momentum of Japan, which will no longer be able seriously to rival the United States. As for the Asian Tigers, they lost their characteristic self-confidence.

The World Trade (dis)Organization

Given the distortions, the imbalances and even the frequent chaos created by global market irrationality, a question comes to mind: why doesn't the World Trade Organization (WTO) intervene to ensure the equitable and harmonious development of trade between nations? The fact is that, contrary to popular belief, the WTO was not created to regulate international trade but rather to deregulate it. Its mission is to regulate the systematic deregulation, not only of the world economy but also of domestic economies.

Birth and death of the International Organization of Commerce (IOC)

Here's another question: didn't the original blueprint of international governance include an agency designed truly to regulate world trade? Indeed, the most insightful pioneers of the new international order, created in the post-war period, wanted to prevent the type of chaos that caused the Great Depression and, indirectly, the Second World War. One of these pioneers, John Maynard Keynes, proposed setting up an agency to regulate and control economic trade flows between nations. The eminent British economist believed that encouraging free trade was not enough: the international circulation of goods and capital needed to be governed by fairness principles. For example, he suggested that buffer stocks be created to ensure the stability of raw material prices. Going even further, he recognized that the price of basic goods should be established taking into account economic as well as human factors such as the diet and quality of life of people living in the countries producing such goods. To ensure monetary stability, he suggested the creation of a world central bank, in charge of issuing a reserve currency called the bancor.[26]

However, other more powerful and better positioned players wouldn't hear of it. In 1946, when talks started to set up an international trade regulating agency, two forums with almost opposing views were held almost at the same time in two different settings. The first one, held in London and organized by the UN Economic and Social Council (ECOSOC), brought the 56 UN member countries together. Convened by the United States, the second forum was less formal and more limited. It took place in Geneva with only 23 participating countries – the richest and most powerful.

At the ECOSOC Conference, the European representatives – less dependent and better prepared than at the Bretton Woods Conference held during the war – won over the Latin American representatives to

Box 2.4   American Erly Rice against Haitian rice farmers

Until 1986, the rice farmers of Haiti produced practically all the rice consumed in their country. Today they produce less than 50 per cent. What happened?

Time magazine sums up the situation in a clear sentence: 'After Haiti lifted its trade barriers under the IMF pressure in 1986, an imported mountain of cheap American rice – subsidized by the U.S. government – buried the island's rice industry.' Over the last ten years, American rice imports grew rapidly from zero in 1986 to close to 120,000 tons per year.

It is worth recalling that this IMF policy followed the 1985 adoption of a US law on agriculture creating export subsidy programmes. American rice producers and traders greatly benefited from this policy. At the time, the price of American rice was far higher than the world market price and rice reserves were growing fast. According to the US Department of Agriculture, this loan and subsidy policy had immediate effects.

The United States is now the second largest rice exporter in the world. Haiti is its largest market in the Caribbean and seventh largest in the world. This policy's greatest beneficiaries are the American Erly Rice company and Riz d'Haïti, its Haitian counterpart, that has imported about 120,000 tons of rice per year over the last ten years. Now established in Haiti, Erly currently imports 40 per cent to 50 per cent of all the rice consumed in the country and holds a de facto monopoly on rice imports since it can sell below the price of locally produced rice, thanks to the US government's help to producers and exporters.

Source: Relations, May 2000; *Time,* 24 April 2000.

support affirmative-action measures in favour of the poorest countries and those left in dire straits by the war. The Americans disagreed. Nevertheless, the majority prevailed and the Charter of the International Organization of Commerce was signed in Havana in March 1948. The American delegation also signed it, not without ulterior motives, knowing full well that Congress would refuse to ratify it. And so it was. Noting that the country controlling over half of all world trade refused to ratify the Charter, the other governments of the world disbanded. The IOC was stillborn.

The GATT and the 'principle of non-discrimination'

In fact, the death sentence of the IOC was signed in Geneva, at the second forum, which had already approved, on 30 October 1947, five months before the signing of the treaty creating the IOC, a memorandum prepared by the United States pertaining only to the reduction of tariff barriers. Presented as a provisional trade protocol, the General Agreement on Tariffs and Trade would hold sway for forty-seven years and progressively extend its jurisdiction to almost the entire world. Since it was only provisional, no parliament ever debated or voted on the General Agreement on Tariffs and Trade.

The GATT strongly reaffirms the 'principle of non-discrimination', which is sacrosanct according to the United States. Supposedly placing all countries on the same footing, this principle means in fact that GATT members must not make any distinction between rich and poor, developed and underdeveloped, countries. In this fool's bargain, African and Latin American peasants are left to compete with agribusiness transnationals. May the strongest win! This game has had catastrophic consequences on subsistence farming in Third World countries, which could not resist the flooding of foodstuffs from the North sold cheaper than local food. Senegal, for example, which was formerly self-sufficient in rice, now must import 400,000 tons per year, since the – more often than not – subsidized TNCs produce it cheaper. In the same way, the Vietnamese and Haitian rice farmers were forced to compete against American multinationals, and lost.

The GATT opened its doors in Geneva on 1 January 1948. Numerous negotiation rounds followed on the gradual suppression of tariff barriers, quotas and non-tariff barriers.

The metamorphosis of the GATT into the WTO

In 1994, as the roadroller of globalization sped up and the IMF was integrating underdeveloped countries into the global market through structural adjustment programmes (SAPs),[27] time was ripe to convert the GATT into a global transnational body. On 1 April, in Marrakesh, some 120 governments signed the Charter of the World Trade Organization. On 1 January 1995, the WTO took over from the GATT with enhanced powers. The new body casts its net further and more deeply.

Its policies encompass all goods and services in the world that are traded or that could potentially be traded, as well as investments and intellectual property rights.

Since the WTO's founding, its 600 technocrats have already obtained the signature of some twenty major agreements that complete and reinforce the General Accord (GATT) inherited by the WTO. Some of the most important are:

- GATS: *General Agreement on Trade in Services*, which tends to include in the market all services, particularly public services such as health, education and entertainment.
- TRIPs: *Trade-Related Intellectual Property Rights*, which are particularly aimed at protecting the interests of the giant pharmaceutical and biochemical industries and efficiently pave the way for the patenting of life.
- TRIMs: *Trade-Related Investment Measures*, designed to prevent governments from exercising democratic control over foreign investments, such as imposing local-content requirements.
- The *Agriculture Agreement*, aimed at creating world competition for agri-food products by forcing poor countries to open up their markets to products from rich countries, which are often subsidized, and prohibiting them from protecting subsistence farming.

Contrary to the GATT, which never tried to meddle in domestic state regulatory policies, nor put into question the pre-eminence of domestic policies over liberalization, the WTO tends to give precedence to international objectives over domestic considerations. This is becoming more obvious with the negotiations on financial services and investments, and, consequently, on production conditions. It should be recalled that it is through direct foreign investments that transnational corporations impose their production systems throughout the world. These same TNCs use their respective states to impose their standards on the WTO and the rest of the world. In the end, WTO agreements express the combined interests of oligopolies and their countries of origin.

Another major innovation is the WTO's Dispute Settlement Body (DSB). The consensus rule used at the GATT has been replaced by a judicial and executive power, in charge of interpreting and enforcing law. A genuine supreme court of international trade, the WTO has the power to assert the Law of the Market in everything and everywhere according to its own interpretation of the said law. It has the power to dictate what is right, what is good and even what is beautiful. It also enjoys executive powers, since it can impose ruinously expensive sanctions on recalcitrants.

It is often claimed that this tribunal puts all countries of the world on the same footing. What an outrageous deception! The facts clearly show that Third World countries, especially the poorest, cannot use DSB mechanisms to their advantage. They lack sufficient qualified personnel. To understand all the implications of complex and multiple topics formulated in gobbledegook and extending to thousands of pages, a country needs considerable financial, technical and human resources. The vast majority of underdeveloped countries, even the more prosperous, have barely enough representatives even to participate in the WTO's countless meetings and receptions. The poorest countries don't even have a permanent delegate. To save appearances, during votes, a single delegate may sometimes represent some fifteen countries. The fact is that, from January 1995 to May 1998, over half of the 122 complaints presented before the DSB were against Third World countries, which are involved in only 27 per cent of world trade. They lost almost all their cases.[28]

On the other hand, each OECD member country has on average ten permanent representatives. In addition, it can hire at will the best specialists in highly specialized fields. The United States staff at the WTO includes dozens of experienced economists, lawyers, technicians and negotiators to defend its cases. And it is backed by the powerful lobbies of transnational corporations which always remain on the alert.

The WTO's bias towards the United States

It is well known that the United States has always been unwilling to give up even the smallest bit of its sovereignty in trade matters. It signed the Charter of the WTO on one explicit condition: that it keep the right of recourse to Articles 301 and Super 301 of its Trade Agreement Act, also called the Trade Act. This law authorizes it to adopt unilateral retaliatory measures should an American lobby or the Department of Commerce consider that certain trade practices are unfair. In concrete terms, trade practices are considered unfair each time a US lobby or multinational believes it will come out behind. The US government's lawyers then bring out the heavy artillery and multiply the ultimatums. Under these conditions, the DSB is seen as a simple negotiation framework that allows the strongest, the United States, to apply unilateral sanctions legally.

An observer of the WTO architecture noticed that it is like the Leaning Tower of Pisa: it always leans in the same direction. Three recent verdicts illustrate perfectly the WTO judges' bias in favour of the United States.

1. *Growth-hormone beef* For public health reasons, European Union countries refused to import meat from hormone-fed beef raised on American farms. When the case was brought before the WTO, it settled in favour of the United States, which was authorized to reimburse itself unilaterally $117 million in duties on European products.

2. *The banana war* Applying the Lomé Convention,[29] the European Union had given preferential treatment to the poorest countries of Africa, the Caribbean and the Pacific (ACPs), from which it bought bananas at slightly higher than market prices; the American Chiquita/ Del Monte/Dole oligopoly, which buys its bananas in Central America at rock-bottom prices, considered that its rights were infringed upon. The case was brought before the DSB, but Washington applied sanctions even before the verdict was announced, which backed the fait accompli against the Europeans and the ACPs. By attacking the Lomé Convention, the WTO has outlawed the correction of market laws in favour of poor countries.

3. *Opening up the Japanese automobile market to American multinationals* Having difficulties in establishing a foothold in the Japanese market, and believing they were being treated unfairly by Japanese laws, American car makers asked Washington to take their case before the WTO. When the DSB was on the verge of settling in favour of Japan, the American authorities, going against DSB rules, withdrew the complaint and insisted on settling the dispute through bilateral arm twisting. Forgetting its own rules, the WTO merely endorsed the dispute settlement in favour of the Americans.

A democratic organization?

The director-general of the WTO tells anyone who will listen that his organization is highly democratic since its rules 'were approved by the parliaments and congresses of its 136 member countries'.[30] In fact, the vast majority of WTO member governments don't have a democratic parliament or congress. At least two-thirds of the WTO signatories represent either dictators, caudillos, military juntas or administrations dominated by a single party. As for the other third, it would be worthwhile seeing to what extent the WTO rules and conventions were subjected to parliamentary debate.

Another correction should also be made: by signing the WTO Charter, governments have to all intents and purposes renounced their sovereignty over international trade and the regulation of domestic socio-economic structures. The bureaucracy at the organization's helm is aware of the great powers thus bestowed upon it, powers enhanced by impenetrable opacity. Neither public opinion nor governments, save that of the United States, has any real effect on it. As we have seen with NAFTA, international economic negotiations are conducted by senior officials, and public opinion is generally kept in the dark until it is too late.

Seattle

On 30 November 1999, the 136 WTO members[31] met in Seattle, the home of Nike and Microsoft, sponsors of the event, for a summit meeting prepared long in advance. Taking advantage of the magic effect created by the coming of a new millennium, the global business elite wanted to make a killing. The summit, dubbed the Millennium Round, was to draw up a daring agenda for a final negotiation cycle designed to accelerate market deregulation and liberalization. Governments were called upon to give up their remaining powers to regulate what was left in culture, agriculture, electronic trade, the environment, the patenting of life and food security.

But for the first time in the history of such meetings, demonstrators showed up in droves to challenge astonished politicians and technocrats and disrupt their peace and quiet. Global civil society, represented by some 100,000 angry citizens cried out 'Basta! Enough!' And the summit failed. The shockwaves were felt everywhere in the world.

Flabbergasted at first, the world leaders rapidly regained their composure. They changed their discourse, but not their intentions or interests. Bargaining has already resumed on the quiet at WTO headquarters in Geneva.

Nevertheless, the blow had its effect. Alerted, world opinion might not ever fall back asleep. The WTO has lost its innocence. Worried, the big bosses are more cautious. They now have a strange feeling that they are being watched. They fear they may no longer be able secretly to settle the world's fate. Sheltered from social realities by its wealth, the proud global elite is starting to sense the crisis of legitimacy afflicting both governments and globalizing institutions such as the WTO.

CHAPTER 3

The Masters of the
Globalized World

The only problem is that most politicians have yet to fully understand
how much they are already under the financial markets' control, and how
much they are even dominated by them.

Hans Tietmeyer, former president of the Central Bank of Germany

Our political leaders take pleasure in constantly repeating that globalization is a force of nature as irresistible and inevitable as the tides. On
18 May 1998, before the representatives of 132 countries meeting in
Geneva to celebrate the fiftieth anniversary of the GATT–WTO, Bill
Clinton proclaimed that 'Globalization is not a policy choice, it is a
fact.' And Tony Blair added: 'Globalization is irreversible and irresistible.'
This chapter sheds light on this obscure misleading discourse and iden-
tifies the actual institutions and people controlling the system.

Who wrote the script of globalization? Who directs the show? Is
there a driver in this mega-machine, this juggernaut whose inexorable
progress seems to crush everything and everyone in its path? In other
words: who are these new masters of the world who dictate the laws of
globalization, plan it, and finance its implementation?

The Empire of the Transnational Corporations

We have entered the age of global giants capable of pushing governments around, comments a columnist of one of the leading US business
magazines.[1] These giants are the transnational corporations. They form

a powerful production, trade and finance network that is the framework and vanguard of globalization. Who are they? How many are there? Where are they located?

Rating agencies, investment banks and business magazines draw up and update lists of the largest companies by sales, assets, market value, profitability and degree of internationalization. There's the *Fortune 500*, the *Forbes 400* and the Forbes *Platinum 100*. The most instructive of these is no doubt *Business Week*'s[2] annual chart glorifying 'The Global 1000, the World's Most Valuable Companies'. This thousand-headed hydra controls the better part of the world's market economy and sets

Table 3.1 Comparative economic size of transnational corporations and states (2001)

State/TNC	US$ billion
1. Wal-Mart	218
2. Exxon Mobil	213
3. Austria	208
4. Turkey	185
5. General Motors	175
6. BP	174
7. Denmark	173
8. Ford Motor	162
9. Poland	155
10. Norway	153
11. Indonesia	145
12. DaimlerChrysler	136
13. Shell/Royal Dutch	135
14. Finland	130
15. South Africa	129
16. Saudi Arabia	127
17. General Electric	126
18. Thailand	126
19. Greece	125
20. Toyota	121

Note: This table presents two sets of comparable figures: corporate sales and country GDPs (total annual amount of goods and services sold and bought in a country by its citizens and foreign residents).

Source: Business Week, 15 July 2002; CEPII, *L'économie mondiale 2002*.

the parameters of globalization. Organized in global lobbies, industry associations or strategic alliances, these corporations represent a formidable and dreaded strike force capable of swaying governments in their favour.

The combined annual sales of these 1,000 mega-businesses reached US$10 trillion in 2000, or 33 per cent of the global GNP (a third of everything that is bought and sold in the world in a year) and twice the combined GNP of Africa and Latin America. The world's top 1,000 together own assets worth $41 trillion – that is, over 80 per cent of the world's developed resources, production equipment and debts. In the fiscal year ended 31 May 2002, the 500 largest TNCs drew $306 billion of profits from all the countries in the world, with a sizeable share from the Third World.

Table 3.1 compares the world's ten largest transnationals with ten countries having a comparable economy. The champion, Wal-Mart, with $218 billion in annual sales, surpasses the GNP of 167 countries individually, or the combined GNP of the 49 least-developed countries ($169 billion). Only 23 countries have bigger economies than Wal-Mart and Exxon Mobil. If the list were extended, Cuba and its GNP of $19 billion dollars would be surpassed by 255 mega-corporations which are managed in a no less authoritarian fashion, *mutatis mutandis*, than Castro's regime.

It is interesting to note that among today's 50 largest transnationals – The World *Super Fifty* – 19 of them were already included in this group at the end of the 1920s. Five of the eight largest corporations in 2001, General Motors, Ford, Exxon Mobil, Royal Dutch–Shell and General Electric, were already at the top of the list eighty years ago. The economic and political might of these global corporations is precisely the product of an uninterrupted appropriation of financial and technological resources. It also stems from their extensive experience acquired from year to year, sometimes from generation to generation, or from designated successor to designated successor, just as in the ancient dynasties.

The ease with which these giant corporations obtain all kinds of favours – removal of trade barriers, tax breaks, tariff reductions, low-interest loans, subsidies, outright gifts, and so on – clearly shows the powerful influence they exert on governments. French sociologist André Siegfried has keenly observed that 'a dominant social class can be identified by its ability to avoid paying its fair share of taxes'.

In 1998, *Time* magazine carried out an in-depth investigation on what it called the corporate welfare system. Its reporters discovered that the American government dishes out approximately $125 billion each year to rich multinationals, an amount 'equivalent to the total income tax paid by 60 million individuals and families'.[3]

The situation is hardly different in Canada. Corporate bums are most imaginative when it comes to avoiding taxes, and what little they pay is amply returned to them in subsidies. Figures obtained from the Department of Finance by the Canadian Centre for Policy Alternatives show that in six years, from 1994 to 1999, Canadian companies received incredible outright payments of $15 billion. This figure does not include all kinds of favours extracted from provincial and municipal governments, estimated at over $30 billion each year.[4]

In 1996, the extremely wealthy Bronfman family of Montreal, founder of the Seagram empire, pulled off a noteworthy feat.[5] Two Bronfman family trusts succeeded, 'thanks to government decisions taken in vague circumstances to say the least, in transferring assets of two billion dollars to the United States without paying any capital gains taxes'.[6] This tax evasion, carried out with help from the Departments of Finance and Revenue, was worth approximately Can$700 million or US$500 million at the time.

What a sad sight to see: politicians appearing as marketing agents brandishing taxpayers' money to appease the blackmailers of globalization, or to attract or keep arrogant and fickle investors. Transnational executives are delighted. A vice-president of McDonald's thinks it is normal to have governments at its feet: 'If I am not mistaken, there is not a single state in the world that has not approached us. Ambassadors and commercial attachés regularly visit my office to praise their country and explain why it is essential that we open McDonald's restaurants there.'[7]

The Money Masters

The financial markets' supremacy puts large bankers at the helm of globalization's juggernaut. More than any other player, these bankers wield decisive influence over governments. Addressing the *crème de la crème* of the global elite meeting in Davos in February 1996, Dr Hans

Tietmeyer, the king of German bankers, thought it useful to put things in their proper perspective: 'The only problem is that most politicians have yet to fully understand how much they are already under the financial markets' control – indeed, dominated by them.'[8]

Central bank governors occupy a prominent place among the kings of finance. *The Economist*[9] does not shrink from a comparison to gods. In an article entitled 'The Central Bankers as Gods', the British magazine notes that 'they have become the central planners of the late 1990s'.[10] A *Financial Times* columnist was only slightly less enthusiastic in his article 'The Money Masters':

> Central bankers are the masters now. Presidents and prime ministers may play at war and peace. They can prance abroad and posture at home. But money is different. Leave the politicians in charge of our money and they will debauch it. They freely admit as much. We are to put our trust instead in greyer men in darker suits.... By and large, central banking remains a society as secretive as it is powerful, a profession that has always prized discretion over its public profile. The relentless accretion of power has gone largely unnoticed in the wider world.[11]

When the central banks were first created by their respective governments, their role was to ensure the smooth operation of the national banking system and monetary circuits. They accomplished this by following government-defined measures, within the framework of national economic and monetary policy. This role has become obsolete due to financial globalization: now the global financial market determines the rules of the game, which are identical for all states. Today, the basic function of central banks is to ensure that the world financial system is operating efficiently, by adapting national finances to global policies. In this context, the total independence of the central banks from national governments has become a necessity, a requirement of the 'international financial community'. The new European Central Bank, for example, is totally protected under its statutes from political influence.

Because bank governors constantly consult one another, they have greatly increased their power. They regularly congregate in Basel, Switzerland, their favourite meeting place, at the headquarters of the Bank for International Settlements (BIS), the oldest and most mysterious international financial institution. Switzerland hands out diplomatic immunity and privileges to this institution's leaders and members. Founded in 1930 as a corporation, the BIS is at once the social club of the rich

Table 3.2   The ten largest transnationals as of 31 May 2002

Company	Headquarters	US$ billion
Sales (12 months)		
1. Wal-Mart	USA	217.80
2. Exxon Mobil	USA	213.49
3. General Motors	USA	175.35
4. BP	UK	174.22
5. Ford Motor	USA	162.41
6. DaimlerChrysler	Germany	136.07
7. Royal Dutch/Shell	UK/Netherlands	135.21
8. General Electric	USA	125.91
9. Toyota	Japan	121.72
10. Mitsubishi	Japan	112.97
Profits (12 months)		
1. Exxon Mobil	USA	15.11
2. Citigroup	USA	14.28
3. General Electric	USA	14.13
4. Shell/Royal Dutch	UK/Netherlands	10.85
5. BP	UK	9.88
6. Philip Morris	USA	8.57
7. Pfizer	USA	7.75
8. IBM	USA	7.72
9. Microsoft	USA	7.72
10. Merck	USA	7.28
Market value		
1. General Electric	USA	309.46
2. Microsoft	USA	275.70
3. Exxon Mobil	USA	271.23
4. Wal-Mart	USA	240.91
5. Citigroup	USA	223.04
6. Pfizer	USA	216.78
7. Shell/Royal Dutch	UK/Netherlands	194.55
8. BP	UK	192.12
9. Johnson & Johnson	USA	186.94
10. Intel	USA	184.67

Source: *Business Week*, 15 July 2002, according to Morgan Stanley Capital International compilations.

countries' central bankers and the central bank of central banks. It has only thirty-three official members, most of which come from industrialized countries. By virtue of its by-laws, the BIS discriminates between its shareholders – that is, among the different central banks of the world. Its board of directors is off limits to all but the central bank governors of the ten richest countries.

Officially, the BIS's role is to organize central bank co-operation and cohesion. In practice, the BIS is a pragmatic system for coordination among the world's major financial networks. At the centre of the system are the presidents of the US Federal Reserve and the new European Central Bank (ECB). Since the end of the 1970s, the BIS has also become an international information agency on monetary issues, gathering statistics on the banking activities of every country in the world, including those of the offshore banking havens which it readily recognizes. This influx of information enhances its influence on the system.

'The best kept secret', comments Jean Baumier, author of an essay on these non-elected bankers that govern us, 'is that of the discussions taking place the first weekend of each month at the headquarters of the Bank of International Settlements in Basel.'[12] On the agenda: topical financial, economic and political issues, monetary crises, currency devaluations, the interbank market, lending rates. Neither international competition, nor political trials and tribulations, nor even wars succeed in disturbing the serenity of these meetings. During the Second World War, the Basel Club quietly carried on its activities, with bankers from both sides meeting under the presidency of Thomas McKittrick, an American who was officially neutral in the conflict.[13]

As we shall see below, central bank governors are at the heart of the financial G8, which must not be confused with the political G8. They also lay down the law at the G20, the new 'board of directors' of the globalized economy created in September 1999.

Better known than the BIS, the International Monetary Fund and the World Bank are the two other international financial institutions that deserve to be counted among the money lords and masters of the globalized world. This is because of the subordinate, but crucial, role they have played, and still play today, in managing the globalization process. Above all, they intervene directly in the integration of Third World countries into the global market. For over four decades, the two Bretton Woods sisters have taken on a leading role in this crusade, planning and imposing development strategies based on foreign aid and indebtedness. In the early 1980s, when the age of globalization began, the aided countries were grappling with serious debt overhang problems, and all the while sinking even deeper into underdevelopment. Taking advantage of the disarray of the countries ruined by debt, the IMF and the World Bank forced them to implement draconian reforms of their economic, social, and even constitutional structures – a genuine bureaucratic *coup d'état* under the guise of 'structural adjustment'. Structural adjustment programmes (SAPs) are still being implemented and consolidated throughout the Third World. Their basic aim is to pry open further the markets of dependent, export-oriented economies, forcing them to compete at a disadvantage with TNCs and industrialized countries.

The IMF provides another well-known contribution to the globalization process: managing the crises created mainly by speculation and the financial markets' hasty deregulation. How ironic that the IMF, originally responsible for watching over the smooth operation of the international financial system, is now in charge of managing its failures.

The New Masters' Powerful Lobby

Since the beginning of industrial capitalism, the big bosses have always tended to get together and consult each other to promote their shared interests. As early as 1776, Adam Smith, the father of modern economic theory, noted:

> Masters are always and everywhere in a sort of tacit, but constant and uniform combination, not to raise the wages of labour above their actual rate. To violate this combination is everywhere a most unpopular action, and a sort of reproach to a master among his neighbours and equals. We seldom, indeed, hear of this combination, because it is the usual and, one may say, the natural state of things which nobody even hears of. Masters, too, sometimes enter into particular combinations to sink the wages of labour even below this rate. These are always conducted with the utmost silence and secrecy.[14]

This is still true in 2002. Global corporate leaders know when to set aside competition and rivalry for consultation and the creation of powerful lobbies[15] we never hear about… unless we listen carefully. In fact, there is no plot or conspiracy, but rather a convergence of shared interests. It is 'the natural state of things', as Adam Smith said. Introducing its yearly report on the world's most active billionaires, *Forbes* magazine notes that all these people know and protect each other:

> Whether opposing one another on deals or facing off in the boardroom, the world's richest inevitably cross paths. They're trustees of the same museums, alumni of the same colleges. They can be co-investors and co-conspirators. In France there's an expression, 'tour de table', to describe this penchant to maintain power amongst themselves.[16]

The lobbies of the global elite are generally highly structured associations, coalitions or forums working behind the scenes to influence governments and international organizations. They do not aim to exercise power directly, but rather to change economic, social and cultural policies in their favour. They intervene vigorously in the legislative and administrative processes of governments and international organizations but always discreetly and secretively. They exert pressure, blackmail, engage in intrigues or offer bribes. This circumventing of democracy rarely causes any problem, for the lobbyists work to develop a strong consensus with politicians and senior officials ready to sell or trade part of their power for financial or 'future considerations', or simply because of a servile mindset.

Let's take a brief look at a few of the most active of these brotherhoods by which the power of the TNCs is magnified.

The Trilateral Commission

Created in 1973, the Trilateral Commission[17] considers itself as an organization focused on defining policies regarding the operation of the international system and on issues related to the expansion of world trade. It was created during the oil crisis as 'anti-Western agitation' was raging in Third World countries demanding a new international economic order. As Samuel Huntington put it in a seminal study for the Commission, the world was suffering from 'excesses of democracy'. Today, the Trilateral Commission monitors the globalization process and periodically updates its strategy.

The Commission's main founder is none other than David Rockefeller – grandson of the oil baron – when he was president of the Chase Manhattan Bank. Its members, approximately 350, are chosen from among the most dynamic personalities in business, politics, the media, major universities and conservative think tanks. The Commission's name reflects the fact that its members are from the three poles of late capitalism: North America, Western Europe and Japan. They include senior executives of Coca-Cola, Exxon Mobil, Nestlé, Toyota, Sony, Alcoa, Hollinger, Banque de Paris, Chase Manhattan Bank and Barclays Bank. Among the former heads of state are Carter, Bush, Giscard d'Estaing, Barre and Nakasone. Brzezinski and Kissinger, former US government strategists, are prominent members. Acting heads of state and government are not admitted. The Commission has offices or contacts in every country of the Triad. Its reports, circulated in influential circles, set the tone for major economic and political decision-makers.

Business Roundtable (United States)

Founded in 1973, the Business Roundtable brings together the leaders of the 200 largest corporations in different sectors of the American economy.[18] Its objective is to influence political decision-making and public opinion. This highly reserved group never takes a public stand on any issue. When it does choose an option, it succeeds in imposing its view. It was at the heart of an impressive network called the Alliance for GATT Now, which succeeded in winning over important union and congressional leaders opposed to the 1994 agreement that created the World Trade Organization. It managed the same feat with the North American Free Trade Agreement by creating a powerful organization called USA–NAFTA. In a fascinating book entitled *The Selling of 'Free Trade': NAFTA, Washington, and the Subversion of American Democracy*, American journalist John MacArthur reconstructs this lobbying operation, which he considers to be the biggest of all time.[19]

Americas Business Forum (ABF)

The first Americas Business Forum took place in Denver, Colorado, in July 1995 at the first ministerial meeting of the Free Trade Area of the Americas (FTAA) project. Made up of representatives of the largest corporations in the three Americas, the ABF has an official consultative status. It participates in all the trade-related ministerial and negotiating meetings alongside senior government officials. American Business Roundtable delegates play a predominant role in this group due to their numbers and strong lobbying experience. The ABF makes detailed

recommendations on all topics under negotiation, particularly those pertaining to deregulation and direct foreign investment.

European Roundtable of Industrialists (ERI)

The European Roundtable of Industrialists is a replica of the American
Business Roundtable. Founded in 1983, it brings together forty-six of
the most important bosses of the global European corporations such as
Krupp, Fiat, Olivetti, BP Amoco and Renault. This powerful lobby
group is active mainly at the European Commission. All of the Commission's major policy decisions benefit from the advice of these globalization crusaders. The ERI also lobbies national governments whenever
necessary to speed up market liberalization, deregulation and privatization.

Business Council on National Issues (Canada)[20]

The BCNI is the Canadian equivalent of the American and European
business roundtables. It was created in 1976 by corporate leaders 'anxious
to exert more influence over a state that they felt had grown too large
and interventionist'. According to an unconfirmed secret members' list,
it brings together 150 business leaders whose assets total Can$1.7 trillion,
and combined annual income is estimated at Can$500 billion. They
employ 1.5 million Canadians.

   The stated objective of this pressure group, the most important in
Canada, is to contribute directly 'to the development of public policy
and the shaping of national priorities'. It has shown itself to be remark-
ably effective in pursuing this objective. The hand of the BCNI is
unmistakable behind the high-level manoeuvring to reform unemployment insurance, erode public health care and deregulate the financial
services sector. This powerful lobby has convinced politicians that what
is good for multinationals is good for Canada.

The Bretton Woods Committee

The superbureaucrats of the World Bank and the IMF need guidance
and supervision in sticking to the script drawn up by transnational
corporations and the financial markets. The mission of the Bretton
Woods Committee is to see to it that American interests maintain their

'leadership within these institutions', which, by intervening in developing countries, create favourable conditions for the 'strategic interests and national security of the United States'.[21] Most of this committee's members also sit at the Business Roundtable. It also includes former American Treasury, Defense, and State Department secretaries, university and business school presidents, members of major law firms, and a handful of union establishment leaders.

The Davos World Economic Forum

Founded in 1970 by economics professor Klaus Schwab, the World Economic Forum brings together the cream of the global elite at the end of January each year, in a Swiss ski resort. Modest in its infancy, the forum today is a politician-friendly world business club that brings together about a thousand senior executives and owners of transnational corporations. The event is steeped in an atmosphere of self-importance. Other participants include economists, professors, journalists, finance ministers and some fifty heads of state and government, mostly from the Third World, but also from the richest countries.

In an editorial entitled 'In Praise of the Davos Man', *The Economist* wrote: 'It is not every day that 1,000 of the people who run the world gather under a single roof. But every year 1,000 of the people who think they run the world congregate in Davos.' This new elite that 'share beliefs in individualism, market economics, and democracy, control many of the world's governments, and the bulk of its economic and military capabilities, ... are singularly unrepresentative'. In their defence it must be said that they are 'a different kind of elite'. These businessmen aren't there 'to butter up the politicians; it is the other way around. The Davos man, finding it boring to shake the hand of an obscure prime minister, prefers to meet Microsoft's Bill Gates.'[22] Private rooms are set up for high-level meetings. While economists and distinguished speakers hold forth before sparse audiences, the global movers and shakers make serious decisions.

The International Chamber of Commerce (ICC)

After leaving his position as CEO of Nestlé, Helmut Maucher decided to share his extensive experience with his colleagues by devoting himself to high-level lobbying. Since 1997, he has been president of the International Chamber of Commerce (ICC), an organization that promotes the interests of transnational corporations throughout the world. In a speech before the heads of state and government of the European Council in Cologne in June 1998, he declared the ICC 'the only organization that speaks authoritatively on behalf of companies from all sectors throughout the world'.[23]

Already recognized as an instigator of the Davos Forum, Maucher is today working to broaden the horizons of the ICC, which lobbies governments, the European Union, the G8, the OECD and the WTO. It is now aiming at having 'privileged access to the United Nations'. Objective: to get the United Nations family – the numerous specialized organizations working with underdeveloped countries – to co-operate more closely with TNCs in promoting globalization in the Third World.

The Fellow Travellers

Swiss writer Jean Ziegler calls them the 'crime lords'.[24] They are the white-collared leaders of transnational criminal organizations (TCOs), who, with the globalization of financial markets, have become the inevitable fellow travellers of the bankers – whom the latter either cannot get rid of or can't do without. Just like the other kings of finance, these crime lords are taking advantage of the lawless space created by the deregulated markets. They don't consider themselves outlaws but rather above the law. Jean de Maillard, author of several works on new forms of criminal activity, describes the intimate relationship between the criminal economy and the global economy:

> One thing is obvious: modern finance and organized crime strengthen each other. To grow, they both require the abolition of regulations and the suppression of state controls…. Dirty money goes through the same channels as that of speculative finance.[25]

TCOs are contributing in no small way to the fabulous volume of capital circulating in transnational financial networks. The United Nations estimates their annual sales in excess of $1 trillion. The world's gross criminal product (GCP) represents 15 per cent of world trade. These figures include profits from drug trafficking and contraband, illegal arms trade, misappropriation of public funds, tax evasion by the rich, casino slush funds, secret bankrolling of political parties as well as various mafia-controlled activities such as prostitution and gambling. All this dirty money needs to be laundered – that is, injected into the legal banking system. Such large-scale money laundering cannot be achieved without the complicity of the financial system and the politicians. Commenting on an article published in the *Journal of Money Laundering Control*, economist Christian Chavagneux writes: 'All large-scale criminal financial transactions depend on the principle of bank secrecy and the possibility of creating dummy corporations.'[26]

Money laundering

Now, it just so happens that the fabulous spoils of organized crime and corruption can magically become undetectable, and thus unseizable, by slipping them into today's deregulated and uncontrolled global financial markets. A June 1998 United Nations report shows that money laundering has become a global threat against the integrity and stability of financial and trade systems. In many respects, the global financial system 'is a money launderer's dream, offering considerable scope to imitate the patterns and behaviour of legitimate transactions'.[27] Indeed, it is now impossible, in international finance, to distinguish illicit from legitimate funds.

A sign of the times is that even Wall Street, the world's prime stock market, is becoming a top-drawer money launderer. In recent years, *Business Week* has regularly reported cases of organized crime penetrating the New York Stock Exchange. The cover page of the 16 December 1996 issue headlined: 'The Mob on Wall Street: An Inside Look at How Organized Crime Influences the Market.' This shocking report did not prompt any significant intervention by the authorities. As an indication that nothing had changed, in its 10 August 1998 issue the same magazine came back with another report whose title asked a troubling question: *Money Laundering on Wall Street?* The report showed how easy it is to launder dirty money in that respectable institution.[28] Not until June 2000 did the US justice system decide to act on what the federal attorney called 'the biggest stock market fraud of all time'. Ten members of the Cosa Nostra and some one hundred brokers and managers were charged. The trials are likely to drag on for years, because the mafiosi have lots of (laundered) money with which to defend themselves.[29]

Large commercial banks, even the most reputable among them, cannot let such lucrative business opportunities go by. On 27 August 1999, the *New York Times* and the *Wall Street Journal* revealed, to everyone's surprise, that the Bank of New York was involved in the laundering of at least $10 billion-worth of proceeds from Russian organized crime. To crown it all, a substantial part of this sum – $2 billion?, $4 billion? – came directly from IMF loans designed to stabilize the (mafia's) rouble. Another revelation: Citibank (now part of Citigroup) laundered several hundred million dollars transferred by Omar Bongo, president of Gabon, and by Raul Salinas, the imprisoned brother of the former president of Mexico. American political circles feigned surprise, but the fact is that the FBI had long been investigating this case, which is only the tip of a gigantic iceberg.

Aside from these somewhat risky traditional channels, current financial system innovations, such as derivatives, private banking, and electronic transfers, are other instruments used by the TCOs to launder their proceeds. It is' well known that a sizeable share of the 700,000 electronic transfers made each day carry funds at one stage or another of the 'wash cycle'.

Private banking in tax havens

In the age of globalization, banking havens, or offshore centres,[30] have become so important that it is worth taking a closer look at them. Almost half of the world's financial flows, as against 5 per cent in 1975, pass through these centres. This is where so-called private banks are headquartered, which manage an estimated $16 trillion in assets worldwide.[31]

Banking havens are better known as tax havens because, since their creation at the beginning of the twentieth century, their main role has been to harbour large fortunes on the run from the tax authorities in their home country. Financial globalization has changed all this. Today, offshore centres have broadened their range of services and clientele, offering privacy through private banking – that is, business anonymity. A 'private wealth advisor' based in the Cayman Islands sums up the value of his services: 'Offshore assets allow an individual an opportunity to pursue global opportunities in an anonymous manner, free from onerous regulations.'[32] In short, the tax havens have become the prime meeting place of TNCs' leaders, Mafia dons, corrupt politicians and terrorists, who all share a desire to circumvent laws in the pursuit of shameful objectives.

Offshore centres are officially recognized by the international financial establishment. They are defined as economic entities – countries, colonies, principalities, bailiwicks – where fiscal and monetary regulations regarding banking activities are lax, if they exist at all, and whose acknowledged purpose is to receive unlimited amounts of anonymous capital.[33] American law, for example, allows US-based multinationals to create subsidiaries called foreign sales corporations (FSCs) in banking havens, where they can deposit their foreign earnings and then transfer them, at will and tax-free, to their headquarters.[34] Michel Chossudovsky notes that in these centres, 'legal and illegal business are more and more intertwined, introducing a fundamental change in the structure of post-war capitalism.'[35] Two-thirds of the hedge funds are set up in banking havens. Almost all the large commercial banks have subsidiaries there, often under a nominee company. The Royal Bank of Canada is no exception. In the banking havens, it manages a subsidiary called RBC Global Private Banking (RBC stands for Royal Bank of Canada) specializing in private offshore business. In an advertorial published in *Offshore Finance Canada*, Senior Vice-President Michael Lagopoulos proudly announced to its distinguished customers that, as of 20 July 1998, RBC Global had acquired a Swiss private banking company in order to take advantage of 'highly experienced people trained by a world leader in our industry'.[36] The Swiss bankers' extensive experience in the money-laundering 'industry' is well known indeed.

There are 70 banking havens throughout the world, located in the Caribbean, of course, but also in Europe (Switzerland, Monaco, Liechtenstein, Luxembourg) and in Asia. Luxembourg (pop. 400,000) has 220 such banks. In Mauritius, the number of offshore institutions jumped from 10 in 1993 to several thousand today. The Cayman Islands (pop. 39,000) are, with their 450 banks, the fifth largest offshore centre in the world behind the City of London, New York, Tokyo and Hong Kong. Of the 50 largest financial institutions in the world, 45 have subsidiaries there. It is worth noting that this small haven is not a sovereign country, but rather a British colony, very properly administered by a governor representing the Crown, which is normally thought of as above suspicion. Nevertheless, fishy things are going on there, so much so that at its 1999 summit, the G7, of which the United Kingdom is a member, expressly named the Cayman Islands banking system a 'black hole of international regulation'.[37] Disturbing, yet the G7 – now G8 – and the United Kingdom still put up with it.

Spoils of corruption

Corruption has doubtless always existed, but, since the beginning of the 1990s, we are witnessing the globalization of corruption. Peter Eigen, a former senior official at the World Bank, had the courage to sound the alarm. In 1993, disgusted by what he saw daily within its walls and in field projects, he quit and founded *Transparency International*, a Germany-based organization specializing in anti-corruption work. He explained:

> I worked a long time for the World Bank and, at the end of my career, I concluded that all the projects I had worked on had been undermined, and even destroyed, by corruption.... Totally useless projects would be created because it was more lucrative for some to build a 50-million dollar highway than to give wheelbarrows and shovels to peasants to repair the existing roads.[38]

Peter Eigen mentions the case of multinational corporations that 'pay huge sums of money – millions of dollars – into the Swiss account of politicians who will find the arguments to defend an unjustifiable project'. Electronics transnational Siemens, for example, has admitted having paid over $100 million to a Singapore intermediary in order to land World Bank and other contracts.

When the media describe corruption in the Third World, they usually focus on the beneficiaries – that is, politicians and senior officials from underdeveloped countries. Mr Eigen thinks that the source of corruption lies on the supply side: 'The corruption wreaking havoc in these countries is a direct consequence of the behaviour of multinational companies based in rich industrialized countries that do not hesitate to hand out generous bribes in order to land contracts.'

Instead of fighting bribe payments abroad, the governments of rich countries encourage this practice by making these large sums tax-deductible. It was recently discovered that the French oil company Elf Aquitaine used a slush fund to bribe Third World leaders – to the tune of $20 billion over a twenty-year period. The costs were passed on to the consumers at the rate of one cent per litre of gas. Canadian companies behave similarly. Former Superintendent of Financial Institutions Michael Mackenzie was dismayed to observe that 'Canadian companies "buy" foreign governments as intensely as any other companies on Earth; almost all the money offered in bribes is subsidized by Canadian taxpayers.' About 95 per cent of the bribes given to foreign governments are declared as legitimate business expenses and deducted from federal taxes.[39]

International bodies are starting to worry about this phenomenon, observed in all industrialized countries. On 15 February 1999, the OECD, after years of bargaining and compromises, finally got its twenty-nine members to sign the Convention on Combating Bribery of Foreign Public Officials in International Business Transactions. But the agreement will not be implemented as long as parliaments do not implement it with laws criminalizing such behaviour.

As for the IMF, the official watchdog of the international financial system, it makes a pretence of denouncing such illicit operations. And what does it suggest as a solution? Stricter regulations might be expected, but in fact it prescribes the opposite. IMF experts believe that the 'ultimate source' of corruption lies with government restrictions and intervention, 'including trade restrictions (such as tariffs and import quotas), favoritist industrial policies (such as subsidies and tax deductions), price controls...'[40] Their reasoning is simple: if corruption is defined as breaking the law, it can be eliminated simply by eliminating the laws.

Rating Agencies

The role of financial rating agencies is to measure and anticipate the risks incurred by lending institutions on the thousands of loans extended each year to companies and governments. Their sole objective, assures the director of one of these agencies, 'consists in evaluating the chances that the capital and interests of a state, municipal or corporate issue will be honoured completely at maturity'.[41] Their assessments are based exclusively on economic and financial criteria. Although they take care not to give any social or political advice directly, they manage to do so indirectly. If a budget is too generous with social programmes or if its tax system is too compassionate towards low-income earners, it will receive a lower grade.

There are rating agencies in most countries, but for governments and large global market creditors, only two really count: Moody's Investor Service and Standard & Poor's (S&P). Both are headquartered in New York City, the financial hub of the world. Thousands of port-folio managers, currency speculators, finance ministers and government heads take their decisions based on Moody's and S&P ratings. These agencies closely scrutinize governments. Their organization chart in-cludes a division for rating sovereign nations.

Commenting on the latest Moody's ratings, the *New York Times* head-lined: 'The Man from Moody's Rules the World'.[42] A pithy statement, but no exaggeration. Every finance minister is haunted by the spectre of having his rating cut. Many go on a pilgrimage to New York just before or after tabling a budget to head off such an eventuality. A negative evaluation inevitably causes a rise in interest rates, and hence a larger debt service. This can cause panic on the financial markets. In April 1998, a rumour that Moody's was examining the advisability of main-taining Japan's 'Triple A' rating spread fear among investors and caused a mini-upheaval on the Japanese financial markets; the yen fell to its lowest level in seven years.

Contrary to what one would expect, borrowers, not lenders, pay the ratings agencies' fees. Almost all these borrowers are highly indebted and constantly in need of credit. In other words, governments pay the agencies to issue an opinion on their ability to pay, and thus on their capacity to manage public finances properly. Why do governments go to the trouble of having an external agency, completely foreign to the public interest, judge them? Because they are major borrowers and can expect no consideration from the lenders without an assessment by the two raters. An unrated government is like a college student without an academic transcript. This compulsory but voluntary subordination of governments was gradually brought into effect in the 1980s and 1990s, as governments lapsed into a culture of debt. The indebtedness was trivialized, even fostered, by national and international banks and financial institutions. Admittedly, despite declining deficits, the huge public debt is still there, and debt service and refinancing remain the largest budget items. This puts politicians in a vulnerable position with respect to decisions taken by creditors and their rating agencies.

Anxious to extend and consolidate their assessment monopoly, ratings agencies consider it their right to issue even unsolicited ratings. Thus a Colorado board of education that did not find it useful to submit itself to an assessment learned at its expense that it is not advisable to refuse to pay one's contribution to the judge (agency). It received a bad rating that more than one observer interpreted as an order to appear.

The USA, Capital of Globalization

The claim stated above that globalization transcends states needs to be qualified. There is one exception to this. The headquarters of globalization's mega-machine is more and more located in the United States. Everything is unfolding as if the American elite had long ago foreseen the advent of corporate transnationalization and had prepared itself to control the process without missing a turn. As during the Second World War, when the United States was convinced that the world needed its leadership, it is today imbued with a sort of calling to globalize.

The American political class and the transnational corporations have joined forces in order to prescribe the rules and rhythm of globalization. In the higher reaches of the American administration, politicians and big business give each other mutual support in the promotion of free trade and capital market liberalization. The Treasury Department, the Department of Commerce and the US Trade Representative have taken the lead in this crusade.

The United States has considerable tools and means at its disposal with which to implement this hegemonic project:

1. The dollar, established as the world currency at the Bretton Woods Conference in 1944, has since remained the international monetary system's sole reference currency. All other currencies fluctuate around the American dollar; this puts the United States in a privileged position compared with all other countries, allowing it to finance its foreign debt as well as lessen the impact of its huge trade and current-account deficit (around $400 billion in 2001). Two-thirds of the world's monetary reserves are in US dollars.[43]
2. The Federal Reserve exerts an undisputed influence on all financial markets; nobody on Earth has more power than its president, Alan

Greenspan. His decisions and hesitations affect the value of all currencies, your savings, your mortgage, and your pension fund. One word from Greenspan can send seismic waves through all the world's stock exchanges. His role as protector of the world currency – the dollar – makes him the tsar of the global financial system.

3. The IMF and the World Bank are headquartered in the capital of the United States, not far from the Treasury Department and the Federal Reserve. Throughout their careers, senior managers go back and forth between these four financial institutions. Under an unwritten agreement, the president of the United States appoints the president of the World Bank, and approves the appointment of the managing director of the IMF.

4. American companies dominate cyberspace. Financially and politically supported by the federal government since the Internet's inception, they have a commanding lead in new information technologies, a sector that remains the driving force of the global economy despite temporary setbacks.

5. American transnational corporations dominate every sector of the world's productive system, without exception. This includes five key sectors: finance, energy, pharmaceuticals, life industry, and new information technologies. The most recent figures show that the largest global firms tend to be American. Among the top 1,000 global giants by market value, there are 480 American companies. Among the 200 largest, 53 per cent are American; of the 100 largest, 57 per cent; of the 50 largest, 66 per cent; and of the 5 largest, 100 per cent.[44] Merger dynamics clearly favour American transnationals due to the well-known principle that big fish eat small fish and not the other way around.

6. The largest, most influential and active stock markets in the world are all located in the United States. In 2001, they represented 55 per cent of the world's total market capitalization of 21 trillion dollars, while European stock markets accounted for 29 per cent and Japanese 10 per cent.

7. The US military budget reached $380 billion in fiscal year 2002/3 – almost twice that of all the other industrialized countries combined. (In comparison, the United Kingdom's military budget is US$35 billion and Canada's is under US$7 billion.) And if 'homeland defense' spending is included, the American war budget is $650 billion.[45] This

overwhelming superiority allows the US to intervene at will any-where in the world – something it does not shy away from doing – and impose on its allies its military doctrine and strategies. The objective of US strategists is to prevent the resurgence of a power capable of challenging the United States and its status as the sole superpower.

8. As the dominant member of the North Atlantic Treaty Organization (NATO),[46] the United States has shaped this organization into its international military arm and a tool to control Europe. The Kosovo crisis and the Yugoslav war became the opportunity to supplant the United Nations as the world's official policeman and peacemaker in international conflicts.

And so the United States of America stands unchallenged. A trilateral world, in which Europe and Japan counterbalance American might, is a thing of the past. The enormous economic and political weight of its transnational corporations, together with its monetary and military arsenal, have converted the United States into the only real global power and the capital of globalization.

The Board of Directors of the Globalized World

On 25 September 1999, on the initiative of US Treasury Secretary Lawrence Summers, the financial G7 met in Washington, where it cre-ated 'the first board of directors of the global economy', in the words of Canadian finance minister Paul Martin, who participated in this historical meeting.[47] Not to be confused with the political G8, the financial G7 brings together the central bank governors and finance ministers of the seven richest countries in the world.[48] It quietly meets four times a year to assess the world's economic and financial situation. Its members also meet when there is an emergency, but in that case Canada and Italy are excluded. The financial G7 and the G5 are the link between financial circles and political bodies.

On its own initiative, and without prior democratic debate, the financial G7 decided to broaden its consultative base. It set up an entity comprising the central bank governors and finance ministers of 18 countries (11 OECD members including the G8 countries, South Africa,

Saudi Arabia, Argentina, Brazil, China and India), as well as the IMF and the World Bank. This group was christened the Group of 20 or G20. Its founders guaranteed that the private sector would be closely involved in the Group's discussions. It will be, insisted Mr Summers, 'an informal mechanism for an on-going dialogue'. A dialogue about what? All aspects of the world economy, in particular the 'architecture of the international financial system'.

Be that as it may, the G20 should only be considered an advisory council, because the real decisions are made elsewhere, in more exclusive circles, either at the monthly meetings of the Bank of International Settlements, or within the Financial G7 and, when all is said and done, in the various transnational lobbies, because the true centre of power is in the hands of those who own and manage mega-corporations. They are the main agents of globalization. The other players mentioned in this chapter are either fellow travellers such as the TCOs, or integrators such as international financial institutions, rating agencies and the WTO. As for the US government, it is globalization's attorney, police, central bank and bogeyman.

This is the first time in history that such a small number of traders and merchants, bankers and speculators, without any representation or responsibility, if only towards their anonymous shareholders, have succeeded in amassing so much financial, technological, organizational, ideological and political power that they have taken on the de facto leadership of the world.

John Jay, one of the founding fathers of American democracy, who, a short time after the independence donned the gown of Chief Justice of the Supreme Court, liked to claim, 'The people who own the country ought to govern it' – a statement which the masters of the new world order have taken to heart.

Box 3.1   Globalization takes a militaristic turn in 2001

2001 marked a turning point in world geopolitics. Shaken by the shock wave of 11 September, corroded from within by greed, and disturbed by the rise of dissent, global capitalism needed drastic changes. But rather than reform, it called upon the military–industrial complex to ensure its protection and further development. The government of the United States has resolutely taken the leadership of this militarization. Four symbolic dates mark this change in course:

11 September: Terrorists attack the WTC and the Pentagon   The blind jealousy of a band of desperadoes struck two of the Empire's most powerful symbols of triumphant globalization. By brutally attacking the wealth of the privileged world, this extremely perverse feat laid bare the unbearable inequity of a system that mercilessly impoverishes the poorest and outrageously enriches the wealthiest. President George W. Bush showed rare perspicacity in his on-the-spot analysis of the event: 'They are jealous of our success', he stated. Quite. This civilization of technology and mercantile individualism is too fragile to be surrounded by a sea of angry people.

7 October: The endless war against terrorism begins   The most powerful country in the world deployed its formidable military arsenal against Afghanistan, one of the most destitute countries in the world. And the leaders of America warn that they will wage this war against all countries that harbour terrorists – that is, throughout those underdeveloped regions where the opulent elite has severed its destiny from that of its unfortunate general population. In the rich countries, the new, hastily passed, anti-terrorist laws shall be used to repress the rising dissent of civil society. First heralded as a 'crusade', then as a 'war without end against terror', this campaign is in fact aimed at all opponents of globalization. It militarily buttresses a system whose excesses have made it both abominable and vulnerable. Words and ideas no longer suffice to sway the masses. The globalizers are now resorting to arms.

2 December: ENRON implodes   The US transnational Enron collapses, swept away by the greed of its corporate managers. Acting in complicity with the most prestigious investment banks and a leading financial auditing firm, these executives misappropriated funds to their advantage, thus sacking the company and pillaging its small-wage-earners. All this was done with the collusion of the political class and the guardians of the Stock Market temple. From Enron to WorldCom, the endless scandals shaking the megacorporations all have the same root: the unchecked ambition of the global power elite to hoard ever more and ever faster, in fealty to the slogan 'Get rich quick!' As economist Paul Krugman wrote, 'the Enron scandal, even more than 9/11, shall be a pivotal moment in the history of the United States.' Indeed, 2 December shone a light on the congenital defect of global capitalism: 'infectious greed'. That, at any rate, is the pithy assessment of Alan Greenspan, the president of the US Federal Reserve.

20 December: Crisis of the neoliberal model and popular uprising in Argentina
In Argentina, a popular movement beyond all political parties and social categories forced three unworthy presidents to resign in short order. Armed with pots and pans, the angry population rejected the entire political and economic class that had brought ruin upon the country, by slavishly espousing the dogmas of neoliberalism. Formerly one of the most prosperous nations in the world, Argentina is now bankrupt and living proof that the agents of globalization, the IMF and the World Bank, have led the Third World countries into a blind alley. This crisis demonstrates the faulty nature of a development strategy based on trade liberalization, uncontrolled foreign investment and external debt. It also poses an unprecedented challenge for civil society, that of reconstructing a country on new foundations, that of inventing new forms of democratic participation and self-development.

Another, no less significant, date also marked the major turning point that was the year 2001: On 30 January, in Porto Alegre, the first World Social Forum was inaugurated with countless representatives of civil society arriving from everywhere on Earth. They were there to announce that another world is necessary and possible.

CHAPTER 4

The Overseers

They are addicts of pure power, quite simply divorced from the questions of morality. This amoral quality of our leadership is essential to understanding the nature of our times.

John Saul

The masters of the globalized world – the hyper-oligarchy described in Chapter 3 – can't do it all on their own. All by themselves, they cannot manage the global economy's mega-machine, establish favourable production conditions, protect private property, ensure the social peace required for a smooth running economy, and control population flows. No matter how powerful this small group might be, to rule over such a large estate – the Earth – it needs faithful allies and assistants. These masters need obedient, efficient, intrepid and loyal managers who, just like them, are ambitious and eager to get rich quick. Without these overseers, not only would the global oligarchy fail to manage the new economic system, it would also find it socially and politically impossible to defend its own interests. As a result, it must pay a premium price to a large administrative class.

Who are these indispensable assistants? How does the global oligarchy win over the dedicated services of this army of overseers to manage globalization? What are the features of this rich but subordinate planetary overclass, which might also be called the global bourgeoisie? (see Box 4.1).

Box 4.1   Social classes and globalization

Social classes are large interest groups differentiated from one another by their position in the economic system, their role in the social organization of work, and their greater or lesser share of collective wealth. Any full-scale reorganization of an economic system necessarily entails a reconfiguration of social classes.

As a result, the globalization of the economy has given birth to a new social class, or, rather, to two new global social classes sharing the same interests. At the top, one finds a global oligarchy: the masters of the globalized world. Below them, a new type of bourgeoisie is emerging, a global bourgeoisie made up of globalization's overseers: corporate executives, top-ranking technocrats and high-level politicians. Just like all governing classes, the global oligarchy and bourgeoisie show great cohesion and vigorously defend their share of the economic pie. And that share is never big enough to satisfy their appetite.

Most members of the global bourgeoisie come from national bourgeoisies that have dumped their former allies, the middle classes, to forge an alliance with the global oligarchy. These two global hyperclasses do not overlap with the national bourgeoisies; they are, instead, replacing them. In this new situation, the middle classes have become redundant. This is why we are witnessing the gradual decline of the middle classes and the emergence of an underclass composed of the downtrodden, outcasts, migrants, the working poor, temporary workers, and all the other 'damned of the Earth'.

The International of Global Overseers

There are three main categories of global overseers: chief executive officers (CEOs) of large corporations, senior bureaucrats and high-level politicians. They are the taskmasters in charge of putting labour to work, maintaining order and efficiency and handing collective wealth over to private transnational interests. They are all people of power, technocrats that control the three sources of power: information, organization and technology. Their position establishes them as essential intermediaries between the people, including the middle classes, and the real holders of power, the transnationals.

Supporting each other and at the same time often competing for the same promotions, CEOs, mandarins and politicians can easily switch from one category to another.

Former corporate executives commonly head regulatory agencies. When bureaucrats quit government service they are often hired by corporations – many go on to lobby their former colleagues on behalf of their new employers. Corporate executives serve in cabinets and ministries. Advisory committees appointed by many governments are dominated by corporations and industry associations, linking private interests to public authorities.[1]

Larry Summers' story is a case in point. Chief economic adviser at the World Bank (1991–93), he was named US Treasury Undersecretary and Deputy Secretary in 1993 before being anointed Treasury Secretary in 1999. Forced to leave in 2001, after the Democrats lost the presidential elections and George W. Bush's team took office, he soon became president of Harvard University.

The global oligarchy secures the loyal and devoted services of these mercenaries of globalization by giving them a sizeable share of the economic pie; by seeing to it that they are generously compensated and by fostering their ambition of being ever better paid, rewarded and promoted. This is how mutual co-operation is created and why certain interests are shared between the masters and the overseers of the global village. Their common objective is to 'get rich quick'. Although overpaid, the overseers constantly compare their situation with that of better-paid peers to demand ever more.

In 1999, Royal Bank president John Cleghorn received $6.7 million in compensation – the same as the total income of the bank's 420 worse-paid employees. Facing questions from journalists, the bank's communications director stated that he understood the astonishment of ordinary people when they hear such figures taken out of context. But, he explained, 'when you look at what some of the new economy CEOs and the market cap that some of these companies are commanding these days, I think Mr. Cleghorn's compensation and that of our senior executives actually compares quite favourably.'[2]

When it comes to money, the nouveaux riches lose all sense of proportion. Their class consciousness having freed them from any obligation towards civil society, they all stand together in their amorality. This solidarity is revealed by the zeal with which they protect each other. They jealously see to the maintenance of a written or unwritten no-fault system protecting them from any social responsibility. In a *Time* magazine interview on the series of corporate crimes made public after the collapse of Enron, activist Ralph Nader explained that the most surprising aspect of the saga was the complete collusion between all of the business world's actors:

> What amazes me is that there are thousands of people who could have been whistle-blowers, from the boards of directors to corporate insiders to the accounting firms to the lawyers working for these firms to the credit-rating agencies. All these people! Would a despotic dictatorship have been more efficient in silencing them and producing the perverse incentives for them all to keep quiet? The system is so efficient that there's total silence. I mean, the Soviet Union had enough dissidents to fill Gulags.[3]

John Saul, author of *Voltaire's Bastards*, notes that globalization technocrats 'understand events within the logic of the system.... They are addicts of pure power, quite simply divorced from the questions of morality. This amoral quality of our leadership is essential to understanding the nature of our times.'[4] And to understand our elite's amorality, one must realize that they are in the service of a global plutocracy whose sole value is profits.

The Global Economy's Supermanagers

Among the overseers of globalization are, first, the giant corporate supermanagers, or chief executive officers. These are employees hired by a corporation's board of directors to manage the company and its numerous subsidiaries. Whatever their title might be – president, chief executive officer, director or production manager – the fact is that they don't own the corporation. It is of little importance whether they own company shares or not. As army chiefs of staff, they are not admitted in the exclusive club of the true masters of the world, that of the large corporations' main shareholders.

These supermanagers have a clear mandate: maximize profits. They are assessed only according to the company's performance – that is, its profits, its sales, the growth of its assets and, above all, the dividends paid to its shareholders. They behave differently from the real owners since they can be fired at the first sign of a dip in profitability. This makes them more zealous, more ambitious and more ruthless. In other respects, the competitiveness requirements imposed by globalization make the board of directors more demanding. CEOs are called on to deliver the goods in the very short term. Some 58 percent of American CEOs last no more than five years at the head of a company, compared with 46 per cent in 1980. Furthermore, only 23 per cent stay between six and ten years today, compared with 41 per cent in 1980.[5]

However, this lack of job security does not depress them. There will always be another company ready to hire them, because once they become members of this prestigious caste, they enjoy lifetime protection. A fired CEO never leaves empty-handed. Witness the mediocre CEO who, in 1998, caused the spectacular collapse of the transnational corporation Waste Management. When dismissed, he left with a handsome termination allowance of $14 million. How could an employee having reached the height of incompetence succeed in leaving with such a large portion of the shareholders' assets? The answer: as very sophisticated technocrats, CEOs never sign a contract if it does not include a valuable severance package. The scandals that led to the recent dismantling of Tyco International revealed unscrupulous methods practised by its senior executives. The corporation's general counsel, Mark A. Belnick, indicted in September 2002, even had a provision in his contract giving him 'a hefty termination payment – up to $10.6 million – even if he were to be convicted of a felony'.[6] One wonders how the board could ever agree to such a thing. The answer: infinite complicity.

CEOs are also richly rewarded in hard cash for good performance of their duties, earning 500 times the average wage of their employees.[7] Their compensation includes a basic salary, bonuses, production bonuses and, especially, share options. As Business Week notes, 'salaries and bonuses are now an afterthought compared with the potential wealth that options represent' for this class of wage-earners. 'Once a minor perk, options have come to account for 80% of the executive-compensation pie.' In 2001, American CEOs received an average of $11 million in compensation. The CEO of Oracle was the best paid with an incredible $706.1 million. The tenth best paid CEO on that list received $64.6 million.[8]

This compensation model, involving the granting of shares or stock options, was developed by large American corporations to stimulate manager productivity to the utmost. Acting on the advice of the compensation committee, the board assigns a certain number of shares to the corporation's senior managers at a very preferential price, often

completely free of charge, allegedly according to merit. The beneficiary
is free to resell these shares on the market at the right time – that is,
when he deems the moment is ideal to maximize his profits. Should
the share price stagnate or slump, the beneficiary loses nothing; he can
simply wait. As a critical-minded small shareholder noted: 'It's sort of
heads I win, tails let's flip again.' This practice, which has spread throughout the world, encourages executives to adopt a short-term management style. By rapidly increasing dividends paid to shareholders, *ipso
facto* they maximize their own earnings, since as a result the compensation committee hastens to grant them more stock options.

What justifies such lofty compensation packages? The interested
parties simply answer: the market. They claim that they turn down,
almost every day, far more generous job offers from other institutions.
The fact is that these great management strategists form a caste, a social
class whose members, imbued with hubris, grant each other undeserved
privileges. CEOs earn so much because the compensation committee is
made up of senior executives from the same company or affiliated companies. In a word, everyone's stratospheric compensation is due to a
buddy system rather than to the law of supply and demand – buddies
who, given the chance, become inveterate scoundrels. A case in point,
the looting of Computer Associates International by three of its executives, shows how greedy these executives can be. On 22 July 1998, the
corporation's CEO, president and senior vice-president together cashed
in over $1 billion by selling, at current market price, their options. In
all, they had received 21 million shares free of charge. This was an
entirely legal operation approved by the annual general meeting. How
could the shareholders be so generous towards their employees? A *Business Week* analyst explained that 'pay proposals are often written in language that's difficult even for the pros to fathom.' Executive pay critic
Graef 'Bud' Crystal said he would have had to do a day's worth of
computer modelling to figure out the [Computer Associates] plan's
impact.' This confirms yet again that the annual general meeting of large
corporations is a farce.[9]

As the entire world observed in the recent scandals of highly
renowned corporations such as Enron and WorldCom, the craving for
prestige and getting rich quick is so strong within this overclass that
some executives don't shy away from increasing their already exorbitant
income through totally fraudulent practices. A worldwide study of 11,000

Box 4.2 Envy, greed and corruption

In the 1980s, through relentless work, Ivan Boesky, an expert super-manager in speculative trading, raider and arbitrageur by profession, had just barely succeeded in making it onto one of the numerous lists of multimillionaires that American business magazines regularly publish. Although he was at the very bottom of the list, he had finally succeeded in appearing among the wealthiest people in the United States. Now, as it happens, soon after receiving this honour, he participated in one of the most important criminal conspiracies in Wall Street history, a misdeed that landed him behind bars. What demons could have driven this already rich and talented financier to indulge in criminal acts? Sure enough, the demon of greed. But also envy, that terrible disease that consumes the upstarts of the global petty bourgeoisie. His wife later related that the very day her husband's name appeared on the *Forbes* list, he arrived home depressed and in a very bad mood. In front of his wife, surprised to see him react so badly to such good news, he thundered: 'We're nothing. We're nowhere. We're at the bottom of the list and I promise you I won't shame you like that again. We will not remain at the bottom of that list.'

Source: The story of Boesky and his associates is detailed in James B. Stewart, *Den of Thieves*, New York: Simon & Schuster, 1991. The interview with his wife Seema was reported in *New Internationalist*, April 1997.

multinational executives carried out by the Ernst & Young accounting firm found 'that fraud is commonplace in large corporations'. Over 60 per cent of serious frauds against these corporations are committed by senior management. The head of the study explained that 'accountants and managers have always relied on internal controls', but 'in today's competitive environment' this is no longer enough.[10]

In a recent report entitled 'Why corporate crooks are tough to nail', *Business Week* wondered if 'the rogue gallery of irresponsible execs who have populated the business pages over the past several months will finally go to jail?' before answering: 'Don't count on it.' The reason: 'The laws regulating companies are ambiguous, juries have a hard time grasping abstract financial concepts, and, well-counselled executives have plenty of tricks for distancing themselves from responsibility.'[11]

CEOs must meet their corporation's efficiency requirements. If they still retain any personal values, they are torn between their own code of ethics and the corporation's code of efficiency – a recipe for chronic schizophrenia. In the end, it is always and without fail the corporation's code that prevails, as demonstrated by the following classic example of a model CEO's pathetic moral flip-flop.

Warren M. Anderson was managing Union Carbide[12] in India when the most deadly industrial and environmental catastrophe in history occurred. In 1984, a factory in Bhopal owned by the chemicals multinational released extremely toxic gas into the atmosphere, poisoning some 500,000 people, of which at least 16,000 died in atrocious conditions. Today, some 200,000 other victims are still suffering from the effects of this disaster. At the time, Anderson was so shattered that he stated to the media he was willing to dedicate the rest of his life to repair the damages caused by his company to the community and stricken families. But barely a year later, he had changed his mind. Still at the helm of Union Carbide, he indicated that his initial reaction had been exaggerated and that he was now ready to lead the corporation's legal battle against the damage claims of Bhopal's citizens and the government of India. What happened? At first, Warren Anderson had simply reacted as any other normal human being would. But on further consideration and after his superiors admonished him for being too sensitive, he was forced to choose. Had he persisted in upholding his personal values and acknowledging the harm the company had caused, he certainly would have been dismissed.[13]

The Mandarins in Power

The second category of overseers includes the senior executives or mandarins[14] of the state apparatus – ministries and public agencies – and of international organizations. Since most cabinet ministers have but a superficial knowledge of the matters in their charge, and being as busy as they are in preparing their re-election, they must always depend on their deputy ministers. These ambitious but discreet lieutenants work behind the scenes, their power stemming from their complete and often exclusive knowledge of issues. As is well known, whoever controls information controls power.

Let us not forget that, in the British parliamentary system, the prime minister rules by using two channels within the government machine: that of the elected ministers and that of the technocrats appointed at his discretion. He chooses and appoints both kinds of servants. However, while he must spare the feelings of ministers, who are after all elected public officials, and take into consideration their nuisance potential, there is no need for him to take similar precautions with the mandarins, who have no legitimacy beyond the fact that they were chosen by him. Depending on the circumstances, he uses one or the other channel, and if need be, he has them compete against each other. Nevertheless, mandarins remain the most reliable and most efficient of the two, as long as these indispensable overseers are treated properly.

Senior civil servants are either graduates of prestigious business schools or, in many cases, have acquired their expertise on the job. Most of them are careerists who work hard to keep their position and continue their climb up the professional ladder. They attend senior management development courses given by their corporate associations. Some of them travel widely, sharing their management experience and methods with foreign colleagues. The most prominent mandarins maintain close ties with major international organizations, including the Organization for Economic Cooperation and Development. Recognized as the club of rich countries, the OECD's main mission is to harmonize the policies of its member countries. Since the early 1990s, this has mainly consisted in adapting national policies to the imperatives of globalization. To this end, the OECD has paid special attention to the training and development of top-ranking civil servants. By the hundreds, they file into the lecture halls of Château de la Muette, the headquarters of the OECD in Paris, to attend conferences, seminars and a plethora of negotiation and information sessions.

The mandarins' influence can also be felt in international economic negotiations. They are the only ones within the government to grasp thoroughly the key issues of global trade, finance, technology, commodities, and so on. They inform their ministers in a timely fashion and convince them to adopt solutions according to the requirements of the moment. Public opinion is usually informed only when it is already too late. And it is only when well-organized and worried citizens raise their voices that ministers take some of their demands into account.

The loyalty and devotion of this army of senior civil servants is secured through salaries, fringe benefits, job security and hopes of receiving a rewarding promotion or appointment to a prestigious institution. While governments hold back on unemployment insurance benefits, parental leave and pay equity, mandarins get the VIP treatment: rises, in some years, of up to 15 per cent, especially for the select group of five or six senior civil servants in charge of keeping the government apparatus on side with globalization. The remuneration pecking order is a major issue in these circles. The media take care to propagate the myth that the quality of public service depends directly on the total payroll granted to the mandarins. As for the mandarin's job security, it is bullet-proof. Changes of government bring about the reshuffling of the upper reaches of the civil service, but a senior civil servant is never fired or demoted. If he or she must be excluded because of flagrant incompetence or lack of allegiance towards the party in power or his boss, a promotion is offered by way of compensation.

Politicians Subservient to Globalization

High-level politicians – that is, heads of state and government, finance ministers and treasury secretaries – make up the third category of globalization overseers. As objective allies of the global hierarchy, these politicians are far from being innocent victims of globalization. On the contrary, they have become its attentive servants, surrendering voluntarily to the very forces they are supposed to control. And this is happening not only in Third World dictatorships or in countries undermined by corruption, but also here, in our venerable and respectable Western democracies.

Indeed, those in power are themselves organizing their own capitulation. In treaty after treaty, in law after law, governments and parliaments are clearing whatever obstacles may impede the concentration of wealth and power in the hands of the masters of the world. From the liberalization of currency markets, in the 1970s, to NAFTA, to Maastricht, and the recent piecemeal ceding of nation-state sovereignty orchestrated by the WTO, the politicos themselves created a situation they no longer can or wish to control. Under their guidance, the state now stands against the nation in promoting the reduction of wage-earners' purchasing power, cuts in the social safety net, the privatization of health care, lax environmental laws, and the fire sale of public state-owned companies. Transnational corporations now consider those in power as simple tenderers in charge of auctioning off their country piece by piece.

Two political leaders exemplify this abdication for the benefit of the masters of the global economy: Margaret Thatcher, elected prime minister of the United Kingdom in 1979; and Ronald Reagan, who took office as president of the United States in January 1981. The almost simultaneous rise of these two politicians was no accident of history. At the time, the two countries were the centre of gravity and anchor point of 75 per cent of the world's multinationals and transnationals. The Thatcher–Reagan duo would show government leaders throughout the world what the new words 'privatization' and 'deregulation' really meant. And to complete the abdication, they would prescribe public spending cuts particularly in health, education, housing and the environment, in order to reduce the role of the public sector.

Whenever Mrs Thatcher's government had to choose between these prescriptions and the welfare of its own citizens, she had the habit of saying 'There is no alternative!' This phrase would be repeated so often in her speeches that some satirists christened her Mrs TINA. In a special issue celebrating 'the 100 revolutionary leaders of the twentieth century', *Time* magazine called her a revolutionary and paid tribute to her deeds as 'Britain's biggest contribution to practical economics in the world since John M. Keynes invented Keynesianism or even Adam Smith published *The Wealth of Nations*'.[15] This is somewhat exaggerated since she simply carried out orders at the behest of Great Britain's giant corporations. And she did it with an iron hand, by first attacking the so-called 'uncontrolled power of the unions'. By simply outlawing the coalminers' strike, she taught an object lesson to all of Great Britain's stunned unionists.

A staunch defender of private enterprise and fervent admirer of Margaret Thatcher, Ronald Reagan followed her advice and example. He too started by bringing the unions to heel by unceremoniously firing every single striking air traffic controller. He then initiated a deregulation process involving the elimination or de-fanging of antitrust and labour legislation enacted throughout the twentieth century. The

Thatcher–Reagan counterreform would be copied by practically every political leader in the world.

In the Third World, the complacency of the 'aidocracy', the new political class created by official development assistance, is no less blatant. Recently, the president of the Securities and Exchange Board of India called on his government to follow 'the Thatcherite model of privatization'. Recalling the Iron Lady's wisdom, he urged concerned ministers to sell, even at a discount price, state corporation shares in order 'to make the public sector really and truly owned by the public'.[16] This emulator of the Western overseers fails to add that when public corporations of underdeveloped countries are put on the auction block, transnationals, and not ordinary citizens, get their hands on them first.

What drives globalization's political overseers to emasculate themselves voluntarily? Salaries are not the only reason. If one compares their remuneration to the compensation of CEOs, they pass for the volunteers of globalization. In fact, power and prestige mean a lot to them. Closely covered by the media, prime ministers and finance ministers have become television stars. Moreover, for many of them, politics, which is in itself gratifying in many respects, only represents a springboard, a launching pad for more lucrative positions. Look where the former prime ministers and ministers who were the least bit ambitious are today. They have all secured positions where they can grow rich a lot faster than if they had skipped their tour of duty in politics.

In these times, it is hard to find political leaders governing on the basis of the public interest and taking into account the Earth's future. Ours is an age in which politicians don't seem to see or understand the huge environmental and social problems piling up in a context of unlimited economic growth. Unconditional defenders of globalization, they follow the advice of the IMF, which never misses an opportunity to restate that the current international economy is bringing about 'a profound evolution in views about the relative roles of government and market forces in the economic process'. From now on, what will be the mission of heads of government? The IMF oracle is unequivocal: 'The role of government is to allow and support, not to restrain and compete with, private initiative.'[17]

Whereas the political leaders' role in the globalization process is simply to act as servants, they set themselves up as genuine potentates within the government machinery. Observers of the contemporary political scene have concluded that the prime minister and the finance minister today have monopolized all power. Political scientist Donald Savoie spent six years in the corridors of power in Ottawa to flesh out his recent work on the concentration of power in the Canadian political system. He found that

> The idea of Cabinet as a collective, confederal-type decision-making body no longer applies. The notion was invented at the time the prime minister was *primus inter pares* and both concepts now belong only to our history books. Only the prime minister and the minister of finance, through the budget, can decide when and how to land on a policy issue or even a new spending commitment.[18]

In the British parliamentary system, party discipline forces members of parliament and ministers to submit to official orthodoxy. If, by chance, one of them dares to vote against the leader's motion, he is sure to be excommunicated. In 99 per cent of the cases, they chose to follow the party line rather than their own conscience. In the American presidential system, where party discipline is less coercive, it is the lobby groups, the official representatives of the campaign fund backers, who do most of the work in compelling senators and representatives to toe the line. Everything is happening as if our political systems had used up their democratic potential and were gradually slipping into 'democratic centralism', a system created long ago by Bolshevik totalitarianism.

During the last US presidential election campaign, the 1,000 largest US companies donated over $187 million to the candidates from the two main parties, an increase of $20 million compared with the 1996 campaign. Those who give such sums to a candidate or a party obviously expect favours in return in the form of administrative decisions that are favourable to them. Nobody wants to look at the consequences this has on the system because it is clear that it has perverted representative democracy as it is practised today.

Throughout Europe, one can also observe the corrosive effect corruption has on democracy. And most of the time, it is the heads of state who set immoral examples. It seems as if no political party that holds power or that has a chance of holding power is spared.

Ralph Nader, a long-time US consumer advocate and defender of democracy, eloquently demonstrated how elected officials vote on the key issues of globalization without realizing what they are doing. In 1994, when Congress was about to ratify the agreement creating the WTO, Public Citizen, an NGO founded by Nader, offered $10,000 to any senator or representative who would meet two easy conditions: (1) sign an affidavit stating that they had read the 500-page agreement; and (2) successfully answer ten simple questions about its contents. Only one senator took up the challenge of this unique contest. He signed and, before the Senate Committee on Foreign Relations, correctly answered Public Citizen's ten questions. He then stated that he had originally intended to vote for the agreement, but, after having read the text, he was against it. Congress submissively ratified the agreement creating the WTO under the terms dictated by international senior civil servants and the Business Roundtable.[19]

In the end, whether there is a party line or not, a parliamentary or presidential regime, a conservative or socialist party, all systems and all political families are following the imperatives of globalization so well that they have all come to look the same. Once in office, the politicos adapt themselves. The party programme doesn't matter any more. A cynic has observed that two members of parliament where one is conservative and the other socialist have more in common than two socialists where one is a member of parliament and the other a grassroots member.

Why be surprised, given these observations, that citizens have completely lost faith in the political class? They don't believe in it any more. John B. Judis, one of the most insightful political commentators and most committed observers in Washington, shows how this situation has come to be: 'Together, the irresponsibility of the nation's elites, the power and proliferation of special interest groups, and the paralysis of Congress and the executive have contributed to a corrosive public cynicism.'[20]

The G8 Superstars of the Political Scene

Every year, the heads of the eight richest countries in the world meet to discuss the big issues of the day. The Group of Eight (originally Seven), or G8, is made up of Canada, France, Germany, Italy, Japan, Russia, the United Kingdom and the United States. Originally designed as a 'fireside meeting' of good and wise political leaders preoccupied by the world's economic and financial problems, the G8 summit gradually became a solemn high mass intended prominently to display the majesty of its celebrants. Hundreds of bureaucrats burdened with thick files assist the world political superstars in the wings. Some 2,000 reporters, technicians, analysts and other sycophants bustle about to give maximum media coverage to the spectacle and broadcast the images of these great politicians, so deserving of all honours, to every home on the globe.

What should one think of this exclusive club? Doesn't the G8 represent a world government of sorts? The unofficial objective of these luxurious annual summits is precisely to demonstrate in a dazzling way that there is indeed a world political leadership, embodied in this self-proclaimed directorate. Nevertheless, to the keen observer, the spectacle has the opposite effect. It demonstrates the impotence of these eight important politicians, who instead seem to be actors following a script written elsewhere. For they decide nothing. They offer no solutions to the dangers threatening the planet, nor to the outrageous poverty afflicting four-fifths of the world's population, nor to the destruction of the ecosystems, nor to pollution, nor to the proliferation of organized crime. All they do is support what others have already decided, taking care to announce only that which may enhance their public image.

Why the G8? Why these costly summits? (The 2000 summit cost the Japanese $750 million.) This question invariably resurfaces at each annual celebration, usually held in July. 'This so-called "directorate of the world economy" is never anything else but a meeting of heads of state primarily worried about their own interests', deplores *The Economist*. The G8 has demonstrated that it is totally incapable of providing leadership by solving the serious problems within its reach. The British magazine detects the cause of this helplessness in the 'emergence of new factors, and particularly of globalization ..., which has taken all economic power away from governments.'[21] Here we have a very conservative magazine acknowledging the antidemocratic character of globalization.

Here are a few examples of the G8's distressing vacuity. In 1994, it voiced its support for the 'flexibility' of labour and of labour costs, taking its cue a few months earlier from the OECD and the global economy's big bosses. In 1995, in Halifax, the final communiqué, prepared as always by bureaucrats, was leaked to the media two days before the summit, seriously undermining the significance of this social gathering. In 1996, looking into the underdeveloped countries' debt problem, the eight urged their Third World colleagues to 'create a favourable environment' for direct foreign investment; and, clearly showing their colours, claimed in their final communiqué that 'economic growth and progress are closely linked to the globalization process'. In 1997, they expressed their 'strong concern' regarding the debt of the least advanced countries. In 1998, in the middle of a disastrous financial crisis, they urged Asian countries, ruined because they had followed the IMF's advice, to closely observe the instructions of the very same organization. The director of the IMF was there in person to prompt this piece of advice to the politicians. Indeed, since 1996, the director of the IMF, the president of the World Bank and the secretary-general of the WTO all participate discreetly but efficiently in the economic sessions of the G8.

The most concrete decision of the G8 in 1999 was a promise to cancel the debts of the poorest countries. Meeting in Okinawa a year later, the same leaders renewed the same promise, confessing in this way that they had not met the preceding year's commitment.

In July 2001, in Genoa, 150,000 demonstrators representing thousands of civil society organizations gathered to expose the hoax that these sumptuous meetings really are, meetings whose sole objective is to support the progress of globalization. As has been the case since Seattle, the Great Powers called an aggressive police force to the rescue, producing one death and hundreds of wounded, and ransacking the alternative media's offices. All this to announce in a final press release that 'the G8 is committed to boosting growth'.

The Secession of the Global Elites

Globalization has created a new global class. 'Their members', write Andrew Simms, 'see themselves as avant-garde, living in a brave new world of performance-driven individualism and the unrestrained operation of market forces.... Their identity is built around a quasi-religious belief in orthodox economics. Pushing the universal truism of unrestrained free-market economics on a global scale as the ultimate organizational principle for a rational human society.'[22]

In *The Work of Nations*, Robert Reich explains that globalization euphoria has resulted in the separation of the selfish interests of the super-rich classes from the larger interests of the population in general. Reich contends that the three categories of globalization overseers have formed a sacred and supranational alliance in which their professional and personal interests hinge on the objectives of globalization, which is so profitable for them. This has created for the global overseers a virtual reality floating above the daily existence of local communities. Reich is shocked and worried by what he calls the 'politics of secession of the new elites'.[23]

CHAPTER 5

The Ideology of Globalization

The system's real strength lies not in the violence of the dominant class nor in the coercive power of the state apparatus, but rather in the citizen's acceptance of the world-view of those who rule them.

Antonio Gramsci

To be accepted by the general public, and even by its victims, globalization needs to be presented in a discourse making it credible, legitimate, benevolent and, above all, inevitable and irreversible. This discourse is called 'neoliberalism', which is the ideology of globalization. What are the origins of neoliberalism and its founding dogmas? Who develops this ideology with its apparently implacable logic? Who disseminates it? Who preaches it?

Behind any ideology, there are always interests, the interests of a dominant group. The ideological discourse is created and sponsored by the group holding power and capable of imposing its world-view according to its interests. This group also has the means to hire ideologues: philosophers, intellectuals, sophists, moralists, theologians, communicators, journalists, and others skilled at handling ideas and words. Economists are the most important manufacturers of neoliberal ideology. They are the ones who, historically, designed and built this system of ideas and values, based on quantified observations and statistics, of course, but also and above all on a certain view of humankind and society — that is, on postulates.

A Brief History of Liberalism and Neoliberalism

The history of liberal and neoliberal ideology closely parallels that of economics. Both liberalism and the new science of economics emanated from nascent capitalism, which they tried to rationalize. They followed its evolution and its numerous upheavals up to and including globalization. The following short historical overview describes the visions of the six most important theorists in the history of political economy and its underlying ideology.

Adam Smith, the father of liberalism and modern economic thought

In the beginning there was liberalism, or classic liberalism, developed by Scotsman Adam Smith (1723–90). Smith intervened when the new capitalist mode of production was taking shape in England, a mode featuring mechanization, an innovative way of organizing the workplace and a considerable influx of capital from the previous period. He witnessed the birth of capitalism, which marks a true revolution in production and trade. He would become the theorist of this revolutionary economic practice and its effects on social structures.

Smith was no economist, nor a businessman, nor a company manager. He was a quiet professor of logic and moral philosophy who succeeded in gaining the favour of a certain aristocracy. At 40, he was appointed tutor to the young Duke of Buccleuch, for which he would receive a relatively comfortable lifetime pension, allowing him to write and travel, to France in particular.

Many authors before Smith had pondered on the economic organization of society. For example, at the same time, the French physiocratic[1] school of thought maintained that agriculture was the supreme form of economic activity as a source of wealth for the kingdom. The physiocrats also advocated the free circulation of agricultural commodities throughout the national territory, without state intervention, to liberate the forces of the land. They invented liberalism's well-known slogan: 'Laissez faire, laissez passer.' They claimed that the state should not control the market but should let its subjects enrich themselves. During his trips to France, Smith met with the physiocrats Quesnay and Turgot, with whom

---

Box 5.1   What is ideology?

Ideology is the programming of thought. It is a system of ideas, beliefs and values spread by a dominant social group better to establish its hegemony over all of society. Ideology provides a world-view and exudes a universe of values that suggest standard conduct. It is both a description and a prescription: it describes reality by interpreting it in a given manner and prescribes what should be thought and done to be normal. Once the system of thought is set in people's minds, they feel their submission to the regime as the product of their own judgement and conscience. A distinctive feature of ideology is that it functions incognito, presenting itself as basic common sense. The most dangerous ideologues are those who believe they are free from all ideologies. In short, in modern society, ideology plays the same role as that of religion or mythology in previous eras.

When necessary, ideologies coin new words and expressions to interpret the world in favour of dominant interests. Unemployment insurance becomes 'employment insurance'; the sick, 'beneficiaries' or 'clients'; and massive layoffs, 'rationalizations'. 'Words are the body armour of the established order' according to Herbert Marcuse.

Ideologies are so powerful that even the system's victims end up believing that their situation is inevitable and considering their lot as normal. Submitting oneself is perceived not as a disgrace but rather – supreme alienation! – as a fair distribution of roles in the best of worlds. If there are so many unemployed, poor and outcasts in our rich industrialized societies, it is because public opinion has ended up accepting and deeming it normal that the system – the best in the world! – produces so many losers.

Submission to the dominant ideology is obtained in a thousand ways, particularly through education, sermons, advertisements, political discourse and media conditioning.

---

he compared the state of France's economy with that of his own country where the new industries were producing an unprecedented abundance of wealth. He challenged their main thesis that agriculture must predominate over industry but borrowed from them an idea he considered fundamental: the free circulation of goods in the domestic market.

Back in England, Smith wrote his main work, in which he ex-
pounded a view contrary to that of the physiocrats: the new factory
production mode, he asserted, is a country's main source of wealth. He
aimed at rationally explaining this 'factory economy', which, regulated
by the market, has the virtue of multiplying goods and rapidly enriching
the new industrial classes and the entire nation. In a nearly 1,000-page
book published in 1776, Smith analysed in fine detail the workings of
factory manufacturing and the commercial flow of mass-produced goods.
His fascinating essay _An Inquiry into the Nature and Causes of the Wealth
of Nations_ thoroughly describes these workings, and above all provides
a global interpretation that remains to this day the cornerstone of all the
economics treatises used in our universities, even though most economists never even read it.

When Smith started writing this economics treatise, he already had
strong views on the morals of individuals, human passions, society and
private property. In his famous _The Theory of Moral Sentiments_,[2] he
conceived society as a set of rational and perfectly selfish individuals
driven by an innate desire to improve their lot – that is, to enrich
themselves and lead more comfortable lives. Moreover, Smith was part
of the Enlightenment. For him, as for Hume, Rousseau and Voltaire,
individual freedom is a fundamental element which necessarily involves
the right to own, produce and trade. This freedom, like security, is
inconceivable without state protection. And the state's main role is just
that: to defend individual freedoms and private property. This is an
absolute, inviolable and sacred right, which is essential for the entrepreneur's and merchant's freedom to manoeuvre. Such are the postulates
underlying Smith's economic and political theory.

Starting from these premisses, Smith wanted to demonstrate that
economics and social questions are intertwined in a functional movement, similar to the mechanical workings of heavenly bodies subjected
to the law of universal gravitation, which his compatriot Isaac Newton
had discovered and brilliantly explained several decades earlier. A great
admirer of Newton, Smith sought an equivalent explanation in the
field of human endeavour, where he believed a universal law must exist
accounting for everything else. He saw the market as this regulating,
universal and infallible mechanism ordering and structuring all economic
activity and, by the same token, the entire social system.

The mechanism operates on the domestic market, where the suppliers and purchasers of goods and services meet. For Smith, all human beings are producers, and the goods and services they produce are marketable commodities. Smith stresses that free and fair competition, in the market, between all the perfectly selfish individual interests determines the best possible price for the seller and the buyer, since each of them trades freely and makes a fully informed decision. Consequently, the optimal price ensures maximum production in quantity and quality, since it is obvious that everyone tries to offer and acquire the best products at the best price, according to their talent and means.

Smith's economic philosophy is summed up in a famous passage of *The Wealth of Nations*:

> It is not from the benevolence of the butcher, the brewer, or the baker, that we expect our dinner, but from their regard to their own interest. We address ourselves, not to their humanity but to their self-love, and never talk to them of our own necessities but of their advantages.[3]

'Economic rationality' and the famous law of supply and demand, which are at the heart of the mechanism regulating economic trade, are based on this individualistic postulate. It is clear that behind the economist Adam Smith has become, there is a moralist, a psychologist before the term was invented, whose theory is based on a specific interpretation of human nature – that is, that individuals are mainly motivated by their own interests, an attitude which is particularly manifest in the market-place. Smith generalizes and interprets this self-interest as the height of rationality. Other behaviour, such as altruism, co-operation and seeking the common good, are not really rational. These exist but they are neither constant nor decisive. They are only feelings, subjective by nature and often irrational.

Since labour itself is a commodity, the market also determines the optimal distribution of wealth and income. The labour market determines everyone's wage and, all things considered, a fair income for each thanks to the same law of supply and demand. It is income that determines each person's place in the socio-economic structure. As a result, the market has the virtue of converting the sum of perfectly selfish individual interests into the general interest – a surprising but undeniable result. In Smithian logic, any sensible person can see that the market is not only an infallible regulation mechanism of price and income distribution but also the main agent of an optimal spontaneous order.

To explain such an amazing effect, which is beyond the reach of his science, Smith introduces a mysterious 'invisible hand'. In a famous passage, he states that the entrepreneur 'by directing [his] industry in such a manner as its produce may be of the greatest value, he intends only its own gain, and he is in this, as in many other cases, led by an invisible hand to promote an end which was no part of his intention'.[4]

Here is the main thrust of Smith's theory, which remains the foundation of modern economics:

- *The psychological basis*: the selfish desire of each individual to improve his or her lot to the exclusion of all social or simply altruistic considerations.
- *The motor*: personal gain – that is, to increase one's assets, which, for the entrepreneur, are created through profit.
- *The regulating and structuring mechanism*: the market ruled by the law of supply and demand requiring free competition, and the freedom to invest and trade.
- *A sacred and inviolable right*: the unfettered right to own and hoard property, recognized by a legal framework guaranteed by the state.

David Ricardo, the father of free-trade ideology

The Englishman David Ricardo (1772–1823) is the co-founder of original economic liberalism. He still is recognized today as the theorist of free trade, a topic that Smith did not study in depth. Indeed, as we saw earlier, Smith's horizon was the nation, the national market composed of small buyers and sellers. His anti-mercantilist position even prompted him to oppose the colonial system, which he viewed as an unproductive and costly system (the American Revolution was in full sway in 1776): 'Under the present system of management, therefore, Great Britain derives nothing but loss from the dominion which she assumes over her colonies.'[5] (Note that, on this point, the English political and economic elite did not agree with Smith, since his theory did not support their interests; colonization continued for almost two more centuries after Smith.)

Ricardo came on the scene some forty years after *The Wealth of Nations*. The context had changed. Capitalism had matured. Factories had multiplied. England had an abundance of products it needed to sell on the international markets. After its victory over Napoleon in 1815, it consolidated its rule over the seas. Moreover, having ensured the development of its agriculture through two centuries of protectionist laws, it now found it advantageous to relax these laws in order to promote a drop in the cost of foodstuffs and, by the same token, of factory labour, which, all things considered, worked for its food. This new context prompted Ricardo to take a stand on a key international trade issue: free trade.

When Ricardo published his *Principles of Political Economy* in 1817, the English political class was divided into two hostile camps. On the one hand, the old agrarian aristocracy, protected by the famous Corn Laws, took advantage of the population explosion and expansion of the national market to enrich itself rapidly. On the other hand, the new industrial class, hard-working and innovating, an ally of the financiers and merchants, accused the large landowners of enriching themselves too easily, sheltered from free competition.

Ricardo, a talented businessman and broker on the London Stock Exchange, intervened in the debate by supporting his capitalist class. He called for the outright abolition of measures protecting national grains.[6] To back his point, he developed a theory demonstrating, with apparently irrefutable logic, that, for the welfare of the nation as a whole, free trade is preferable to protectionism. His 'law of comparative advantage' basically states that a country must specialize in the production of goods it can produce more efficiently compared with other countries and import what its competitors can produce at a lower cost. A classic illustration of this law was Portugal, which could produce wine at a better cost than England, and which acknowledged the advantage of specializing in this field rather than developing textile production, a sector where England already had a huge lead. If wine and textiles were to circulate freely between the two countries, their citizens would enjoy lower prices than if each protected its weaker sector. As a result, by eliminating customs tariffs throughout the world, all of humanity could share more products at a lower cost.

This theory makes Ricardo the ideological father of free trade and international division of labour. What he and his successors do not say is that the countries that unfortunately specialize in less structuring sectors, such as that of basic goods, run the risk of remaining for a long time producers of those less profitable commodities. 'History shows', writes economist Dimitri Uzunindis, 'that there are impoverishing and discriminating specializations.'[7]

Karl Marx, the most radical critic of liberalism

After a hundred years of triumphant capitalism, the liberal theory developed by Adam Smith and completed by David Ricardo was radically questioned by a brilliant German intellectual who had taken refuge in England: Karl Marx (1818–83). This stateless Jew appeared at a time when mechanization and the highly efficient factory production system were being challenged by those who operated the machines: the workers. Underpaid, badly protected, exploited by long hours of work, they started rebelling. Around the middle of the nineteenth century, the revolt spread throughout Europe. There were numerous riots. Not allowed to organize into unions, the 'damned of the factories' protested against their subhuman working conditions and miserable wages.

This is the context in which Marx published, in 1867, the first volume of *Capital*. Smith and Ricardo had developed economics into the science of wealth by rationalizing the new system of enrichment. Through a detailed analysis of the system, Marx aimed to convert economics into the proletariat's liberating science. He praised capitalism's prodigious productivity as well as the market's efficiency but insisted that the workforce is not a commodity. He determined the capitalist system's predisposition for crises and unemployment. He predicted, long before their emergence, the creation of monopolies and oligopolies that, he foresaw, would challenge and destroy all competition. He even predicted, without giving a date, the system's self-destruction. As for the 'invisible hand' metaphor, he ridiculed this ghostly entity and demonstrated the unscientific character of Smith's and Ricardo's theories.

Venerable American economist Robert Heilbroner considers that Marx's critical work clearly 'remains the gravest and most penetrating examination the capitalist system has ever undergone'.[8] He was the first to develop a theory of economic cycles and crises as consequences of the system's logic. He provided tools to understand the economy to generations of both right-wing and left-wing analysts. He explained to wage-earners that their only strength against the masters' excessive power is worldwide unity, a basic observation that contemporary trade unionists, shaken by globalization, are starting to make themselves.

Léon Walras, father of neoclassical liberalism and mathematical economics

After such devastating and thorough criticism, which won over many followers, economics needed a new lease of life. French economist Léon Walras (1834–1910), one of the first to recognize this, would become the leader of a new neoclassical economic theory. Without reneging on the broad outlines of Smith's and Ricardo's classic liberalism, this school of thought tried to correct its flaws by developing more rigorous analytical methods. Walras firmly believed that 'pure economics is exactly the same as physical-mathematical sciences' because, in fact, it is 'a physico-mathematical science like mechanics or hydrodynamics'.[9] In his *Elements of Pure Economics* (originally published in French in 1883), Walras recognized that Smith had avoided crucial problems with his 'invisible hand' metaphor. He took pains to mathematize the theory, propping it with sophisticated equations and statistics. His calculations were systematized in a theory of general equilibrium according to which the free operation of markets suffices to ensure full employment, the optimal development of resources and a just and fair distribution of income.

Walras's works earned him the title of father of mathematical economics and econometrics, which are today thriving in universities and business schools.

John Maynard Keynes, the champion of 'liberalism with a human face'

Barely fifty years later, in 1929, the certainties of mathematical economics were shattered by a crisis that shook the very foundations of the capitalist system. Monopolies, speculation, corruption and the concentration of wealth got the better of the national and world economies. The cataclysm's epicentre was located in the United States, the world's most prosperous country, whose success, it was believed, was due to its exemplary compliance with the principles of orthodox capitalism. The New York Stock Exchange collapsed, bringing down with it all the world's financial markets. Unemployment and misery moved in. Demand fell. Harsh reality bluntly belied the claims of the 'general equilibrium theory'.

Caught off guard, economists muddled and spluttered. Week after week, they announced the end of the crisis. According to the classical and neoclassical theories, neither the underutilization of the industrial capacity nor unemployment could last. Unemployed workers would eventually bring themselves to offer their services at a lower rate, and industrialists would then find it profitable to rehire them. If the factories produced too much, prices would drop, thus attracting purchasers. Competition would convince recalcitrant industrialists and force them to drop their prices. Consequently, production, sales and hiring would pick up. This is what theorists preached. Yet months and years passed, and nothing showed a rise, except unemployment and misery.

In 1932, a pragmatic political leader not without courage, US president-elect Franklin D. Roosevelt faced the crisis by prescribing massive state intervention. The theory, as always, would come later.

It came in 1936 with the publication of *The General Theory of Employment, Interest and Money* by British economist John Maynard Keynes (1883–1946). In this authoritative work, Keynes developed a thorough critique of the system, not to destroy it but rather to save it. He castigated and corrected the classical and neoclassical theories that support market self-regulation. His conclusions and prestige supported the US president's initiatives and dispelled the generally accepted notions prevailing since the beginning of the capitalist era. This was a genuine intellectual revolution. Keynes did not believe in the 'invisible hand' parable, that unspeakable Providence expected to transform the sum of businessmen's selfish interests into the public interest. He proposed a controlled capitalism, which would be improved by government interventionist policies when necessary. His message can be summed up in three points:

1. The market is an efficient productivity and price-adjustment mechanism but, alone, it cannot ensure full employment or effective and fair income distribution.
2. Political institutions must intervene to remedy market deficiencies whenever there is a drop in employment and income, and, consequently, in demand; in times of crisis, governments should boost demand by increasing the nation's purchasing power.
3. The state must regulate competition.

Less radical and more optimistic than Marx, Keynes rehabilitated politics. And facts support him: given free rein, pure capitalism produced underemployment, and the economy's deterioration and self-destruction. The state's saving intervention, first during the Great Depression, then during the Second World War, confirmed his novel view of the economy. Supported by thorough analysis, his message is clear: the success of economic and social endeavours depends on politics and, in the end, on a community that makes its decisions freely, not on the market's blind mechanisms. Pressed by the crisis, most of the world's governments acted accordingly. Keynesian thought would become the norm in public administration and universities for several decades. In the wake of Keynes, a new generation of economists would emerge proposing a renewed view of the relationship between politics, society and economics.

Milton Friedman, the guru of neoliberalism

Nevertheless, orthodox liberal ideology survived in bastions such as the London School of Economics, in England, and the Chicago School of Economics, in the United States. Its most constant, outspoken and renowned standard-bearer is Milton Friedman (1912–). He is the guru of the ultraliberal gurus. Already in 1947, he participated with Friedrich von Hayek in founding the Société du Mont-Pèlerin,[10] which brought together right-wing intellectuals in order to fight Keynesian ideas. In 1962, Friedman published *Capitalism and Freedom*,[11] his main work, seen as the manifesto of neoliberalism. This essay sums up the essence of his credo, which is based on an unshakeable faith in the liberating power of the free market. The market is presented as the most perfect modern application of the concept of liberty.

In his numerous works, Friedman takes pains to demonstrate the superiority of the market over the democratic political system, even in the case of a proportional electoral system. Indeed, having to choose between political democracy and the market, the true 'liberal' would choose the market, for the market is the supreme arena of liberty and, therefore, of democracy. The market, he writes, 'permits unanimity without conformity; it is a system of effectively proportional representation'.[12] Whereas the political system allows people to vote only once every four or five years, the market represents a kind of daily referendum where the consumer-citizen can exercise his right to vote several times a day, if he so desires, by buying or not buying this or that commodity. More importantly, political democracy, 'far from permitting unanimity without conformity, tends toward ineffectiveness and fragmentation. It thereby operates to destroy any consensus on which unanimity with conformity can rest', whereas 'the widespread use of the market reduces the strain on the social fabric by rendering conformity unnecessary with respect to any activities it encompasses.'[13] After this demonstration, the professor does not hesitate to conclude: 'We are thus led to accept majority rule in one form or another as an expedient. That majority rule is itself an expedient rather than a basic principle.'[14]

One would probably conclude that this is an overstatement that Friedman would in due time qualify. Not at all. Twenty-five years later, in Vancouver, Friedman was a speaker at a Fraser Institute symposium on 'Liberty, Democracy, Economics and Social Assistance'. In conclusion, a participant claimed that it goes without saying that 'democracy is an ultimate value, giving protection of minority rights and basic fundamental rights'. Friedman bounced to correct him: 'You can't say that majority voting is a basic right.... That's a proposition I object to strenuously.'[15] For ultraliberals such as Friedman, the only fundamental right is the limitless right to property. And the state's main role is to protect it.

Friedman proposes income tax reductions for the rich, because they are the ones who save, invest and create jobs. He believes 'corporate taxes should be abolished'. He is against graduated income taxes: 'I find it hard, as a liberal, to see any justification for graduated taxation solely to redistribute income. This seems a clear case of using coercion to take from some in order to give to others and thus to conflict head-on with individual freedom.'[16]

As for unemployment, which sometimes may reach painful proportions, Friedman has a scientific explanation for it. There exists, according to his calculations, a 'natural rate of unemployment' caused by the market's normal imperfections, a rate that can reach 5 per cent, 10 per cent or even 20 per cent and that no government policy can change, if not by worsening it. It is the natural rate of unemployment law.

What about corporate social responsibility, a topic that emerged in the 1980s? Friedman thinks that it is part of an idealistic discourse that has nothing to do with the reality of business. 'The social responsibility of business is to increase its profits.'[17] The reasoning is always the same: by increasing their profits, businesspeople create jobs, and so on.

Friedman firmly believes in the virtues of the market's invisible hand,
which makes the selfishness of large companies converge towards public
interest. As is the case for any other fundamentalist, his faith provides
him with an answer to everything. How did prosperity reach such
heights during the thirty years of post-war Keynesian policies? According to Friedman, if the situation of abundance and progress was maintained during the years of Keynesian dominance, it is because 'the
invisible hand has been more potent for progress than the visible hand
[of government] for retrogression'.[18]

When, in 1973, Pinochet violently overthrew the democratic, social-
istic regime of Salvador Allende, Friedman eagerly accepted the dicta-
tor's invitation to help him restore a truly liberal economy in Chile. He
believed that the social and political conditions existed for this, and
consequently sent his best team. The first practical country-wide application of Friedman's principles was carried out in Chile. This experiment proved that neoliberal capitalism does not need democracy to
prosper. The Chicago Boys would later be called upon to travel throughout the world, starting with the Third World, to advise governments on
the proper implementation of liberalism.

The advent of globalization represents a triumph for the guru of
ultraliberalism. Always at the forefront, the Chicago School justifies and
glorifies the global economy's new practices: massive lay-offs, keeping
democracy out of the way, monopolistic control over the market, unbridled speculation – nothing seems to upset it. Its logic has become
dominant in international financial institutions. Ultraliberalism super-
sedes Keynesianism as the main current in the business schools and
universities, and feeds think-tanks and the media. The OECD, the IMF,
the World Bank and the WTO adopt its most radical theses to justify
their decisions in favour of the globalizing economy. Even the Nobel
Foundation backs this school of thought by lending its name to an
economics prize created by bankers.

The Nobel Prize of Ultraliberalism

Since its creation in 1969, two times out of three the so-called Nobel
Prize in Economics has been awarded to economists from the Chicago
School. Among its winners one finds the founders of neoliberalism,

Hayek (1974) and Friedman (1976), both of whom taught at the Chicago School of Economics. To illustrate the jury's dubious choices, we shall mention Robert William Fogel (1993), another Chicagoan, rewarded 'for renewing research in economic history' by mathematically demonstrating that traditional historians had exaggerated the problem of American slave exploitation; on the contrary, slaves were treated rather well, since their masters allocated to their upkeep no less than 88 per cent of what this free labour produced. Not as free as it seems: slaves' work was subjected to an expropriation rate of only 12 per cent, a rate three to four times smaller than the fiscal expropriation rate practised by current governments on the average wage earner. What about personal freedom? Well, this is an imponderable factor impossible to calculate, which economics need not take into account.

In a moment of euphoria, Friedman revealed the mysterious selection criteria used for choosing the Nobel prize-winners in economics: one's chances of receiving the prize are the highest if one is a US citizen, male, and has taught or studied, at one point in one's life, at the University of Chicago.[19]

We can only be surprised by the complacency of the Nobel Foundation, which tacitly agreed to lend its reputation and fame to enhance the prestige of an 'Economics Prize' that has nothing to do with the Foundation. For Alfred Nobel had in no way planned to have his name attached to a science that is not one, and much less to a specific economic ideology. The objective of the Foundation named after him is 'to reward persons that have rendered the greatest services to humanity'; economics is not included in the list of five fields clearly indicated in the famous Swede's will – physics, chemistry, medicine, literature and peace. Consequently, the Nobel Prize in Economics does not exist.

As for the 'Prize in Economics in memory [sic] of Alfred Nobel', it was created by the Royal Bank of Sweden, and is entirely funded – to the tune of approximately $1 million annually – by this banking institution and not by the A. Nobel Foundation. The usurpation of the Nobel's prestige was a complete success: the 'Nobel Prize in Economics' is considered by the media on an equal footing to the genuine Nobel prizes. The idea was obviously to reinforce the scientific status of economics.

In 1997, however, the Bank's éminence grise simply went beyond the pale of scientific farce by awarding their prize to two 'golden boys',

Myron Scholes and Robert Merton, for developing a mathematical formula which, in theory, accurately predicted changes in the price of derivatives. The financial world marvelled at this clever formula that converted the haphazardness of speculation into pure science. Bolstered by the 'Nobel Prize' award added to their résumés, the two mathematical economists were offered senior management positions in a company specializing, as it happens, in financial speculation: Long Term Management Capital (LTMC). The prestige of the two Nobel prize-winners and the promise of fabulous profits allowed LTMC rapidly to recruit large investors with an initial placement of at least $10 million each. With a contributed capital of $2.3 billion, LTMC invested $1,200 billion of borrowed capital, of which $1,000 billion was invested in derivatives. In September 1998 the fund collapsed, dragging with it the credibility of the Nobel Prize in Economics.[20]

A few months later, to clear its name from such a huge blunder, the Swedish bank's jury set its heart for the first time on a Third World economist – Amartya Sen, whom *Business Week* ironically called 'the Mother Teresa of economics',[21] noting that 'he will not threaten the world financial system'. While the vast majority of economists develop get-rich-quick formulas for the already rich, this Indian economist is worried more about the growing impoverishment of underdeveloped countries. For over thirty years, his studies have focused on famine, poverty and inequality. He has demonstrated that, in our age, famines cannot be attributed to a lack of food, but rather to poor distribution of the social right to food. 'Famines', he writes, 'kill millions of people, but never affect the leaders.' Amartya Sen is one of the few well-known economists to do field work, not only mathematics and computerization.

Box 5.2   Is economics a science?

The bottom line: despite its scientific pretensions, economics still remains more of an art than a science. The future, by definition, is unknowable, as the geniuses at Long Term Capital Management discovered. Anyone who simply extrapolates past trends, however elegant the algebra, is an educated fool. Economics needs nothing so much as a little modesty.

Robert Kuttner, *Business Week*, 6 September 1999.

The Economists' Escape into
Mathematical Modelling

The greatest flaw of economic thought is without a doubt its escape into abstract mathematical modelling. This trend is not new. Walras paved the way over a hundred years ago. What is new is its excess. Investigations carried out at the end of the 1980s show a surprising trend: over 50 per cent of articles published in the most prestigious economics magazines present formalized theories and mathematical models without any data.[22] In political science, the share of purely abstract articles is only 18 per cent; in physics, 12 per cent; in sociology, 1 per cent; and in chemistry, 0 per cent. Modelling and formalization – that is, the abstract construction of equation systems that are perfectly coherent because they are abstract – have become fashionable among conventional economists, precisely because of their mystifying effect. By sheer repetition, theoretical models end up seeming like reality itself.

As a result, deplores Georges Corm, another Third World economist, in order to rise into the prestigious sphere of physical sciences, economic thought tends to 'escape into the construction of abstract mathematical models which are more and more incapable of explaining the complexities of reality'.[23] In France, economics students at the largest universities recently rose up against the excessive mathematization of economics. Their revolt was expressed in a petition denouncing studies unable to help them understand economic and social realities, 'stuck in mathematical formalism and dominated by the dogmatism of the neo-classical approach'.[24] Indeed, by escaping into mathematics, professors avoid expressing their point of view on the fundamental features and likelihood of the original hypotheses.

Super-powerful computer programs are reinforcing this evasive trend into abstract modelling. Yet it is known, or should be known, that a computer's verdict can only reflect the quality of the data it is fed. As the American saying goes, 'Garbage in, garbage out.' 'The bigger a model is, the stupider it gets', notes Bernard Maris. 'And as more equations and exogenous, endogenous and stochastic variables are added, it will produce stupider results.'[25]

Broken up into numerous specializations, disconnected from the complexities of social reality, contemporary economics is focused on specialized topics, seen through a fragmentary and reductive lens, whereas the economic life of human beings can be understood only through its social, cultural and environmental complexity. In other respects, the so-called scientific economics literature, which is growing by an annual rate of several tens of thousands of pages, has become so abundant that nobody can acquire a reasonable knowledge of it all. So where do the economists won over to the neoliberal current find their inspiration and references? In the publications of the great gurus, the reports of international institutions such as the OECD, the World Bank, the IMF, the WTO, and from a few commentators reflecting the views of the Chicago School.

Curiously, very few economists acknowledge the need to question the global economy's stated objective — growth — as the focus of contemporary economic thought. When all is said and done, all their calculations, equations and forecasts are based on a false postulate: that the material resources feeding the mega-machine of economic globalization are inexhaustible.

Fortunately for this discipline, there is a growing number of dissenting economists, such as John Kenneth Galbraith, Amartya Sen, Georges Corm and David C. Korten. Peter Eigen and Herman Daly left senior positions at the World Bank to devote themselves to promoting alternative economic practices. Many others, in universities and schools, are teaching the principles of social economy and debunking the myths of liberalism.

Funders of Right-wing Ideas

During the ten years that followed the Second World War, the growing popularity of Keynesianism demonstrated to the American business community how important ideas are in preserving and promoting their interests. They realized that political lobbying does not suffice to change tack. This is when they set forth to transform the intellectual landscape infested with Keynes's ideas and occupied by the new generation of progressive economists. Who would have thought that the right would end up believing in ideas more strongly than the left?

As we have already seen, resistance was organized around the School of Economics of the University of Chicago. The participation of American economists in the Mont-Pèlerin founding seminar in 1947 was financed by the William Volker Foundation, one of the United States' oldest fortunes. Afterwards, conservative businessmen started recruiting right-wing thinkers to produce books, articles, magazines, seminars and conferences.

Funders abounded. Foundations set up by old and noble fortunes were eager to finance the creation of institutes dedicated to promoting right-wing ideas.[26] The most remarkable are the Volker, Ford, Bradley, Coors and Olin foundations. They create and support think-tanks, the most important of which are located in the United States. The American Enterprise Institute was created in 1943 to oppose economists supporting Roosevelt. Founded in 1973, the Heritage Foundation is the best financed; it is also the best known for having openly supported President Reagan; renowned for its media savvy, it publishes a yearbook listing the names of thousands of right-wing economists available for interviews and talk shows of all kinds. The Manhattan Institute for Policy Research specializes in the scientific criticism of governments' social programmes. The Media Institute keeps track of major media coverage of the business world. Life industry transnationals lavishly finance the Hudson Institute to promote biotechnologies and discredit organic agriculture.

Think-tanks are mushrooming daily everywhere. Recently, American petroleum giants united their efforts to create the American Petroleum Institute (API), whose mission is to develop an alternative to the too pessimistic findings of the United Nations Intergovernmental Panel on Climate Change (IPCC) regarding greenhouse gas emissions. IPCC studies show that global warming exists and is mainly caused by the consumption of fossil energy sources but that doesn't matter! API 'researchers' received $5 million in advance to prove the opposite... with an obligation to yield good results.[27]

In Canada, the Fraser Institute claims to be the most important advocate of neoliberal thought. Set up in Vancouver's business centre and sponsored by the great names of finance and industry, it employs two dozen full-time researchers. Its publications are widely distributed. It also works closely with its peer institutes from the United States and the United Kingdom, with which it has formed a kind of international of ultraliberal think-tanks. A faithful disciple of Friedman, its founding director, Michael Walker, also sees himself as an eager admirer of the liberating market that, together with his colleagues, he considers to be

a superior form of democracy. 'The market is a kind of daily referendum on production, though one where every taste may be represented,
not only the majority', writes one of his experts.[28] In an interview with
journalist Philip Resnick, Walker was delighted with his think-tank's
results. The documents provided to the different media, he explained,
have contributed to the production of 'more balanced' news bulletins
and public affairs shows.[29]

The Broadcasters of Neoliberal Ideology

At once theorists and preachers, conventional economists work at the
top of the broadcasting chain. They play their role in universities, business
schools, public administration schools, international organizations and,
often, directly in the media. Many are hired by banks and multinationals
as soothsayers and prophets in speculative operations.

Once developed by economists and other idea manufacturers, neoliberal globalization ideology is reflected and broadcast to all layers of
society and throughout the world. It creeps into news bulletins, interviews, editorials, entertainment shows and commercials. By reading,
seeing and listening to the same message over and over, the general
public ends up considering globalization a truly inevitable and beneficial force. Of the many broadcasting networks used, the three most
important are the media, the public relations industry and advertising.

First, the media. The information and communications technologies
explosion in the early 1980s produced fundamental changes in the media.
The business world rapidly understood that the transformation of information into a commodity could represent an important source of
enrichment. This observation caused a phenomenal flow of capital into
the media and an unprecedented concentration in this sector. While in
1982, 9.5 per cent of the 400 largest American fortunes were made in
this sector, this proportion now exceeds 20 per cent. A major share of
all the information broadcast throughout the world is now controlled
by ten transnational corporations dominated by four colossal empires:
AOL Time Warner, Disney, Viacom/CBS and News Corp.

Not so long ago, information was guided by certain values, particularly that of seeking the truth. But with the advent of globalization, it
is the exchange value that counts – that is, the sale of advertising space

related to information. What is a daily today if not a collection of readers–consumers sold to advertisers? What are the objectives pursued by large television networks and electronic media owners? To capture the greatest possible number of eyes and ears and sell them to retailers at the highest possible price. In short, they sell the public to advertisers, while feeding the former a low-calorie diet of information. It is claimed that the editorial and advertising departments are independent from each other. However, all media owners know that advertisers will cancel their contracts if the media become an 'unfriendly environment'.

The media's main sources of information are the major press agencies – three or four – and government and corporate press releases. This creates an ideological symbiosis between the media and those who feed them. In this context, it is easy to understand that journalists have very little freedom and space in which to manoeuvre. They are barely needed at all. In the United States they have been given a new name: media workers. Disillusioned, a freelancer confesses: 'Contemporary journalism is 90 per cent recopying.'[30]

Public-relations consultants are gradually taking over from journalists. In recent years, a full-fledged industry – the PR industry – has been set up to offer its services to companies, business leaders and politicians in creating an image that has little to do with reality or the truth. Their objective is no longer to convince public opinion but rather to change it. Not to persuade but to manipulate. 'The new development this century is that propaganda has become a profession. It is now called public relations.'[31] In the United States, the major public relations agencies have 200,000 full-time employees. The same situation prevails, relatively speaking, in the other industrialized countries, where, as in the United States, there are more image makers than journalists.

Moreover, each government department, each major corporation, each international organization has its communications branch. One would like to believe that the mission of a corporate or government communications director is to inform the public as precisely as possible and in the clearest terms about what is occurring in his institution. Not at all! The communications director is the propaganda chief. Using credible half-truths, he is responsible for presenting the most flattering image of his employer.

Finally, there is advertising, a powerful propaganda machine which calls on human-behaviour specialists to induce citizens, considered

> **Box 5.3**   The love of servitude
>
> A really efficient totalitarian state would be one in which the all-powerful executive of political bosses and their army of managers control a population of slaves who do not have to be coerced because they love their servitude. To make them love it is the task assigned in present-day totalitarian states to ministries of propaganda, newspaper editors, and schoolmasters.
>
> Aldous Huxley, foreword to *Brave New World*, New York and Evanston: Harper & Row, 1946, p. xvi.

exclusively as consumers, to desire and buy what companies produce. Every year, the latter spend the astronomical sum of US$1,400 billion, or 70 per cent of the combined debt of all Third World countries, or 50 per cent of all the public funds earmarked for education throughout the world. Since the beginning of the 1980s, advertising budgets have grown phenomenally, particularly in underdeveloped countries: 1,000 per cent in China, 600 per cent in Indonesia, 300 per cent in India, Malaysia and Thailand. These investments are designed to convert the population in these countries to Western consumerism, to encourage them to drink Coke, to smoke more, especially American cigarettes, to buy more cars, and so on.[32]

Researchers have demonstrated that advertising, in addition to promoting the sale of a specific brand, has far broader and more profound consequences: 'It bears the apology of consumer society and mass culture.' It globally moulds minds and consciences.[33]

The Neoliberal Faith Propagation Office

The Organization for Economic Co-operation and Development has become the essential reference in the dissemination of globalization ideology. Its image has long been that of a publisher of voluminous and more or less reliable, and more or less useful, statistics reports. But its total commitment to promoting market globalization shows its true colours: it is a research and development department for spreading ultraliberal policies that targets senior public administration technocrats.

Created in 1948 to monitor the distribution of Marshall Plan credits and promote economic co-operation between European countries, the OECD changed in 1961 into an exclusive club bringing together all industrialized countries, now numbering twenty-nine. Its members are co-opted rather than chosen according to objective criteria. To be part of the club, it is important to meet three sets of criteria regarding economic liberalism, human rights and democracy. While the Organization is inflexible regarding the first condition, it has shown itself to be very flexible concerning the other two, especially since admitting Mexico, in 1994, and Turkey's failing democracy during recent years.

As indicated in OECD publications, its mission is to advise its members to help them define their economic policies. Economic policy obviously includes employment, taxation and the distribution of tax revenue, and, indirectly, education, proper administration of public affairs and the entire social field, including health. OECD bureaucrats know what are the best economic practices, what is the correct social policy to be followed and how properly to administer public affairs. Where did they acquire this wisdom and perceptiveness? From scientific calculations made by numerous economists working in the Organization's offices, permanently connected to the needs of globalization and fed by the gurus of the ultraliberal school of thought.

The OECD's secretary-general, Canadian Donald Johnston, gives countless interviews, writes editorials and organizes conferences to outline the policies to be followed. In an interview to *La Presse*, a major Montreal daily, he specified that the OECD's mission is to defend 'all the economic liberalization initiatives' and 'the labour market's flexibility'.[34]

Sadly, observes Mr Johnston, many people do not understand this and are opposed to globalization. He wonders why and answers with a rather shrewd diagnosis: 'In part because they have yet to see the benefits. They see the Wall Street financier get richer, but not necessarily the man on the street.' And he prescribes the remedy: educate and persuade the people of the benefits of globalization. In a word, indoctrinate. In a recent article, this high mandarin confided what he really thinks about the inevitability and benevolence of globalization:

> Globalization is not a policy; it is a process which will affect all aspects of our lives. We may not always like it; after all, it can compel us to give up cosy habits. But to stand against it would be sheer folly.... Those who do not

adapt quickly to this new environment will find it hard to survive. Those
who do adapt will lead the world in the twenty-first century.[35]

What means does the OECD have to meet its ends? Training and
development programmes through meetings, symposia and seminars, as
well as its innumerable publications. It has an annual budget of US$500
million and 2,000 employees led by clever and extremely dogmatic
economists. Each year, some 60,000 senior civil servants and politicians
of all kinds file into its Château de la Muette offices in Paris to retrain
themselves in neoliberal policy and management. An OECD promo-
tional brochure explains that the organization is a place of 'consensus
building through peer pressure'. This system of peer pressure 'encourages
countries to show transparency, accept explanations and justifications
and criticize themselves. This encouragement to practice self-criticism
among the representatives of its member countries is the OECD's most
original feature.'[36] Wait a minute! Self-criticism, pressure from the most
knowledgeable and powerful... Aren't these the good old methods that
totalitarian regimes developed in the past to create consensus?

The Seven Articles of the Globalization Creed

From Smith to Friedman, liberalism has undergone many alterations
and refinements to become present-day neoliberalism. Its critics call it
ultraliberalism to show clearly that the neoliberal discourse pushes to the
limit, and goes well beyond, the doctrines of liberalism. Liberalism is
the basic founding doctrine, which, from the Industrial Revolution to
the information revolution, has never ceased to transform and adapt
itself to all forms of capitalism. Today, neoliberalism is the discourse that
justifies and glorifies global oligopolistic capitalism.

Liberalism, which has become neoliberalism, exploits, even in its
own name, the notion of liberty. In the final analysis, the entire liberal
and neoliberal argument is based on a subtle distortion of that fundamental value, ever recognized as an essential dimension of the human
adventure: liberty. With the ideal of liberty in the background, neoliberal
ideology is structured, in an apparently implacable logic, around seven
dogmas presented as incontestable and irrefutable truths. These articles
of faith appear as self-evident facts based on common sense. But this

common sense is itself based on unsophisticated appearances (just as it was common sense and unsophisticated appearances that made the predecessors of Copernicus and Galileo believe that the sun revolves around the Earth).

Here, in order of importance, are the seven fundamental dogmas of globalization, which overlap and complete each other in a coherent and seemingly flawless system:

1. *Supremacy and infallibility of the market*   The market is the best place for exercising all freedoms: consumers' freedom of choice, which is superior to political democracy; freedom to trade, characterized by free competition; freedom of enterprise and of production; freedom to invest anywhere and anytime. Thus conceived and respected, the market, which includes labour, ensures the optimal distribution of income, wealth and resources better than any political body would be able to.

2. *Unlimited right of appropriation and property*   The right of property, sacred and inviolable, is the sole fundamental right. It is invoked whenever necessary to justify the hoarding and concentration of wealth by individuals or institutions. Protecting private property is considered to be the state's primary function.

3. *Primacy of private interests over the state and public interests*   Public interest is guaranteed by Adam Smith's old 'invisible hand'. The social state went astray when it usurped the attributes of divine providence and set itself up as the defender of public interest. When private interests are freely expressed – even though they are perfectly selfish – they combine, in a mysterious but undeniable way, to realize and protect public interest.

4. *Competition at all costs*   In a free-competition system, each company needs to become more productive – that is, produce more at a better cost – to vie with its competitors and, if possible, to buy them out or ruin them. This policy sometimes requires massive lay-offs and wage decreases, but, according to the theory, these temporary sacrifices are necessary to save the company from bankruptcy and, consequently, save jobs.

5. *Labour flexibility*   In this permanent economic war, labour flexibility, without which neither companies nor countries could remain competitive, becomes an absolute necessity. As a result, preachers urge

workers to make reasonable demands, accept wage decreases and renounce social benefits of another age, now untenable in the age of globalization.

6. *Everything is a commodity*   Neoliberal globalitarian ideology stipulates that the public interest is best served if all human activities, including culture, education and information, are treated as commodities. Even humanity's common goods such as air, water, and the plant, animal and human gene pool must be commodified, so the highest-bidding companies may appropriate them in order to manage them better and guarantee growth.

7. *Infinite growth*   According to neoliberal theory, the globalized economy's sole objective is infinite growth. Moreover, capitalism cannot give itself any other objective, for the regulating and self-regulated market itself determines the best objectives for the economy and society. Growth is the key to solving the serious problems afflicting our society, such as unemployment, poverty and underdevelopment. This dogma postulates that the planet's resources are infinite and inexhaustible.

It is easy to observe that, in practice, things are done in a very different way. What makes the champions of unbridled capitalism tick is not liberty but private property and hoarding. Profits rather than liberty represent the system's real objective.

CHAPTER 6

The United Nations, Patroness of the Third World

The UN Charter is a pre-atomic age document. In this sense it was obsolete before it actually came into force.

John Foster Dulles, former US Secretary of State (1953)

Does the United Nations play a leading role in the government of the globalized world? Have the new masters of the world assigned it a primary function in the management of world affairs? As the prime political body bringing together all of the world's sovereign states, is the UN not called upon to preside over the destiny of humanity? Is it not the universal institution best positioned to exercise world leadership, preside over the peaceful resolution of conflicts, and ensure the fair and harmonious use of the planet's resources? With its solemn Charter, its General Assembly comprising representatives from 189 sovereign countries, its Security Council, its dozens of agencies, commissions and institutions specializing in all fields of human existence, its hand-picked leaders, its peacekeepers and its legions of high-priced international experts, does it not represent a sort of world government?

Alas, the answer to all these questions is *no.* There is no world authority in charge of managing wisely the world's resources and promoting a worldwide social contract for the age of globalization. To understand why world leadership escapes the UN, it is necessary to examine the circumstances that brought about its creation.

The Dashed Hopes of the Human Community

In 1945, when the ordeals of the Great Depression and the wounds of the Second World War were still fresh in everyone's minds, humanity dreamt of a world free from the calamities of military conflicts, want, intolerance and inequality. The politicians who had confronted these catastrophes realized that to save their credibility they had to meet the peoples' legitimate aspirations. Such was the setting in which the United Nations was created, succeeding the deceased League of Nations in October 1945.[1]

The preamble of the United Nations Charter echoes a universal ideal of peace, justice and prosperity, promotes the end of the 'scourge of war, which twice in our lifetime has brought untold sorrow to mankind', proclaims 'the equal rights of men and women and of nations large and small', and promises 'the economic and social advancement of all peoples'. These promises are embodied in the UN's two basic missions, duly stated in its Charter: (1) ensure collective security and peacekeeping throughout the world; and (2) promote the economic and social progress of all peoples.

With such a clear mandate and apparently considerable means, why has the UN been a disappointment? The answer can be found in its origins. Despite what the first words of the preamble say – 'We, the peoples...' – the UN is not the outcome of a worldwide public debate, but rather that of selfish bargaining between the leaders of the two superpowers who haggled over its functions and reduced its effectiveness to a minimum. As a result, the very foundations of the UN bear traces of doubletalk: on the one hand, the rhetoric of the preamble echoes the wishes of the citizens of the world; on the other, the wording and omissions of the rest of the Charter meet the imperatives of a world order defined by the economic and geopolitical interests of the powers that be.

This is why the UN was born an impotent, bureaucratic and theatrical organization. It has remained so because this is what those who negoti-ated its structure wanted, as they reorganized their spheres of influence in the world and a new international economic order was taking shape.

Box 6.1 Preamble of the Charter of the United Nations

We, the peoples of the United Nations determined:

- to save succeeding generations from the scourge of war, which twice in our lifetime has brought untold sorrow to mankind, and
- to reaffirm faith in fundamental human rights, in the dignity and worth of the human person, in the equal rights of men and women and of nations large and small, and
- to establish conditions under which justice and respect for the obligations arising from treaties and other sources of international law can be maintained, and
- to promote social progress and better standards of life in larger freedom,

and for these ends

- to practice tolerance,
- to live together in peace with one another as good neighbours, and
- to unite our strength to maintain international peace and security, and
- to ensure, by the acceptance of principles and the institution of methods, that armed force shall not be used, save in the common interest, and
- to employ international machinery for the promotion of the economic and social advancement of all peoples,

have resolved to combine our efforts to accomplish these aims.

Accordingly, our respective Governments, through representatives assembled in the city of San Francisco, who have exhibited their full powers found to be in good and due form, have agreed to the present Charter of the United Nations and do hereby establish an international organization to be known as the United Nations.

Signed 24 October 1945

The Congenital Defects of the UN

In the summer of 1944, fifteen months before the end of the Second World War, aware of his country's 'manifest destiny' as world leader, US President Franklin D. Roosevelt convened two super-conferences to lay the foundations of a new international order designed almost exclusively by his own services: economic in nature, the first conference was aimed at setting up institutions to promote foreign investment and regulate financial transactions and trade between nations; the other conference pertained to the creation of a universal political organization bringing together every sovereign state in the world.

The United Nations Monetary and Financial Conference was held at Bretton Woods, in the New Hampshire mountains, on 1–22 July 1944. Fictitiously held under the aegis of the United Nations – which still did not exist, except in the files of the US State Department – this meeting was prepared well in advance by senior American and British experts and civil servants. It brought together 169 official delegates – among whom there was only one woman! – from the forty-four Allied countries, including representatives of the USSR, who would refuse to sign the final agreement creating the so-called Bretton Woods institutions. This is how the three pillars of the new world economic order – the International Bank for Reconstruction and Development, commonly called the World Bank, the International Monetary Fund (IMF) and the GATT, which would later become the World Trade Organization (WTO) in 1995 – were set up under the care of the United States rather than the United Nations.

The second conference convened by Roosevelt focused on the creation of the United Nations, christened as such a few years before it came into existence.[2] This conference took place in the unpretentious Dumbarton Oaks manor near Washington DC, and extended over a period of two months, from August to October 1944. It was more like a secret meeting where the three great powers of the moment – the United States, the United Kingdom and the USSR – engaged in epic underhand dealings to delimit, each to its own advantage, the powers and scope of the future international political institution. This unofficial tripartite committee was chaired by US Undersecretary of State Edward Stettinius and negotiations were based on a US memorandum containing a well-defined proposal. During the conference, Chiang Kai-shek's

China was invited to take up an unassuming role in order to warrant the project's universal nature. In fact, there were only two conflicting positions, the Soviet and the American, the USA having won Churchill's support several months, if not years, earlier. Distrustful at first, the USSR soon saw it had an opportunity to advance its cause in a prestigious world forum. Facing three opponents on its own, it cleverly manoeuvred to have the future institution reflect the new power relationship between the consolidating communist system and the capitalist forces boosted by the war.

At their meeting in Yalta in February of the following year, the heads of the leading victorious powers, Roosevelt, Churchill and Stalin, endorsed the Dumbarton Oaks plan and officially convened all Allied states to the UN's founding conference in San Francisco, on 25 April 1945.[3] Fifty states took part in sessions that lasted two long months, in which the Charter of the United Nations was debated and approved point by point. But in the end, the delegates did nothing more than rubber-stamp what had already been decided by the Dumbarton Oaks conference. These negotiations produced a system that faithfully reflected the strong will of the Big Three – particularly that of the biggest of them all – not to surrender any of their political, military and economic hegemony to the new supranational institution officially founded on 24 October 1945.

Designed and negotiated under these conditions, the UN was born with four congenital defects that to this day have affected and undermined its entire operations and explain its powerlessness:

1. *Jealous preservation of political and military hegemonies resulting from the balance of power established by the war* First came the United States, promoted to the status of greatest industrial and military power; facing and opposing it, the USSR, which the conflict confirmed as the leader and standard bearer of the non-capitalist world; then the United Kingdom, the only Western European power to have resisted the Nazi onslaught without wavering, but not without massive aid from the United States; and, finally, France and China, which were included for tactical and strategic reasons. These five powers ensured their absolute domination over the organization by claiming a special status as permanent members of the Security Council with veto rights.

2. *Decentralization and compartmentalization of specific areas* such as culture, science and education (UNESCO), agriculture and food (FAO), children (UNICEF), health (WHO), labour (ILO) and a few dozen more. In each area, an organization, a programme, an institute or a commission was created over which neither the Secretariat nor the General Assembly would have real supervisory, or even co-ordinating, power, and this, in order to 'avoid politicization', as required by the conventional wisdom of the time. This is how specialized, autonomous and extremely bureaucratized agencies directed by technocrats and experts were created.

3. *Exclusion of economics from the authority of the General Secretariat and the UN's main bodies*, separating the economy from political and social concerns, and giving free rein to major economic players to determine all on their own the rules of the game. As a result, despite their formal inclusion in the United Nations' organization chart, the World Bank, the IMF and the WTO are completely autonomous and independent. From the outset, these powerful bureaucracies refused to yield in any manner whatsoever to the United Nations' authority.

4. *The lightness of the General Assembly*, which is more like a theatrical stage than a deliberating or legislative body. It was designed as a forum, at most as an arena for confrontation rather than negotiation, or as a verbal war zone where each government tries to impress world opinion favourably.

Powerless Bodies

At the heart of the UN system, there are six main bodies, of which only three are really important: the General Secretariat, the General Assembly and the Security Council.

The *General Secretariat* is the UN's executive, a body practically devoid of power, except for that of managing its own personnel. It reigns over its 9,000 employees but not over the affairs of the world. The masters of the globalized world like their secretary-general to be as harmless as possible. Elected by the General Assembly for a five-year renewable mandate, the secretary-general is in fact chosen by the major powers, who bargain their support to a given candidate. The first two secretaries-general, the Norwegian Trygve Lie (1946–52) and Swedish

Dag Hammarskjöld (1953–61), were active. This interventionism apparently cost the latter his life, as the victim of an aeroplane 'accident' in 1961 during the Congo–Kinshasa war of secession.[4] After that, the great powers took care to designate less obtrusive secretaries-general. In 1972, they chose a very discreet Austrian technocrat, Kurt Waldheim, known by American intelligence agencies for his Nazi past, but recommended by the American ambassador in Vienna as being 'co-operative and helpful in promoting US interests'.[5] This was not the case of Egyptian Boutros Boutros Ghali (1992–96), ousted by the Clinton administration after his first mandate for having demonstrated some unwillingness to yield to American designs. At the beginning of his mandate, the current secretary-general, Kofi Annan, tried to find a peaceful solution to the conflict opposing the United States and Iraq since the Gulf War. Secretary of State Madeleine Albright did not appreciate his zeal. According to *Time* magazine, 'Albright blasted him and told him not to forget how he got his job – a blunt reference to the fact that the U.S. had eased Annan in after despairing of working with his predecessor Boutros Ghali.'[6] It seems that this warning had its effect on the secretary-general, who thereafter behaved in a more 'diplomatic' fashion.

The *General Assembly* is made up of the member states' permanent ambassadors, who represent all forms of government, from democracies to murderous dictatorships to pseudo-democracies. The General Assembly operates on a one-state, one-vote basis. The massive influx of Third World countries in the 1960s and 1970s tipped the Assembly's majority in favour of underdeveloped countries. This prompted the United States to complain about the 'tyranny of the majority' and led Uncle Sam to haggle constantly over the payment of its contributions, with arrears now reaching $1.5 billion. Yet, most of the time, the Assembly only votes on very general or totally insignificant issues. Its sole power is to pass resolutions, some of which are very important, such as those pertaining to the Palestinian territories, but it has no mechanism to enforce them.

According to the terms of the Charter, the *Security Council* is responsible for peacekeeping and international security. To fulfil this role, it can impose economic or other sanctions and authorize military interventions. It has fifteen members, five of which are permanent and hold unconditional veto rights, as seen above. Throughout the Cold War, from 1947 to 1991, the repeated vetoes of the two superpowers – the

United States and the USSR – completely paralysed the Security Council. In all, 233 resolutions were vetoed. The situation has only worsened since the demise of the bipolar world: the United States now controls the Security Council, making it vote at will for the resolutions that suit it. Having succeeded the USSR as a permanent member of the Council in 1991, Russia no longer has the strength or the political will to stand in the way of its former rival. China abstains from time to time – which is not considered a veto – and, when serious crises arise, it ends up yielding to superpower pressure. The Security Council, the only UN organ with real executive power, is now openly dominated by the United States.

What are the consequences of the Security Council's subjection to the five great powers and particularly to American interests? Inertia. Since the creation of the United Nations, over 150 conflicts have been waged with impunity throughout the world, almost all of them in the Third World, causing 22 million deaths and leaving hundreds of millions crippled, refugees, displaced or starving. Could it be otherwise today, now that international security is threatened no longer by superpower rivalries, but rather by arms proliferation? The answer lies in another question: Which countries are supplying the arms? The end of the Cold War caused an important drop in military spending throughout the world... except in the Third World. So who supplies military equipment to underdeveloped country leaders, who use them first and foremost to control civil populations and protect private interests? The five permanent members of the Security Council, who produce 86 per cent of all the arms sold to the Third World.[7] This fact alone clearly demonstrates that the powers controlling the Security Council are not interested in resolving these armed conflicts peacefully.

Whenever a serious crisis arises, we witness the laborious creation of an ad hoc peacekeeping force, beginning with the bargaining over the force's mandate and leadership. This is followed by delays and, finally, tragic inefficiency. From Somalia to Rwanda, Angola, Bosnia and Kosovo, what a disaster! Yet the Charter of the United Nations is clear: it provides for a permanent peacekeeping and collective security system. Chapter VII of the Charter expressly prescribes the creation of a Military Staff Committee made up of representatives from the Security Council's five permanent members and in charge of carrying out peacekeeping missions and coordinating national contingents. This committee was never created because the five never agreed to set it up... and never even tried. When war broke out in Korea (1950–53), the first major conflict after the creation of the United Nations, the Security Council authorized the sending of troops under US command. This is how the United States succeeded in wrapping itself in the United Nations flag to lead a war on its terms, just as it has shamelessly done many other times in the last fifty years.

In the 1999 Kosovo war, a new, even more radical, solution was found. Admitting its powerlessness, the UN let NATO, the armed hand of the rich Western countries, take over its peacekeeping mission. Originally created to fight the Communist threat, the North Atlantic Treaty Organization has been desperately searching for a new calling since the demise of the Eastern socialist bloc. It is perfectly suited to act as sheriff in the service of the TNCs' interests. However, this new mandate needed to be legitimized. The Security Council did it by passing resolutions or simply remaining silent. As a result, the United States now dominates both the UN and NATO.

The Withdrawal of the Economic and Social Council

The Economic and Social Council (ECOSOC) was created to fulfil the second component of the UN's mission: the economic and social progress of peoples. Its mandate pertains to all economic and social issues, but its role has become purely consultative. As Ian Williams recalls in his illuminating *The U.N. for Beginners*, 'the Economic and Social Council is the Cinderella of the Organization'.[8] The IMF and the World Bank chose and ran off with its most important functions.

Officially, ECOSOC is responsible for managing and coordinating all of the UN's specialized economic and social bodies, but it has neither the authority nor the means to carry out this task. The huge bureaucracies of the UN Food and Agriculture Organization (FAO), World Health Organization (WHO), United Nations Development Programme (UNDP) and United Nations Children's Fund (UNICEF), each totalling over 6,000 employees, refuse to be coordinated by anyone. Yet, there is an acute need for coordination. Several of these organizations duplicate, overlap and fight each other on the backs of the populations they claim to help. It is in the agriculture and food sector that one finds the most outrageous case of multiple organizations treading on each other's toes: the FAO encroaches on the World Food Programme (WFP), which bypasses the efforts of the International Fund for Agricultural Development (IFAD). All three organizations are supposedly supervised by the United Nations World Food Council (WFC).

The greatest duplication, however, is the United Nations Conference on Trade and Development (UNCTAD), which overlaps ECOSOC itself. UNCTAD was created in 1964 on the initiative of underdeveloped countries as an alternative to the inertia of ECOSOC, and the obvious bias of the GATT in favour of industrialized countries. Established in the context of the non-aligned movement and hailed by many as an anti-GATT, the new UN organization was to correct the damages caused by unfair trade and propose a development model based on import substitutions in which imports were to be replaced with domestically produced goods. What happened? Confronted by the enormous financial means and political clout of the Bretton Woods institutions, UNCTAD had no choice but to give up. Today, it is reduced to producing paper, just like ECOSOC.

Adding to this resignation, UNCTAD has recently been placed under the supervision of the International Trade Centre (ITC), a new organization completely dominated by the WTO. The ITC's main objective is to promote exports.

What kind of coordinating or supervisory power does ECOSOC have over the World Bank, the IMF and the WTO, theoretically under its jurisdiction? None whatsoever. An agreement between the Bretton Woods institutions and the central organization grants full autonomy to the former. The 'three sisters' even refuse to transmit any relevant information to the UN. But this does not prevent them from imposing the laws of economic and social orthodoxy on the rest of the world system.

It should be noted that the Council is partly to blame for its powerlessness, since it shunned its responsibilities when it faced its first challenges. The withdrawal happened in the early 1950s, when the issue of financing underdeveloped countries arose. Instead of taking on its full responsibilities by reinforcing and adapting its own intervention mechanisms, the Council handed the problem over to the World Bank, asking it to conduct a study on development financing. The Bank complied and took advantage of the situation by proposing the creation of a finance corporation under the jurisdiction of... the Bank. In 1955, at ECOSOC's request, the General Assembly approved the proposal. The International Finance Corporation (IFC) started operating the following year as a component of the World Bank Group with the mandate of encouraging private investment in underdeveloped countries. Today, the World Bank Group comprises four main branches that are very active in the Third World: the International Bank for Reconstruction and Development (IBRD), the International Development Association (IDA), the Multilateral Investment Guarantee Agency (MIGA) and the IFC. The latter, whose mission is to promote private foreign investment in underdeveloped countries, has become a tool to help transnational corporations take root in the Third World.

In the mid-1970s, the creation of a code of corporate behaviour was put high on the agenda of the UN after several TNCs played a leading role in overthrowing Allende and other democratically elected political leaders. This is when ECOSOC set up a centre to analyse the activities of foreign companies in the Third World, the United Nations Centre on Transnational Corporations (UNCTNC). This centre published embarrassing reports on the negative role of transnational corporations and suggested a code of conduct and environmental regulations for big business. But, since it is easier to change an ECOSOC research centre than transnational corporations, pressure was exerted to transfer the troublemaker to UNCTAD, which had never challenged the ideology of globalization. The transfer completely tamed and marginalized the UNCTNC.

With ECOSOC reduced to impotence, the World Bank Group and the IMF assumed alone the flagship role of the development aid industry. The latter now has a free hand to define the criteria and objectives of 'the economic and social progress of peoples', henceforth called 'development'. Since the beginning of the 1980s, their new mission consists in adjusting Third World economies to the global market.

The Bank's and Fund's structural adjustment policies wreaked havoc on the social fabric of the 'adjusted' countries, entailing countless consequences: impoverishment of the population, deterioration of the health and education systems, renewed outbreaks of malnutrition and epidemics, decay of the most vulnerable states. This is when the UN organizations in charge of palliative care come to the rescue. And we are now witnessing a new division of labour in the dispensing of the

so-called aid. While the IMF, the World Bank and the WTO are busy
globalizing the economies of Third World countries, sowing devastation
among their populations, the United Nations family provides the services
to the victims.

Rescuing the Victims of Globalization

Powerless on all fronts, even in carrying out its own mission, the UN
has gradually turned to the Third World, where it has more and more
specialized in social assistance and humanitarian aid. It has become the
patroness of the 'global village's' slums. Like all patronesses, its usefulness
lies in easing the conscience of the big bosses and overseers. Obviously,
the Third World needs more justice than charity, but the idea of justice
is simply beyond the UN bureaucracy. The UN has accepted being
replaced by the self-regulating free market in its mission of promoting
the peoples' social and economic progress. At a United Nations Conference on Social Development held in Copenhagen in 1994, the United
States and its key allies were against holding a debate on the growing
gap between rich and poor countries, alleging that any discussion on
economic issues 'will be best handled by the appropriate institutions',
namely the IMF and the World Bank. Former IMF director Michel
Camdessus considered that 'the UN is just one of the four pillars of the
world system',[9] not to say a fourth leg to the IMF, World Bank and
WTO tripod.

Today, 90 per cent of the UN's activities are concentrated in underdeveloped regions where almost all the UN agencies jostle to treat the
symptoms and consequences of underdevelopment. Five fields of work
attract them in particular:

- *reducing poverty*, under the care of the United Nations Development
  Programme (UNDP), the FAO, the WFP and the IFAD;
- *aiding refugees*, organized by the High Commissioner for Refugees
  (UNHCR);
- *assisting malnourished and exploited children*, run by UNICEF;
- *improving sanitary conditions* and epidemic control under the care of
  the World Health Organization (WHO);
- *humanitarian aid*, a constantly expanding sector not defined in the
  Charter, managed since 1992 by the Office for the Coordination of

Humanitarian Affairs (OCHA), under the responsibility of the General Secretariat. The Office recently created a new unit to co-ordinate work with the 45 million people that have been 'internally displaced' within their own country.

The Tragic 'Restore Hope' Misadventure in Somalia

A three-act drama illustrates in exemplary fashion the dead end in which the UN is stuck as it abides more and more by US dictates and yields to pressure from the new masters of the world. The events take place in Somalia, in the Horn of Africa. Until the early 1980s, this country of nomadic cattle farmers and small peasants was almost self-sufficient in agricultural products: foodstuffs, leather, wool, wood. The main charac-ters in this tragedy are the UN, the World Bank, the IMF, the American administration and Somalia's warlords. The supporting cast is the popu-lation of Somalia, reduced to famine and subjected to all kinds of atrocities. The audience: television viewers throughout the world.

FIRST ACT   Around 1980, the IMF and the World Bank impose their structural adjustment programmes (SAPs) in Somalia, completely disrupting the balance between the economy's nomadic and sedentary sectors. The SAPs' objectives are to adjust the country's economic structure, considered to be backward and obsolete, to the needs of the global market, and, above all – 'First things first!' – to help pay Somalia's foreign debt contracted following the advice of international experts.

SECOND ACT   Around 1990, the Somali economic system is para-lysed, the social fabric is torn apart, and the state has broken down. Famine sets in and world opinion is moved. The warlords resume fighting to seize the UN-sponsored air-dropped humanitarian aid packages and what is left of the political power in disarray. The UN's different organizations and programmes recognize the urgent need to intervene on the ground but consider that the situation is too delicate. Meanwhile, in New York, the members of the Security Council debate, calculate and fight over the idea of sending a police force.

THIRD ACT   In December 1992, outgoing US president George Bush needs a well-covered feat to end his term in office on a high note. The Security Council authorizes him to organize a strong-armed humanitarian expedition to Somalia. The detachment, made up of 36,000 soldiers all wearing the UN's blue helmets, including 24,000 Americans, lands under the UN banner, but under the orders of the American staff. Operation Restore Hope is broadcast live by CNN and rebroadcast by every other television network in the world. Then things start going wrong. The humanitarian contingent becomes an occupation force. As if in a Western movie, the occupying authorities divide the warlords into two camps, the goodies and the badies, and gives chase to the bad guys. As a result, twenty-three peacekeepers are killed, and eleven air attacks are launched that kill and terrorize civilians. Racist soldiers, including a good number of Canadians, play Rambo, capturing young Somalis and brutalizing them to death.

EPILOGUE   Amnesty International severely blames the patroness: 'The UN killed or arrested hundreds of persons in Somalia ..., it made prisoners without indicting them, defining their legal status or allowing them to see their family.'[10] Ten years later, internal wars are still devastating the country, sporadic famines persist, and the 'international community' is courting the warlords in the hopes of seeing the Somalian state reconstructed – and repaying its debt.

The UN Says 'Yes' to Globalization

What is the UN's position on globalization? In late June 2000, Secretary-General Kofi Annan clearly stated where he stands. In an address to NGOs in Geneva on the eve of the five-year review of the World Summit for Social Development (WSSD+5), he declared: 'I would say people are suffering not from globalization itself but from the failure to manage the adverse effects.' And he went on to conclude: 'They are poor not because they have too much globalization but too little.'[11]

How did the United Nations come to share the outlook of the promoters of globalization? We have seen in Chapter 3 how global lobbies are working at convincing the secretary-general of globalization's benefits and enlisting the United Nations family in opening up underdeveloped countries to the global market and direct foreign investment. Two specialized lobby groups were created to this effect: the Geneva Business Dialogue and the Business Humanitarian Forum. But the two most active lobbies pursuing this objective undoubtedly are the International Chamber of Commerce and the Davos Forum.

In January 1997, the Davos Forum created an Economic Council designed to advise the secretary-general of the United Nations. Five months later, on 24 June 1997, Kofi Annan and his staff solemnly hosted for dinner the CEOs of ten transnationals, the secretary-general of the International Chamber of Commerce, and a few government representatives including the American Undersecretary of the Treasury. After warmly greeting this impressive delegation, Mr Annan stated that he foresaw numerous avenues of co-operation between the United Nations and the business world.[12]

Not long after this meeting, ICC secretary-general Maria Livanos Cattaui, who for many years helped organize the Davos events, wrote in the *International Herald Tribune*: 'the way the United Nations regards international business has changed fundamentally. This shift towards a stance more favourable to business is being nurtured from the very top.'[13]

At the beginning of 1998, Helmut Maucher, ICC president, former CEO of Nestlé and Davos *éminence grise*, led a delegation of twenty-five leaders of the global economy to the UN headquarters. According to the joint press release issued after the meeting, the two sides committed themselves to 'forge a close global partnership to secure greater business input into the world's economic decision-making and boost the private sector in the least developed countries'. The ICC president summed up the meaning of his work by recalling that 'governments have to understand that business is not just another pressure group but a resource that will help them set the right rules.'[14]

In January 1999, Kofi Annan appeared at the Davos meeting to propose a 'joint venture' to TNC leaders. The Global Compact was formally launched in July 2000 at a meeting at the United Nations chaired by Kofi Annan and attended by senior officers of some fifty TNCs, including Aventis, British American Tobacco, Nike, Royal Dutch/Shell, Nestlé and DuPont, all of which are making every effort to undermine the UN's efforts on climate change, toxic waste, tobacco, child labour, and so on. This *sui generis* agreement encourages all UN agencies to enter into partnerships with the world's richest corporations. Participating corporations can use a UN label if they commit to respecting some ten principles of the Charter of the United Nations, but this partnership is a purely voluntary contract, with no control mechanisms, enforcement or sanctions for violators. Kofi Annan made a point of indicating that 'the Global Compact is not a code of conduct, neither a disguised effort to raise minimum standards'.[15]

Taking its new role in the globalization process seriously, the UN, together with the World Bank, the IMF and the OECD, signed a report in June 2000 on world poverty. The title of this joint report was *A Better World for All*. The document stresses the need for the four signatories to harmonize their poverty-fighting strategies. This strange co-operation produced the anger of NGOs the world over. Even the Church Ecumenical Council deemed it had to add its voice to the protests. In a letter to Kofi Annan, it criticized his 'participation in a propaganda exercise in favour of the international financial institutions whose practices have caused most of the world's serious social problems'.[16]

Yet the UN Plays a Positive and Irreplaceable Role

Despite its congenital defects and shortcomings, the UN has played a positive and irreplaceable role in building a world community, in two respects: the gradual recognition of human rights and the emergence of a global civil society.

Regarding the recognition of human rights, the UN has, alas, not stopped wars, genocides, military coups, the subjection of women and exploitation of children, still going on to this day in many countries. However, more than in any other period of history, it has furthered the issue of and respect for human rights in the world. The UN has achieved these improvements simultaneously on four different fronts:

1. *It has developed awareness of the paradigm of human dignity*, the inviolability of human rights and the equality of men and women. Through the Universal Declaration of Human Rights (1948), the International Covenant on Civil and Political Rights (1966), the International Covenant on Economic, Social and Cultural Rights (1966), the Declaration on the Right to Development (1986), and its numerous conventions on the rights of women, refugees, children and native peoples, the UN has established standards recognized and accepted by all peoples. Even if these treaties are but words, this is one case 'where big words trap those that use them without believing in them.'[17] Governments gradually realize they could be held account-

able by virtue of these documents they have signed... or refused to sign.

2. *It has legitimized struggles* of individuals and non-governmental organizations fighting to defend human rights and the environment.

3. *It has provided a forum and pressure mechanisms* to a large number of oppressed constituencies.

4. *It has created tribunals to judge and punish* some of the most abominable crimes committed against humanity.

Regarding the emergence of a global civil society, it should be recalled that the civil society phenomenon started taking shape around the famous UN international conferences. Seven of these summit meetings were held in the last decade. The first and probably most spectacular was the Earth Summit (Rio de Janeiro, 1992), which mobilized thousands of NGOs from the South and the North with the UN's encouragement. Together, all these organizations, associations and base communities prepared a common global project and organized a parallel forum where they challenged governments, international financial institutions and transnational corporations. Parallel forums have since become a fixture of all world summits. The emergence of a global civil society is even more significant today because it seems to have become the historical agent of a world democratic order based on citizens' rights rather than market logic.

Can the UN Be Reformed?

After being forced to leave the UN, former secretary-general Boutros Boutros Ghali published *Unvanquished*, a book full of revelations on US ploys to sway him and in the end to kick him out of the institution he directed for five years. It is the story, he writes, 'about the lost opportunity to construct an agreed-upon post-cold war structure for international peace and security'.[18]

This powerlessness and marginalization of the United Nations organization is neither accidental nor transient. Its shortcomings are in keeping with its congenital defects; they reflect the organization's fundamental problem, that of not being an independent actor on the international political scene. These long-standing defects have become

even more obvious since the demise of the bipolar world. Maurice
Bertrand, an insider who worked for a long time to reform the UN, is
no less pessimistic than Boutros Ghali. He notes that the United Nations
is excluded from any fundamental economic issue such as the monetary
system, credit and investments, and, despite the existence of ECOSOC
and UNCTAD, does not participate in international trade negotiations.
Even 'in the fields it has been granted, it has not been really efficient
except in those (including the humanitarian field) that have interested,
in some respect, the governments of rich countries, thus contributing
to the reinforcement of the established order. Its contribution to the
development of poor countries has remained very limited and in many
cases inefficient.'[19]

Can the UN be reformed? In the last paragraph of his book, the
former secretary-general says yes, but on one condition: 'I believe that
such a transformation is still possible and will succeed if the United
States allows it to do so.' This is enough to cast doubt on any chance
of reforming the United Nations system. Indeed, why would the United
States and the powerful interests it represents want to get involved in a
reform project whose objective would be to control their thirst for
power and hegemony?

And yet... The Iraqi crisis has clearly brought to light the current
state of the international system. In March 2003, the United Nations
was brutally and even scornfully excluded from resolving this conflict
stirred up by the greed of the masters of the globalized world. However,
such a flagrant and brazen violation of international law has awakened
people's consciences. The worldwide protests triggered by this crisis
could also reveal a direct challenge to US hegemony over the 'global
village'. One thing is sure: this militaristic turn in the globalization
process is creating problems of such great magnitude that the emergence
of a world democratic order has become more necessary than ever.

Despite its powerlessness, deviations and failures, the United Nations
still stands, and remains the symbol that we, Earth's 6 billion human
beings, are all living in one world that needs a world government freed
from the superpowers and corporate interests coveting its resources.

CHAPTER 7

The Tragedy of the Commons

Earth provides enough to satisfy every man's needs but not for every man's greed.

Mahatma Gandhi

An outright conflict is being waged today between the global economy and the planet. At stake is the commons[1] – the resources that this little planet called Earth provides to present and future generations to protect life and help it thrive. On a planet as small as ours, peopled by such a large number of users, all resources are limited. However, the ambitions of globalization's masters and overseers are limitless. They behave like poachers hunting endangered species. Yet, in the last two decades, the Earth has been sending out more and more serious distress signals.

Six Billion People on an Interstellar Vessel

As long as the Earth seemed to contain more resources than humanity could use, these were seen as inexhaustible. However, over the final decades of the twentieth century, using knowledge accumulated over thousands of years, humanity has developed technology capable of exploiting, transforming, consuming and wasting the planet's resources with formidable efficiency – an efficiency outstripping nature's capacity to renew itself. In the last fifty years, the production of goods and services increased sevenfold. In 1950, the world GNP was $5 trillion.

By 2000, it had reached $35 trillion. From 1990 to 1997 alone, it grew another $5 trillion; in seven years it had grown as much as during the 10,000 years between the Neolithic revolution and the end of the Second World War.

Furthermore, during the same period, the number of humans increased at a remarkable pace. It took *Homo sapiens sapiens* 37,000 years to reach its 1950 population of 2.5 billion; however, only 37 more years were required to double that figure. Only thirteen years were needed to add another billion to these five billion. Today, humanity has surpassed the six billion mark. So many to share such a limited habitat, the common home of all human beings and of all that lives and pulsates. There is nowhere else to go. So far as we know, there is no spare planet spinning out there – neither around the Earth nor around the Sun. Our only option is to share and manage as carefully as possible the fruits that our earthly garden offers us in order to bequeath it unspoiled to future generations.

In 1968, when the first astronauts brought back a photograph of the Earth taken from space, for the very first time, we could see and perceive our planet as it really is: a small blue marble smeared with white clouds, a frail pod travelling in the vastness of interstellar space carrying its precious payload of living creatures. It's impossible to exaggerate how deep this psychological shock was. It made a major contribution to the awakening of a truly global conscience. We became aware that the Earth is small and fragile. And we also understood that we are not simply passengers on this spaceship – 'we are the crew', as astronaut Rusty Schweickart put it.

The tragedy of common goods, such as water, air, land and the gene pool, is that they have long been considered overabundant, inexhaustible and impervious. As such, they were left in the hands of profit-hungry industrialists, with no concern for the public interest, no accounting of social and environmental costs and without adequate monitoring. When, for example, access to public forests is granted to the forest industry in exchange for minimal conditions, to all intents and purposes the only costs accounted for are tree cutting and transportation. Replacement costs are not counted, nor is the loss of biodiversity, the damage caused to water tables, the destruction of recreational areas and the effect of forests on climate systems. Producers thus pocket easy profits, which in turn encourages them to increase logging. The result is a genuine tragedy with catastrophic consequences: the looting and wasting of a rare and precious common public good without any effective state intervention to protect the public interest. And, alas, without the public rising up to defend its rights and those of future generations.

In recent years, the scope of repeated disasters has prompted the general public to ask the real questions regarding the disturbing weakening of ecosystems. Technological 'accidents' such as Bhopal (1984), Chernobyl (1986), the Exxon Valdez (1989) and the Erica (1999), the holes in the ozone layer, acid rain, devastating wildfires, floods, repeated droughts and tornadoes, hurricane Mitch in Central America (1998), devastating winds in France (December 1999) – all these catastrophes taken together did more to raise the ecological awareness of humanity than did all the expert studies and all the major international conferences. It would seem, however, that it still isn't enough.

When explaining the deterioration of the environment, it is all too easy to blame the demographic factor, just as it was in Malthus's time. Put bluntly, it is alleged that the poor, especially in the Third World, tend to multiply faster than nature's carrying capacity. Thus, the brandishing of the spectre of the 'population bomb'.[2] It is true that humanity must control its population growth, and in fact it is doing so with increasing success, as communities acquire the means to do it. That said, the demographic bomb is an alibi used to conceal the overconsumption bomb, a far more dangerous threat.

The Five Spheres of our Spaceship Earth

Our earthly habitat, which allows life to renew itself ceaselessly and flourish in incredible diversity, is neither permanent nor indestructible. Just as with any other living organism, its relative stability is based on a series of balances that are both constantly threatened and undergoing continual re-creation. Overall, it's a huge ecosystem made up of five major spheres, which overlap, influence and mutually enrich each other.

- *The atmosphere* is the gaseous and fluid layer surrounding the planet without which no life on Earth would be possible. This beneficial envelope contains the air we breathe and the different elements maintaining climate balance. In it move the clouds that pour life-giving water on the globe. The atmosphere is clad in its outer reaches – between 15 km and 35 km above the surface of the Earth – with an ozone layer which shields life against the sun's ultraviolet rays.

- *The hydrosphere* includes the oceans, seas, rivers and lakes that cover 70 per cent of the globe's surface as well as groundwater. About 97 per cent of this huge mass is saltwater. Over two-thirds of all fresh water is frozen. In other words, less than 1 per cent of the entire hydrosphere is available for consumption. The oceans play a fundamental role in keeping the major cycles of life on Earth in balance. They help moderate the climate and are the habitat of an infinite number of animal and plant species, including plankton, which, in addition to producing oxygen, are the first link of an indispensable food chain uniting all living creatures. As a result, the future of humanity is closely linked to the health of the oceans.

- *The lithosphere* (from Greek, *lithos*: stone or hard surface) is the dry land or terra firma, which includes arable land, deserts and steppes as well as mountains and rocky landscapes. It also consists of the subsoil, which contains a great variety of underground resources including metals, petroleum, coal and natural gas.

- *The biosphere* is home to all the animal, plant and bacterial organisms that are born, grow and die in the first three spheres. Nature created, over millions of years, an incredible diversity of species in extravagant and luxurious shapes, numbering some 1.5 million animal species and about 300,000 plant species. There are 50,000 vertebrate species alone.

- *The noosphere* (from Greek, *noos*: spirit)[3] or *cyberspace*, is the Earth's thinking layer, its wide web of ideas accumulated since life, having reached the stage of cognizance, started reflecting on the world and itself. The noosphere is humanity's intellectual heritage comprising science and conscience, traditional and industrial know-how, perception and imagination, sensation and thought, analysis and synthesis, observation and information. By providing this immaterial sphere a worldwide infrastructure, crystallized in the Internet and an array of telecommunications technologies, humanity has not only equipped itself with a truly phenomenal tool for exchanging and accessing the entire world's storehouse of knowledge, but also a new space to discover and explore. This permanent electronic structure enables humanity to generate even more awareness. Cyberspace

Box 7.1 Our Mother Earth

The Great Chief in Washington sends word that he wishes to buy our land.

The Great Chief also sends us words of friendship and goodwill. This is kind of him, since we know he has little need of our friendship in return. But we will consider your offer. For we know that if we do not sell, the white man may come with guns and take our land.

How can you buy or sell the sky, the warmth of the land? The idea is strange to us.

If we do not own the freshness of the air and the sparkle of the water, how can you buy them from us.

Every part of this Earth is sacred to my people. Every shining pine needle, every sandy shore, every mist in the dark woods, every clearing, and humming insects is holy in the memory and experience of my people. The sap which courses through the trees carries the memories of the red man. . . .

We are part of the Earth and it is part of us. The perfumed flowers are our sisters; the deer, the horse, the great eagle, these are our brothers. The rocky crests, the juices in the meadows, the body heat of the pony, and man — all belong to the same family. . . .

We know that the white man does not understand our ways. One portion of land is the same to him as the next, for he is a stranger who comes in the night and takes from the land whatever he needs. The Earth is not his brother but his enemy, and when he has conquered it, he moves on. He leaves his father's graves behind, and he does not care. . . .

This we know. The Earth does not belong to man; man belongs to the Earth. This we know. All things are connected like the blood which unites one family. All things are connected. . . .

Man did not weave the web of life, he is merely a strand in it. Whatever he does to the web, he does to himself. . . .

The whites too shall pass; perhaps sooner than all other tribes. Continue to contaminate your bed, and you will one night suffocate in your own waste. . . .

When the last red man has vanished from this Earth, and his memory is only the shade of a cloud moving over the prairie, these shores and forests will still hold the spirits of my people. For they love this Earth as the newborn loves its mother's heartbeat.

Tom Perry, inspired by a 1854 speech by Chief Seattle, of the Duwamish nation.[4]

should be included among the common goods to be protected and developed, along with the atmosphere, land, forests and oceans. This infosphere is part of humanity's common heritage. It belongs to all of us.

In 1979, James Lovelock revolutionized scientific perspectives regarding life on the planet by voicing the Gaia hypothesis, named after the oldest of Greek divinities, who emerged from the original chaos and gave birth to the first gods and the human race. Gaia personified the ingenuity and prodigious fertility of Mother Earth. This British scientist conceives of the Earth as a living organism in which all the spheres are constantly interacting and reacting, in a ceaselessly restored equilibrium.[5] He warns, however, that Gaia's remarkable capacity to adapt and regenerate itself may be upset by the no less remarkable destructive capacity of its children. Globalization just might make this fear come true.

The Earth's Ten Traumas

Time magazine, hardly a radical ecology journal, published a special issue in November 1997 on the threat that globalization represents for 'our precious planet'. The subtitle of this shocking report speaks volumes: 'Why saving the environment will be the next century's biggest challenge.' One of the report's authors summed up in a single paragraph the magnitude of the threat:

> At some point in this century, humanity itself became a geophysical force, able to affect the fundamental systems that run the planet. Educated people have long known that nuclear weapons have the potential to wipe out most life on land. In recent decades it has become clear that humanity could accomplish this same horrific feat inadvertently in the ordinary course of economic development.[6]

While the masters of the globalized village and their economists may forget the vital link between the economy and the Earth's ecosystems, the same cannot be said for the planet. Its exhaustion and wounds are apparent and the resulting catastrophic blowback is a reminder that the globalizing economy is too efficient for its ecosystems. Through its excesses – overexploitation, overpollution, overconsumption – globalization is inflicting on our habitat numerous traumas, which may be grouped under the following ten headings:

1. Global Warming

During the last 10,000 years, the globe's temperature and climate have been relatively stable. Our modern forms of economic development have succeeded in destabilizing them. The last ten years have been witness to dangerous global warming. In its Third Assessment Report, published in March 2001, the Intergovernmental Panel on Climate Change (IPCC)[7] confirmed that Earth's climate is changing – and faster than expected. Global warming is mainly caused by excessive emissions of greenhouse gases (GGs), such as methane (CH_4), nitrous oxide (N_2O) and, above all, carbon dioxide (CO_2), which, alone, accounts for 50 per cent of all GGs. Like greenhouse windows, GGs form a kind of thermal retention cover in the atmosphere that traps solar heat on the Earth's surface and prevents it from reflecting into space. This planetary greenhouse causes the Earth's temperature to rise. The incalculable consequences of this feverish increase in the Earth's temperature are already making themselves felt through phenomena such as the accelerated melting of glaciers and eternal snows, rising sea levels and extreme weather events, including the emblematic El Niño and La Niña couple, both of which were unleashed by global warming. According to the World Meteorological Organization, in 1997 and 1998 El Niño alone caused the deaths of 20,000 people, injured or displaced 117.8 million others, and wreaked over $33 billion in damages in twenty-seven countries. Year after year, the FAO warns that the severe weather disturbances of recent years pose a dire threat on the supply of foodstuffs in many countries.

Since 1987, several dozen climatic disasters, each of which has caused over £1 billion in damages, have hit one world region after another. During the previous decades, no disaster of comparable magnitude (in constant dollars) had ever been recorded. The insurance industry, a sector that is particularly sensitive to climate disturbances, provides conclusive data: 'World-wide, weather-related insurance claims have climbed from $17 billion per year during the 1980s to $66 billion thus far during the 1990s.'[8] It should be added that these figures do not include the incalculable damages suffered by the uninsured poor of the Third World.

Climate change, a widely recognized consequence of the greenhouse effect, is the most obvious sign of the ecological crisis afflicting the planet. It affects in a powerful way all countries and all components of the biosphere. It is a singularly cross-border and global problem. There is no place to hide. Africa as a whole produces less CO_2 than India and eight times less than the United States; nevertheless, it's the continent which is the most affected by global warming. When it comes to environmental degradation, the culprits are not always those who suffer the worst consequences.

2. Depletion of the ozone layer

Humanity has succeeded, via chemical pollution, in perforating the ozone layer, an upper atmospheric protective envelope stretching around the globe, and without which there would be no life on Earth. In the mid-1980s, a hole was discovered in the ozonosphere over the Antarctic, then another one over the Arctic. Like videogame pacmen, certain industrial gases eat up ozone molecules. CFCs (chlorofluorocarbons) and halons used in air conditioning, refrigeration and in all kinds of insulating products are particularly damaging. The production of CFCs has diminished since the signing of the Montreal Protocol, in 1987. However, its substitutes also deplete the ozone layer. In certain respects, the pesticide methyl bromide is forty times more destructive of ozone than CFCs. In short, the holes in the ozone layer are still growing, with destructive effects on flora and fauna, as well as human beings. Year after year, there has been a disturbing increase in skin cancers and eye diseases caused by ultraviolet radiation.

3. All kinds of pollution

Modern industry spews into the air, water and soil 100,000 different chemical products, gases, heavy metals, toxic agents, radioactive elements and particles of every description. These industrial wastes end up in plants and animals, and eventually in human food and people themselves via the food chain. In addition to attacking human, animal and plant health, this pollution contributes to dysfunctions in ecosystems, climate disturbances and the deterioration of buildings and monuments. Cars and other motor vehicles are the main source of air pollution. Their tailpipes belch out 60 per cent of the lead particles, 97 per cent of the carbon dioxide, 62 per cent of the carbon monoxide and 59 per cent of the nitrous oxide that clog the atmosphere. Most large cities are suffocating from motor vehicle exhausts. These disturbing facts don't bother the automobile maker oligopoly that continues to add 35 million new vehicles each year to the 700 million already on the road worldwide.

Of the thousands of chemical substances used to manufacture pesticides, herbicides and fungicides, only a few are subject to testing by the competent authorities. Some of these substances, derived from gases used in the manufacturing of chemical weapons, attack the nervous

---

Box 7.2   Reclaim the global commons

The global commons – everything the human community depends on and shares together – shall not be turned into a mere commodity to be bought and sold in the marketplace.

We are all commoners of the Earth, with a shared past and future. As commoners we declare our collective rights to access and our collective responsibility to maintain the commons for us, for future generations, and for the planet.

AIR is not for sale and the atmosphere shall be cleansed of all poisons; corporations and governments shall not be allowed to sell and buy pollution rights.

WATER, as a public good essential to life, cannot be sold by any individual, corporation or government; it is best protected by local communities and citizens.

LAND to grow food and spaces to live, to shelter and to enjoy as a community shall be considered as human rights.

FORESTS and wild spaces shall not be exploited for private profit at the cost of long-term sustainability.

OCEANS play a fundamental role in keeping the major cycles of life on Earth in balance; the future of humanity is therefore closely linked to the health of the oceans, which should be administered as a trust.

SEEDS & GENES and all living things – food crops, plants, micro-organisms, animals, humans – are part of the genetic commons and shall not be patented.

CULTURE & KNOWLEDGE – from essential medicines to the Internet, from broadcasting to folk tales – is our common heritage and shall be shared by all peoples.

Adapted from a poster published by *New Internationalist*.

system of insects... and of humans too. Recent studies have suggested that organochlorines used in many pesticides are a major risk factor in the development of breast cancer, because they have properties similar to those of oestrogens, which are a natural substance in the hormonal system of women.

The spreading of these chemical products into the atmosphere and stratosphere causes acid rain, the deterioration of forests and the contamination of fresh water. Among humans, they cause cancers and cardiovascular problems, worsen respiratory diseases, produce mental illnesses, reduce fertility and engender various genetic anomalies. Are we fated to make ourselves stupid and sterile? Mercury has been discovered in the breast milk of Inuit women and nobody knows how it made its way to the far north. Lead has been found in the blood of the inhabitants of Mexico City. A quarter of the children in this mega-city, one of the most polluted in the world, have growth problems caused by the smog laden with vast quantities of lead and other poisons.

And what about the mountains of rubbish accumulating around our cities? What about nuclear waste? There are about five hundred nuclear power plants in the world. Each one produces on average 6,200 cubic metres of radioactive waste over its forty years of operation. No safe solution has been found to dispose of this waste, of which the radioactivity will remain a threat to the biosphere for about 500,000 years.

4. Contamination and overexploitation of the oceans

Since time immemorial, the sea has been considered an unfathomable and limitless reservoir which was beyond our power to alter. Today, this deep blue space is showing obvious signs of exhaustion. According to the FAO, each year 20 billion tons of waste, much of which is highly toxic, are dumped into the oceans. Their countless tributaries, in the manner of so many sewerage pipes, discharge their poisonous effluent as they spew out the polluted waters generated by industrial and agricultural production. The lethal effects of oil spills into the oceans, whether voluntary or accidental, are well known. Some governments are so irresponsible that they bury their nuclear wastes in the oceans, in violation of the treaties prohibiting this criminal practice.

Fish stocks are declining at an alarming rate due to overfishing. Extremely efficient technology enables phenomenal catches: 130 million tons in 1998, compared with 90 million in 1990 and 18 million in 1950. Some trawlers can harvest 500 tons of sardines in a single casting of their nets. Two-kilometre-wide drift nets scrape the ocean floor, entrapping every living creature in their fine mesh. Floating factories process selected species on board and throw overboard a third of the catch because it is the wrong species or size. As a result, the FAO notes the decline of the most productive oceans and the growing scarcity of formerly highly productive species, such as the sardine off the coast of California, the anchovy off the coast of Peru, and the cod off the coast of Newfoundland. As a consequence, fish stocks are being ruthlessly run down.

The collapse of cod stocks is emblematic. For over 500 years, Newfoundland's Grand Banks had provided a steady supply of cod to the entire world. In the middle of the sixteenth century, cod accounted for 60 per cent of all fish eaten in Europe. Modern technology and the greed of the transnationals have destroyed one of the most fertile species on Earth. Scientists from Britain's Fishery Institute estimate that nowadays 'the chances of a North Sea cod dying a natural death are almost non-existent'.[9]

5. The growing scarcity of fresh water

The Earth's fresh water is a global common and its supply should be managed as a trust.[10] In theory, resources available for drinking water are largely sufficient to meet the needs of all. However, because of pollution, waste and unequal distribution, many regions face shortages. About 20 per cent of the world's population lack sufficient water to meet their daily needs. In underdeveloped countries, the shortages are also linked to poverty – that is, the lack of infrastructure required to supply and purify water. According to the United Nations Environment Programme (UNEP), 80 to 90 per cent of all diseases and over 33 per cent of all deaths in the Third World are linked to contaminated water. In the North, it is waste and pollution that threaten water reserves. Waste in the domestic use of water is endemic in North America, where the average household consumes 2,000 litres per day. Waste also exists in the intensive agricultural practices that absorb 70 per cent of world demand. Industry uses 20 per cent, which, with a few exceptions, it pollutes and then simply releases back into nature.

According to the World Water Council, of the 500 largest rivers in the world, only two can be deemed healthy: the Amazon and the Congo. UNEP experts estimate that one quarter of humanity will suffer chronic water shortages within the present decade.[11] Many see this situation as a probable cause of conflicts in the coming years. Fresh water is so essential to life that it could well become a major geo-political issue in the twenty-first century and cause more wars than oil did in the twentieth century. The director of the International Water Management Institute, David Seckler, states without hesitation that 'the growing scarcity of water is now the greatest threat to human health, the environment and food. It is also a threat to peace.'[12] Also according to the World Water Council, in 1998 the number of water refugees rose to 25 million due to pollution and scarcity, surpassing for the first time the number of war refugees (21 million).

6. Soil depletion

Desertification is spreading on every continent. Everywhere, soils are being eroded and their productive potential is declining. In rich countries, and in the underdeveloped regions where export agriculture is practised, agrochemical inputs are used on a massive scale to maintain yields. Erosion and heavy machinery are destroying the soil's layer of humus, thus triggering the desertification process. Almost 70 per cent of the world's arable land is already deteriorated to at least some degree. Each year, 10 million hectares of arable land become unfit for agri-culture. Desertification refers not only to the advance of existing deserts, but especially to the conversion of arable soil into a range of semiarid or sub-humid environments where agricultural activities become very difficult or impossible.

To a large extent, this problem is spreading because land is overused and misused. In Third World countries, the IMF and the World Bank are encouraging intensive monoculture practices in the name of 'com-parative advantages'. This simplistic argument, advocated by international experts, encourages the countries of the South to abandon subsistence farming and specialize in cash crops, even if it means buying rice, wheat and milk from the North. The global market's implacable logic fails to take into account the fact that intensive monoculture fosters diseases and soil depletion, which in turn require an even more intensive deployment of the agrochemical arsenal.

7. Deforestation

Forests are receding, victims of the merciless advance of chain saws, timberjacks and torches. This overexploitation is mostly due to the activities of the giant pulp and paper industry and the lumber barons, who clear-cut, with no regard for the environment's regenerative capacity. Gargantuan heavy machinery eliminates all the trees, big and small, over vast tracts of land. Giant 40-ton tree-length harvesters, capable of cutting up to 5,000 trees a day, break up the forests' fragile humus. The worst damage is caused by the timberjacks, whose wheels dig deep furrows that become, under the effect of the elements, metre-deep channels.

In tropical regions, fire is also used. In Brazil, transnational corporations burn thousands of hectares of Amazon forests to raise cattle for hamburgers. In the Far East, in 1997, gigantic fires devastated the forests of Borneo, Java and Sumatra and covered half of the islands of Southeast Asia with clouds of toxic smoke. Most of these fires burned into virgin humid forests that had been spared this kind of disaster before the onset of global warming.

In his book *The Shrinking Forests of Vietnam*, Professor Rodolphe de Koninck states without hesitation that deforestation in Southeast Asia is caused mainly by the development model imposed by powerful political and economic interests and the World Bank.[13]

The Worldwatch Institute estimates that throughout the planet, '16 million hectares of forests are now being cleared of trees each year either by fire or chain saw.'[14] That is the equivalent of two-thirds of the United Kingdom's land area. Over seventy-five countries have completely cut down or burned their ancient forests. In a dozen others, less than 5 per cent of the virgin forests remain. Canada loses about 200,000 hectares of forest per year. Should this destructive trend continue, the head of the UNEP predicts, in forty years in some countries of the South there will not remain a single standing tree fit for human use.

The consequences of deforestation are numerous and often catastrophic. The torrential floods that hit China in 1998 and the landslides in Italy, the same year, are directly related to deforestation. In addition to annihilating a resource and its potential for renewal, deforestation causes excessive water runoff and, by the same token, limits the beneficial infiltration of water into the water table. Deforestation often triggers an almost irreversible erosion process. Moreover, it brings in its wake the destruction of the habitats of numerous species. Tropical forests alone are home to half of the world's animal and plant species.

8. Reduction of biodiversity

The numerous traumas inflicted on the planet, from the greenhouse effect to deforestation, are causing the extinction of a large number of species. A study commissioned by the UNEP, and signed by 1,500 scientists, found that in the last four centuries the annual rate of species extinction has grown a hundredfold. Furthermore, in the more or less short term, this could very well be multiplied by 10,000. Wholesale slaughter. Between 11 and 34 per cent of fish, mammal, bird and reptile species are threatened. Nor are plants spared this deadly fate: 12.5 per cent of seed plants are threatened. At least 27,000 living species become extinct each year. Susan George notes sadly: 'It is as if we were going backwards in the timeline of life on Earth, by losing the benefits of millions of years of evolution in a few decades; for, at this rate, we will have eliminated one-fifth of the Earth's biological diversity within the next twenty to forty years.'[15]

This slaughter is a cause for concern because it means that a large number of precious molecules and genes that could potentially provide food and medicine to humanity have disappeared. It has been shown that the greater an ecosystem's plant and animal diversity, the more stable and dynamic it is. The struggle for species survival does not stem simply from vague ecological romanticism; in itself, the maintenance of biodiversity constitutes an economic resource. However, it is one that is hard to quantify, precisely because its contributions are both countless and immeasurable.

9. Transnational corporations' takeover of the gene pool

Globalization policies are helping transnational corporations take over the planet's gene pool, which is the world's heritage and a moving force of evolution. This hijacking of public goods is being carried out by a handful of giant agrochemical, genetic engineering and pharmaceutical corporations. Monsanto (United States), Novartis (Switzerland) and DuPont (United States) are among the leaders of this clique.

This usurpation is being carried out thanks to the complicity and zeal of the GATT–WTO. Indeed, the major innovation of the Uruguay Round, which converted the GATT into the WTO in 1994, was to have member states accept an agreement on Trade Related Aspects of Intellectual Property Rights (TRIPs) in which the patenting of life is considered an intellectual property right. This is certainly a major innovation since, although intellectual property rights and patents of invention have been recognized for many years, until recently no one had imagined that living organisms, and even life itself, could be patented. Did the discoverers of the atom or the neutron consider patenting the objects they found? The TRIPs explicitly specify that seeds, micro-organisms, plants and animals, which nobody ever invented, are patentable. And, following pressure from the life industry, this patenting right has even been extended to the human genome. For example, the European Patent Office granted patents to Myriad Genetics, an American company, on the BRCA1 and BRCA2 genes. These two genes, which play a role in breast cancer, now belong to this multinational. Confident of its monopoly, Myriad Genetics sent formal notices to competing laboratories throughout the world prohibiting them from pursuing their research on these genes, thus blocking numerous projects that could help improve the health of millions of women.

The TRIPs' fearsome Article 27 protects genetically modified organisms (GMOs) and seeds produced with the new biotechnologies.[16] These techniques involve the transplanting of genes from one species to another in order to give the latter new characteristics, such as resistance to insects, diseases, cold or rotting. Transgenic foods are spreading without the public's knowledge, especially in North America. Over fifty of these 'Frankenfoods', as they are nicknamed, are being introduced in our food baskets and at our tables. 'Roughly 60% to 70% of all processed foods in Canada, from crackers to TV dinners, may contain ingredients from engineered canola, soybeans or corn, for example.'[17] An increasing number of independent studies have demonstrated that transgenic foods present risks to human and animal health as well as to biodiversity. Potential allergenic and carcinogenic effects have been observed. The possible impacts on the genome of viruses and other vectors used to transfer genes are still unknown. The possibility that natural strains of certain plants that are useful for the survival of the human species might disappear has also been mentioned. The president of the European Institute for Ecology admits he fears that genetic engineering could 'throw nature into wholesale disorder'.[18] The risk is that genetic pollution could be far more serious than chemical or nuclear pollution.

The TRIPs' most damaging effect is no doubt the unbridled bio-piracy in the Third World, where the greatest biodiversity reserves are located. Life-industry TNCs are dispatching research teams to stake claims on plants and genes they may later use for making drugs, food-stuffs and other profitable products, while the country of origin will not gain any benefit whatsoever. There are even cases in which a patent on a plant that natives have used for millennia prohibits people from freely using their own resources. This is what is happening to basmati rice grown in India and Pakistan. RiceTec Inc., a US multinational, is claiming ownership and monopoly rights over 'new varieties of basmati rice'. Patent no. 5663484 now authorizes the company to enforce its exclusive rights regarding the commercialization of these rice varieties, which are in fact disguised copies, under the basmati name. It could even claim exclusive rights over the name.

10. Corporate domination over cyberspace

The Internet, whose worldwide expansion continues unabated, represents the first direct and real-time global communications infrastructure, capable of interconnecting all individuals and communities on Earth and of giving them access to humanity's common intellectual and technological heritage. This unprecedented phenomenon could help global civil society sound a rallying cry. How it is to be managed is as important an issue as the stewardship of the other collective goods, such as air and water, which are intrinsic to everyone's welfare and prosperity. The problem is determining who controls Internet use: civil society as a whole or private commercial interests?

Originally managed by the National Science Foundation (NSF) – a body funded by the US government – then by the international community of Internet users brought together in the Internet Society (ISOC), the Internet still bears the markings of its origins. It was designed and created by American academics sponsored by the US government, particularly the Defence Department. Indeed, from the birth and christening of the Internet[19] in 1974, until the launching of the Global Information Structure, in 1993, the US government had largely financed research on the electronic highway's backbone, as well as its construction as such.

But in 1995, the American government withdrew from the backbone business, leaving it in the hands of a few telecommunications giants, all of them American, such as Microsoft, IBM, WorldCom and Sprint, which now own almost the entire Internet infrastructure. It goes without saying that the prime interest of these global corporations is profit rather than the common good of humanity. Although Internet access is still affordable, it is clear that commerce and advertising could very well dominate the network in the near future.

Moreover, the American government insists on imposing its views regarding 'domain names', and thus regarding the very organization of the information highway. And this, in the name of its 'first occupant rights'. A discussion paper published by the White House in 1998 stressed that the Internet was developed as a US government project, and that its first funder still has legal authority over it.

Save cyberspace! could become the rallying cry of citizens around the world wanting to preserve this common good.

The Commercialization of Air under the Care of the UN

Everywhere one turns, resources are plundered and looted. Pollution and overconsumption are the rule. Globalization policies are worsening these evils intrinsic to an economic system based on unlimited growth, competition and deregulated markets. Is there an international body capable of stopping this destructive madness and of healing the Earth's wounds? With cries of alarm sounding in every quarter, the United Nations finally felt impelled to act. After countless expert studies and reports on environmental issues, the UN decided, in the early 1990s, to try a bold move by tackling the environment head-on.

In 1992, twenty years after the first Environment Conference held in Stockholm, the UN convened all the world's heads of state to the Earth Summit in Rio. Over 10,000 participants attended the official summit and a parallel summit organized by civil society. The objective was to launch a new way of managing the planet's resources. The event raised high hopes throughout the world. However, while the speeches were boastful, the results proved rather slim. With great difficulty, the summit succeeded in having two agreements signed: the Climate Change Convention and the Biodiversity Convention. After a great deal of coaxing, the world's worst polluters committed themselves to reducing voluntarily their greenhouse gas emissions to 1990 levels. The Biodiversity Convention has the merit of recognizing the existence of a world gene pool and the need to regulate it. That said, no agreement has been reached on the issue of regulatory standards. Nevertheless, a fund was created to implement the two agreements: the Global Environment Facility (GEF). Ironically, the World Bank, known for having financed the projects that have done the most damage to the environment in the Third World, was given the task of managing the GEF.

Five years later, the UN General Assembly called for an assessment. As a result, in June 1997, the secretary-general convened the signatory governments to the Rio agreements to a follow-up summit called Rio+5 in New York. None of the commitments made at the Earth Summit had been met. Canada, for example, instead of reducing its greenhouse gas emissions, had increased them by 13 per cent. The same held for the United States (+6 per cent), Japan (+8 per cent) and China (+27 per cent). The energy consumption gap between rich and poor countries had widened still more. As for biodiversity, the pace of deforestation had not slowed down. In the face of such negative results, the participants decided not to decide anything. In short, Rio+5 ratified the refusal of the world's main political and economic leaders to choose sustainable development.

Next came Kyoto in December 1997. The UN convened a meeting focused exclusively on the issue of greenhouse gases. For big polluters, this is the most sensitive point as it concerns the consumption of fossil fuels, a key factor in economic growth. It is easy to understand why the United States, which produces 30 per cent of worldwide carbon emissions, would end up being at the centre of the discussions. Its senior representatives, escorted by a powerful lobby of industrial polluters, promoted a novel idea: 'negotiable emission permits'. In other words, pollution permits that amount to establishing a greenhouse gas market. True to pure market logic, the solution is deemed to lie in the market. To start, each country would be given a number of shares of greenhouse gas emission rights proportional to its population. These shares may then be traded – that is, bought and sold. Thus, under-developed countries, which are generally under-polluters, could sell part of or all their pollution rights to over-polluting industrialized countries. This way, the latter could continue their economic growth while underdeveloped countries would use the proceeds from this trade to industrialize. This would also apply to Russia, which, after the fall of Communism, has seen its greenhouse gas emissions fall due to the difficulties encountered in its transition process. Russia is now 'under-polluting'. The sale of its surplus shares to the United States would allow the US to pollute more and at the same time give Russia the opportunity to reindustrialize – and increase its pollution levels up to its allowed limit. The signatories of the Kyoto Protocol promised to reduce their pollution emissions by 5 per cent by 2008, but they made the mistake of accepting the principle of a pollution market.

A final task remained: defining the implementation and control mechanisms of this 'novel' system which proposes nothing less than the marketization of air pollution. To this end, several UN summits were held: first in Buenos Aires (1998), then in Bonn (1999), The Hague (2000) and in Bonn again (2001). The negotiators finally succeeded in establishing quantitative parameters for greenhouse gas emission sur-pluses and deficits to be used for the allocation of pollution permits. As Europe and most of the world's countries had already signed the Kyoto Protocol – yet again diluted by flexibility measures, such as the 'carbon sink' stratagem,[20] – President George W. Bush announced, in April 2001, that the United States was withdrawing from said protocol which it had previously signed. 'Americans won't sacrifice their way of life to conservation', explained Vice-President Dick Cheney in a speech to the annual meeting of the Associated Press in Toronto. And he made it clear that conservation will not figure prominently in the American energy policy, insisting that more oil, gas, coal and nuclear power will be used to meet US energy needs.[21]

A year after these astounding declarations from American leaders, the Energy Information Agency (EIA), a unit of the US Department of Energy, unabashedly announced that in 2002 petroleum consumption was expected to increase by 600,000 barrels a day, and to continue growing at an annual rate of 2.2 per cent. The EIA also predicted that carbon dioxide emissions might increase 62 per cent from 1999 to 2020.[22]

Finally, instead of coming to the rescue of the planet and the vast majority of its inhabitants, the world political leaders brought together under the UN banner have allowed themselves to become tools in the hands of the petroleum and automobile lobbies. In the end, this series of summits were only useful in their supporting and legalizing of the commercialization of air, without helping in any meaningful way to stabilize the climate or clean the air we breathe.

Opportunistic and Irresponsible World Policymakers

Despite the serious distress signals sent by the Earth, despite the health problems afflicting so many, despite the conclusive studies from numerous independent scientists and despite the protests of environmentalists, the economy's big decision-makers remain unperturbed in their cynicism. Are they deaf and blind? Less than one might imagine. The proof is in their advertising and public relations, where they know when and how to take a moralizing environmental stance. Not that this keeps them from doing the opposite of what they promise. They honour good, but do evil.

The world's worst polluters, the petroleum, automobile and chemical industry giants, understand the stakes so well that they have formed a powerful lobby of 230,000 companies: the Global Climate Coalition – a coalition for polluting the atmosphere and deteriorating the biosphere, led by Exxon Mobil, Shell, General Motors, Ford, Monsanto et al. The objective of this Holy Alliance is to oppose all national and international efforts geared towards regulating greenhouse gas emissions and all other chemical pollutants. It turned up in force in the major international conferences aimed at slowing down global warming. At the Kyoto conference on greenhouse gases, this coalition waged an all-out campaign using sophisms, blackmail and threats. 'Any regulation', warned the Coalition's spokesperson, 'is not only unrealistic, but also very dangerous from an economic growth perspective.' A decline in growth, he added, would have adverse effects on employment and international trade. 'Imposing costly premature cuts is not the solution', explained a leader of the pollution superlobby.[23] So what is the solution? The market.[24]

As for the politicians, they have neither the vision nor the courage to face today's challenges. Instead of staunchly defending the public interest, they beat around the bush and yield to the demands of the bosses of big industry and trade. None of today's leading international decision-makers is willing to assume their responsibilities as heads of state or government to address the issue as a whole, taking into account humanity's public interest and the sustainability of the Earth as our one and only habitat. *Time* magazine reported that before leaving for the Kyoto Conference in 1997, President Clinton had first decided to make a stand against global warming. But 'there was a split among his team of advisers. Environmental advocates favoured more drastic actions, but economic aides warned that making companies spend money on cutting emissions might slow the robust economy that has been the best news of the Clinton presidency'.[25] So, yet again, the short-sighted electoral argument won the day. Clinton chose to side with the Global Climate Coalition. 'Clinton's toughest decision', adds the *Time* reporter.

'After us the heavens can fall!' seems to be the economic and political decision-makers' motto regarding ecological issues and the environment.

Globalization's Hidden Faults Exposed by the Environment

The environmental crisis besetting the planet and preoccupying most concerned citizens has emerged as a powerful warning signal. It exposes the limits of globalization and the flaws of ultraliberal ideology. It warns us that the global economic model has hidden faults that discredit the entire system.

Because the environmental crisis is global, obvious and destructive, it helps ordinary citizens put their finger on globalization's three main flaws:

1. The absurd objective of infinite growth

The collapse of cod stocks, soil depletion and climate change are all warning signals. The planet is warning us that the global market has exceeded the limits of sustainable economic activity. Ecologist Edward Abbey accurately notes that 'growth for growth's sake is the ideology of the cancer cell.' Indeed, the cancer grows and spreads, with no concern for the system's overall rules of operation, until it destroys the organism supporting it. Once a system exceeds its sustainable production limit, it can continue only if it eats up natural capital – that is, nature itself.

2. The myth of the self-regulating market

The plundering of the commons is intensifying under the care of the supposedly self-regulating global market. Yet, the more globalization advances, the less regulation there is: nowhere is the market's 'invisible hand' intervening to protect the ozone layer, the oceans, fresh water reserves, the forests, biodiversity, the soil and the air against the predatory hand of transnational corporations.

3. The irrationality of 'externalizing' environmental costs

The uncontrolled market economy provides excessive profits to many companies because it does not factor in environmental costs. In economics jargon, these costs are 'externalized' – that is, left to neighbours, society as a whole, or to future generations. If, for example, the nuclear industry were to assume the costs of the diseases and deaths it has caused – think of Chernobyl – and the costs of managing nuclear wastes, it could never be profitable. If the chemical, mining, forestry, petroleum, automobile, agriculture and food industries took into account the negative externalities of their activities and resource transformation – that is, if they had to cover the costs associated with eliminating said negative externalities – they would be forced to raise the price of their products by a very considerable amount. Consumption would be marked by a return to values such as frugality and voluntary simplicity. Moreover, these industries would be forced to hire more employees. 'I am convinced', maintains Jacques Delors, former president of the European Commission, 'that if we fully addressed this sustainable development issue, there would be no more unemployment, as we know it today. Everyone would find their place in society.'[26]

To correct the situation, the principles of globalization need to be reversed. The paradigm needs to be replaced. Why is the reduction of greenhouse gas emissions so hard to achieve? Because this problem is linked to fossil fuel consumption, a cornerstone of economic expansion and, consequently, growth in sales, profits and GNP. There is a conflict between growth and the reduction of greenhouse gases, a contradiction that cannot be resolved within the current system's framework.

The advent of an economy that respects the commons requires changes on three fronts: (1) the questioning of growth as a finality; (2) the democratic intervention of communities and political authorities; (3) the establishment of a system that accounts for environmental and social costs. These are steps that today's economic decision-makers refuse to take. Quite the contrary: they are ready to change everything so that nothing changes.

CHAPTER 8

The Slums of the Global Village

If rich countries had the courage to look in depth at the source of their wealth, they would realize that it is rooted in the misery of the Third World.

Dom Helder Camara

The most perverse effect of globalization is undoubtedly rising inequalities: widening disparities between countries, regional disparities of all kinds, and the growing gap between the haves and the have-nots within each state. Far from resembling a large, prosperous and friendly village undergoing a unification process, the globalized world seems more like a monstrous Third World megapolis with an explosion of wealth and modernity at the centre and slums as far as the eye can see on the periphery. It is a worldwide Cairo or Mexico City whose centre is being overdeveloped at the expense of the underdeveloping periphery.

Of course, these inequalities and income disparities existed long before the advent of globalization. But globalization has worsened, systematized and perpetuated them, in line with the imperatives of the global market that is imposing its merciless logic of universal free competition in which the poor must compete against the rich, the weak against the strong, and the least advanced countries against the most advanced.

The Scandal of Underdevelopment

The world has never produced with such efficiency such an abundance of goods and services. Never has so much capital circulated so fast between so many companies, institutions and countries. World financial assets have increased more than fourfold since the beginning of the 1980s. All major industrial sectors are showing excess production. Rich countries with agricultural surpluses are fighting fiercely to take a greater share of the global markets. All on its own, 'the United States could meet the entire world's cereal needs'.[1] And yet...

Far from benefiting from this prolific productivity and prosperity, four-fifths of the world's inhabitants are experiencing shortages, destitution, malnutrition and even famine. For, despite all the promises and predictions, 'economic growth' has failed to improve the status of any of the 127 countries deemed to be underdeveloped by the international financial institutions and the United Nations. 'Gaps in income between the poorest and richest people and between countries continued to widen.'[2] Far from shrinking away, the cancer of underdevelopment seems to be spreading and worsening. This shocking situation is reflected today in statistics that, alas, speak volumes:[3]

- 127 underdeveloped or maldeveloped countries form the periphery of an exclusive club of overproductive, overconsuming, overpolluting and ever-richer industrialized countries;
- 4.6 billion people, or four-fifths of humanity, live in the 127 slums making up the Third World archipelago;
- 49 so-called least advanced countries (LACs) are in technical bankruptcy due to their state's overindebtedness or decay;
- the annual per capita income of 100 Third World countries is lower than it was 10, 15, 20 and even 30 years ago;
- 2.8 billion people, almost half of humanity, are forced to live – feed, accommodate, look after and educate themselves – on less than $2 a day;
- 1.3 billion poor and destitute people in the Third World subsist on less than $1 a day – the official poverty level defined by international experts for the damned of the Earth;
- 25 million refugees are officially under the protection of the UN High Commissioner for Refugees;

Table 8.1 Distribution of world income (1997)

	Population		Income	
	million	% of world population	US$ billion	% of world GDP
First World	860	14.7	23,233	79.2
Second World	368	6.3	1,232	4.2
Third World	4,622	79.0	4,869	16.6
Total	5,850	100.0	29,334	100.0

Note: World income is obtained by adding the national income (NI) of all the countries. The NI equals the GDP at factor cost minus capital consumption. *First World* = OECD countries, except for its new members (South Korea, Hungary, Mexico, Poland and Czech Republic). *Second World* = countries of the former USSR and Eastern Europe (former Communist bloc). *Third World* = the 127 underdeveloped or maldeveloped countries.

Source: UNDP, World Bank, OECD and *État du monde 2000.*

- 130 million people have become dispossessed 'ecomigrants', forced to leave their native area because of desertification, scarcity of water, drought, floods and other 'natural' catastrophes;
- 850 million adults, including 543 million women, cannot read or write;
- 250 million children are workers, including 120 million who work full-time;
- 2.6 billion people do not have decent sanitary infrastructures;
- 90 per cent of AIDS victims, 36 million people, live in the Third World with 14,400 new cases every day;
- 1.1 billion people do not have decent housing;
- 1.4 billion people do not have access to safe drinking water.

The Third World's Role in a Globalized World

All these persistent and growing signs of underdevelopment on the periphery of the overdeveloped world represent a scathing condemnation of globalization. But these statistics only reveal symptoms. The real harm lies even deeper, in the very structure of the global economy. The root of the problem is structured dependence: financial and monetary dependence – that is, indebtedness and capital depletion; industrial and technological dependence – that is, an economy of subcontracts; commercial dependence – that is, unfair trade; food dependence – that is, scarcity and famine. Add to all these subjections the Third World economy's outward orientation and the subordination of its political and economic elites to transnational interests and you have the causes of today's world inequalities.

This state of dependence and extroversion is nothing new. It is part and parcel of the Bretton Woods system created in 1944. The deregulated global market has reinforced the periphery's dependence on the centre by institutionalizing an interstate power relationship that reinforces the economic and political power of the strongest at the centre to the detriment of the weakest on the periphery.

Contrary to what the media convey, underdeveloped nations are neither marginalized nor excluded from the global economy. In fact they are an integral part of a global system of unequal interdependence where each country has its role, whether it likes it or not. The cogs of the peripheral economies mesh perfectly into the globalized economy's mega-machine. Although the Third World economies play a subordinate role, they are essential to the proper operation of contemporary capitalism in four different ways:

- as reservoirs of raw materials, they provide inexpensive oil, gas, metals, tropical foodstuffs, precious wood and a host of semi-finished goods;
- as an almost limitless pool of cheap, and sometimes highly qualified, labour, they help keep wages at 'competitive' levels;
- as a vast duty-free zone offering tax and regulatory privileges, they represent a haven for the delocalization of transnationals and the creation of subcontracting companies;
- as a market, the Third World and its 4.6 billion consumers represent a very coveted and increasingly essential outlet for the sale of excess production from industrialized countries.

Of course, several important distinctions need to be made. The Third World is a heterogeneous set of countries with highly varying degrees of underdevelopment. Singapore, for instance, is the very special case of a city-state whose citizens are treated as employees by an authoritarian regime. It separated from Malaysia in 1965 to become an enclave of advanced capitalism in the heart of underdeveloped Asia and the commercial, financial and logistic platform for every country in the region. Its balance-of-trade surplus remains exposed to the ups and downs of the global economy.

As for China, it is in a category all of its own because it never submitted to IMF 'conditionalities' or to official development assistance. Up to the end of the 1970s, it had successfully developed its own means, thanks mainly to the diligent work of its peasants organized in mutual aid groups, semi-socialist co-operatives and production brigades. At the same time, small and medium-sized industry flourished. As a result, this country accumulated material and human capital that put it on the road to independent and self-managed development. But in 1979, the established bureaucracy, embedded in an autocratic political system, made a 180 degree turn and launched a policy to open up the country to foreign investments to accelerate development... and the enrichment of the political class. Opening up completely to transnational corporations, China was forced to follow the neoliberal model. The country's 800 million peasants – 70 per cent of the population – are paying a heavy price for this forced liberalization and deregulation. So are women, who make up most of the sweatshop workers. This frantic race to wealth marks the return of the old sexist and patriarchal hierarchies. The events in Tiananmen Square in 1989 were only the visible part of rising discontent. The government violently crushed this movement and, a few years later, initiated its long march to join the ultraliberal WTO club, making its triumphant entry in March 2002. This was a sad moment for all of humanity. China's embrace of globalization and the neoliberal policy of growth entails the widespread deterioration of its environment, with worldwide implications.

The group of maldeveloped countries includes the so-called emerging nations, such as Korea, Thailand, Mexico, Brazil and Chile, which are located in the first circle of peripheral development. These countries basically have the same subordinate roles described above, while at the same time they try to compete with industrialized countries in certain sectors such as textiles, automobiles, aeronautics and even electronics. But as soon as they start emerging, reaching a certain level of industrial and technological independence, financial crises, devaluations, privatizations and the disruptions caused by unfair trade hinder them, throwing them once again back into underdevelopment. Emerging countries have always had limited autonomy; globalization inevitably worsens their state of dependence.

The outermost circle includes some sixty underdeveloping countries, such as Haiti, Somalia and the Democratic Republic of the Congo; they show to an extreme degree all the features of dependence, extroversion and economic and social disarticulation.

In the former Communist nations, the transition from socialism to capitalism was accompanied by dramatic changes in the distribution of wealth and national income. In its *World Development Indicators 1999* report, the World Bank notes that in one decade, poverty grew tenfold in the former USSR and Eastern European countries, now affecting 147 million people – one out of every three individuals – compared with 14 million before the implosion of the Communist system. In Russia, the number of people living in extreme poverty grew thirtyfold. Ten years ago, there were 2.2 million inhabitants with a daily income under $4; in 1999, this figure had reached 66 million. During this period, the fortune of the nouveaux riches and multimillionaires grew at the same pace as the misfortune of the poor. And all this under the iron rule of the IMF, well established in Moscow since 1991.

Joseph E. Stiglitz, a leading academic economist who has worked extensively on the development of the Third World and who was, for almost three years, a senior vice-president and chief economist of the World Bank, concludes:

> Globalization today is not working for many of the world's poor. It is not working for much of the environment. It is not working for the stability of the global economy. The transition from communism to a market economy has been so badly managed that, with exception of China, Vietnam, and a few Eastern European countries, poverty has soared as incomes have plummeted.[4]

Growing Inequalities Everywhere

Globalization is also causing widening disparities within the richest nations. In the 1999 report quoted above, the UNDP states that in practically all the OECD countries income inequalities have worsened since the beginning of the 1980s. And 'the deterioration was worst in

Table 8.2   The growing income gap between poor and rich countries

Year	% share of world income		Ratio
	Poorest 20%	Richest 20%	
1960	2.3	70.2	1:30
1970	2.3	73.9	1:32
1980	1.7	76.3	1:45
1990	1.4	83.7	1:60
1995	1.1	90.2	1:82

Source: UNDP, *Human Development Report 1998*, New York: UNDP, 1998, p. 29; and *Human Development Report 1999*, New York: UNDP, 1999, p. 36.

the United Kingdom and the United States', stresses the document.[5] (These two champions of inequality are the pioneers of neoliberal policies.) In 1989, in the United States, there were 66 billionaires and 31.5 million people living under the poverty threshold, with an income below US$13,000 for a family of three; ten years later, there were 268 billionaires and 34.5 million poor. One percent of Americans owned more than the combined revenue of 95 per cent of the country's entire population. In nine years, from 1989 to 1998, the proportion of people struggling to feed themselves grew from 16 per cent to 21 per cent of the entire population. Also, the proportion of people finding it hard to clothe themselves rose from 18 per cent to 21 per cent. The deterioration of health care is also striking: in 2001, 27 per cent of the population did not have sufficient funds to access health care, compared with 22 per cent in 1998 and 15 per cent in 1976.[6]

In Canada, 1.5 million children live in poverty. This situation is quite ironic since in 1989 the Canadian parliament unanimously adopted a resolution to eradicate child poverty by the year 2000. Ten years later, the number of poor children had risen by 60 per cent, as if politicians, now the overseers of globalization, were not bound by the promises they make and the laws they pass.

Should one expect to find such contradictions even in our affluent societies? Yes, if one understands that free competition and the free flow of capital imperceptibly, but inexorably, cause global equalization from the bottom, dragging down the North's social, labour and environmental policies to the South's standards.

As we have seen in previous chapters, the concentration of wealth at the top is a general trend of globalization. No matter how hard economists and politicians twist and crunch the statistics, the fact remains undeniable: the rich are getting richer at a breakneck pace, much faster than the economy's true growth rate. Year after year, the profits of transnational and multinational corporations increase by 10 per cent, 20 per cent and 30 per cent. Large banks are reaping just as fabulous profits. As a result, there is less left for the rest; the poor are getting poorer and the middle classes are gradually losing their purchasing power.

The director of the UNDP confirmed these trends in the *1996 Human Development Report*:

> In the past 15 years the world has become more economically polarized – both between countries and within countries. If present trends continue, economic disparities between the industrial and developing nations will move from inequitable to inhuman.[7]

The trend has continued and inequalities are indeed becoming more and more inhuman. The financial crises of 1997 and 1998 that hit the emerging economies of Asia and Latin America caused the price of raw materials from the Third World to drop. In the First World, mergers and all kinds of rationalizations caused hundreds of thousands of lay-offs that have increased job insecurity and exerted downward pressure on wages.

Year after year, in its annual report, the United Nations Development Programme (UNDP) notes that the global market adventure is a disaster for underdeveloped countries:

> Globalization is thus proceeding apace, but largely for the benefit of the more dynamic and powerful countries in the North and the South. The loss to developing countries from unequal access to trade, labour and finance was estimated by *Human Development Report 1992* at $500 billion a year, 10 times what they receive annually in foreign assistance. Arguments that the benefits will necessarily trickle down to the poorest countries seem farfetched. Even less certain than globalization's benefits for poor countries are its benefits for poor people within countries.[8]

Politicians as well as business leaders and economists promise that growth will eventually resolve the problems of unemployment, underdevelopment and poverty in general. This 'convergence' theory states that with GNP growth, the income gap between the rich and the poor, and between developed and underdeveloped countries, will gradually diminish. Of course, they admit, the already rich are well positioned to be the first to take advantage of growth, but the poor will also benefit from it and almost as much.

This postulate is often illustrated by an apparently convincing meta-phor. Everyone is sailing on his boat on the sea of economic activity; when the tide rises, all the boats, big and small, rise equally. Everyone takes advantage of the situation according to his capacity. But beware, this metaphor can also be used to refute the hypothesis it purports to demonstrate. If it is true that a rising tide equally lifts rowing boats and ocean liners, it should be noted that all ships do not resist equally waves and storms. Rowing boats and other small craft take on water more easily. They can also be sucked into the waves produced by nearby ocean liners and sink like stones. The fable of the kettle and earthen pot rubbing against each other better illustrates the tragedy of competition between strong and weak contenders: sooner or later the kettle will shatter the pot.

The facts contradict even more clearly the hypothesis that country incomes are converging towards equality. In an in-depth analysis of this issue, two economists from the Centre français d'études prospectives et d'informations internationales (CEPII) irrefutably concluded:

> This hypothesis is rejected by the findings drawn from statistical tests carried out on a large sample of countries over a period of about forty years: from 1960 to 1997, the economic growth rate of the initially poorest countries was not consistently higher than that of the richest countries. On average, the standard of living gaps between countries actually grew. The various methods used to measure the convergence of per capita incomes all concur in reject-ing the existence of such a phenomenon at the global level.[9]

Serious researchers point out that only countries with identical struc-tural features – such as the European Union countries – may converge over the long term... as long as their 'initial conditions' are similar. However, this doesn't prevent globalization from increasing inequalities within affluent societies, in North America as well as in Western Europe. Everywhere, globalization is feeding on the deepening of inequalities by constantly creating new disparity mechanisms. And the main mecha-nism lies in creating a system of generalized insecurity and casualization of labour. No one is protected from a decline in income anymore. Prompted by big business, the OECD and the WTO, governments are attacking social benefits, unemployment insurance, labour legislation and even pension funds.

Extreme Wealth, Extreme Poverty

The global enrichment system showers fabulous sums of money on the rich, old and new, making the hyperclass of millionaires grow at an incredible pace, thanks mainly to the massive arrival of overpaid overseers. According to investment bank Merrill Lynch, which produces a yearly report on this topic, in 2001 our wonderful globalized world had 7.1 million millionaires, an increase of 200,000 compared with the previous year and of 1.1 million compared with 1998. In 2001, the

Figure 8.1   The staggering increase in wealth of the 200 richest billionaires (US$ billions)

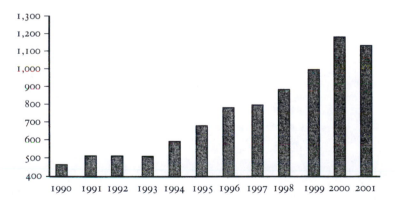

Note: As indicated by *Forbes*, this list only includes the 'working billionaires', excluding the 'non-working billionaires', such as kings, queens, sheikhs and dictators who hide their wealth more easily than the average capitalist. Note that the events of 11 September 2001 only very slightly slowed the progress in the concentration of wealth.

Source: *Forbes*' Annual List of the Richest Global Billionaires: *Forbes*, 5 July 1999; 3 July 2000 and www.forbes.com.

combined wealth of these individuals with at least $1 million of goods, excluding their homes, reached $26.2 trillion, an increase of 25 per cent compared with 1998. In the United States, the number of millionaire households rose by 60 per cent over the last decade to reach 5 million in the year 2000.[10] In this same country, the top 1 per cent of the population pocketed 42 per cent of the stock market gains between 1989 and 1997, and the top 10 per cent took 86 per cent.[11]

At the top of the extreme wealth chart, one finds 497 old and new billionaires who make up today's global aristocracy. The net assets of the 200 richest individuals in the world rose from $463 billion in 1990 to $1,127 billion in 2001 (see Figure 8.1). It is worth noting that nine of the ten richest billionaires in the world are American, as well as almost half of the 200 richest billionaires.

Protected by the sacred dogma of private property, the unlimited hoarding of resources has led to a historically unprecedented concentration of wealth in the hands of a select and insatiable elite. After all is said and done, this is the ultimate goal of globalization: the unlimited accumulation of wealth and power by an elite of fighters. And as a result, the vast majority are impoverished and dispossessed.

In the far reaches of the Third World, the major change brought about by globalization is the emergence of a dispossession process leading to what French economist Michel Beaud calls 'absolute poverty'. In a well-documented article, he explains the novelty of this phenomenon:

In traditional societies, poverty was caused by the low productivity of work, on the one hand, and the levies imposed by the rich and powerful on the low outputs, on the other. Today, in some countries and some rural areas, poverty is caused in part by these same factors; but it is worsened by imbalances between the population and resources and by new needs related to present-day changes. However, it is also accompanied by the destruction of activities and resources that are not compensated by the development of new activities: subsistence agriculture replaced by urbanization and the (state or commercial) development of monocultures; village decline, soil depletion leading to desertification and expropriations.

Hundreds of millions of human beings no longer own their ancestral land; hundreds of millions of others who still own this land can no longer satisfy their basic needs. This is where absolute poverty is setting in: lack of water, soil, firewood, essential resources and food. This absolute poverty is the zero-degree of subsistence with, in extreme cases, unsustainability, destitution, disease and death. The form and scope of this emerging process are new.

In fact, no matter how unequal they were, some societies had in the past allowed the poorest to create ways of living or surviving, redistribution mechanisms or forms of solidarity. Capitalist globalization and the surge of money-based relations are tending to destroy what is left of this.[12]

A Society with Few Winners and Many Losers

In September 1995, against a backdrop of triumphant globalization, the cream of the global elite met in San Francisco's most luxurious hotel to discuss 'labour in the twenty-first century'. About 500 transnational leaders, a handful of famous politicians and a few eminent economics professors attended the Fairmount Hotel meeting to take stock of the re-engineering of labour relations in the global economy. George Bush Sr and Margaret Thatcher made a detour to pay their respects to the new masters of the world. Mikhail Gorbachev, the last president of the Soviet Union, held the place of honour for contributing to the collapse of the Communist regimes which had been slowing the progress of globalization. One of the highlights of the discussions was when John Gage, top executive of Sun Microsystems, astounded the audience by announcing a promising development for the global system: his mega-enterprise now needed only six or maybe eight employees to operate. Obviously including himself among these essential employees, he added: 'We'd be really stuck without them.' The moderator asked: 'How many people are currently working for Sun Systems?' 'Sixteen thousand', answered Gage. 'All but a small minority are rationalization reserves.' And he went on to explain that his corporation hired its staff on a day-to-day basis, according to its needs. Our philosophy, he said, is to find the best brains where they are. Currently, they come from India: competent, not pricey and willing to work long hours. Applications from around the world reach the company by Internet. 'We hire our people by computer, they work on computers and they get fired by computer.'[13] Thunderous applause ensued!

Toning down John Gage's euphoric words, the meeting concluded more realistically, but just as fascinatingly, that a small fifth of the active population would in fact be sufficient to run the globalized economy of the twenty-first century at full throttle. Massive lay-offs will inevitably continue. Computers, robotics, telecommunications and cuts in useless

customer services will continue to increase productivity and, consequently, require fewer workers. A limited, well paid and zealous staff
will be sufficient to produce the goods and services needed for mass
consumption. The others, the remaining four-fifths, will become part of
a useful, but interchangeable, labour reserve. The social and economic
order outlined at the Fairmount Hotel in 1995 and adopted by the
upper echelons of the 'global village' can be summed up in a concise
ratio: 1:4. One-fifth winners and four-fifths losers.

This situation can be explained by the prevailing extreme competition in the global market. The economic war being waged in the labour
market, which is also a battleground, inevitably produces winners and
losers. The CEO of Sun Microsystems and boss of John Gage summed
up his company's philosophy in a terse aphorism, which is also that of
globalization: 'To lunch or to be lunch.' Nevertheless, one cannot conclude that globalization's losers are totally redundant. They represent the
reserve army made up of casual workers, part-timers, McWorkers, working poor, unemployed, welfare recipients, undeclared workers, freelancers
and volunteers. Moreover, the losers remain useful consumers even with
reduced purchasing power. This is not catastrophic anyway since, to
compensate, millions of new consumers can be found in the vast semi-
explored markets of the Third World.

Globalization thus ends the Fordian and Keynesian model applied
during the three decades of prosperity that followed the Second World
War. While remaining capitalist, this model did not refuse to share some
of its benefits with the workers, with the objective of making them
allies of production and mass consumption. It was part of the social pact
designed to create a social equality of sorts by organizing the distribution of wealth. 'Labour flexibility' and other imperatives of globalization
now deny the middle classes and wage earners in general a share of the
profits.

In this globalitarian system, what will happen to the unemployable
and the irredeemable such as the elderly poor, the chronically unemployed, the handicapped, the drug addicts, the insane and the desperate?
Who will take care of these rejects? The global elite of the Fairmount
Hotel clearly indicated that competition and competitiveness do not
allow large corporations to partake in this charitable work. And the
state must no longer disturb the laws of the labour market, through
socialist measures designed to help the so-called destitute, even indirectly

by levying taxes on the multinationals' hard-won income. Is it not the role of the churches, the NGOs, the UN and other charities to take care of the poor? Down with the welfare state! Long live providence!

If such a society creates contented members, like the 500 decision-makers that met at Fairmont Hotel, it is also creating many protesters, dissidents and rebels. The excesses and blindness of globalization are starting to arouse a giant reaction that is crystallizing in various civil society organizations. Seattle could very well have marked the beginning of a worldwide rebellion against the dogmas of global ultraliberalism.

PART II

Reclaiming the Commons

CHAPTER 9

Another World Is Possible

Globalization is a necessary myth because it provokes a sense of political paralysis among those who might otherwise imagine alternatives to an unstable world economy dominated by currency speculators and transnational capital.

Jamie Swift

Is there an alternative to the globalization system and neoliberal logic? Is it realistic to envisage the creation of another social and economic development model ruled not by blind market laws but rather by public interest? In other words, is there a way to put the economy back at the service of society and human development?

It is said that humanity only sets itself problems that it can solve. The devastation of ecosystems, the inequalities dividing humanity between a small number of winners and a majority of losers, the deterioration of democracy, all these plights can be solved with the intellectual, technical and material resources available to us today. To accept this premiss is to accept its consequences: as trustees of our planet Earth, we have the duty to formulate and implement an ambitious world reconstruction project based on new foundations. The important thing is to frame the problem correctly from the outset, in order to size up the task at hand.

The Difficulty of Giving Up an Old Paradigm

Before Copernicus, the Earth was flat and immobile with the Sun peacefully revolving around it. This geocentric view of the universe ordered a system of thought and action that the entire society readily subscribed to. Earth was the centre of the created world. There were an absolute Above and Below – Heaven and Hell – and, between the two, a Here below, the vale of tears of obedient plebeians, who could be exploited at will. Daily life and city structure were organized around this representation of a three-level universe, which gave a prominent position to authorities holding absolute power bestowed upon them by Heaven. By lifting the veil of appearances and demonstrating that it is the Earth that revolves around the Sun, and not the opposite, Nicolaus Copernicus (1473–1543) put into question not only a particular astrophysical model, but also the entire value system of his time. For centuries, the religious and secular pontiffs would fight these Copernican ideas that went against the Scriptures, and the values upon which they had established their domination. As long as the people remained attached to these values, the masters of the world could continue accumulating benefits and privileges.

Nothing is more difficult for the human mind than to change a paradigm – that is, to change mainstream common sense and the worldview provided by those in power. Today's neoliberal religion requires that economic activity, society and life itself be ordered and revolve around the global market. This is without a doubt the most pernicious idea circulating in the world today. It is based on appearances, on an optical illusion of sorts that is distilled into people's minds by the new world masters and their preachers. Like the popes of times past, they claim that the market-centred system is an indisputable and unavoidable natural phenomenon, and is thus devoid of alternatives.

In an extensive interview for Mexico City's *El Financiero*, Mike Moore, WTO director-general and the high priest of free trade, recalled neoliberal orthodoxy and accused of 'idealism', not to say heresy, those who stray from it: 'The globalization process driving the world's economic life is irreversible: there is no other option', he states. Why is this so? the journalist asks. Because 'globalization is not an option designed and planned by a political party [or any human institution]; it is a mechanism [the market] fostering improvements in the standard of living everywhere in the world.' Lenient, he concludes that the Seattle demonstrators are 'good … but idealistic people'. Of course, Mr Moore admits, the global market produces losers, but that's their own fault: 'Certainly, the poorest, the least developed countries, have not been able to benefit from trade liberalization', not for lack of protection, they don't need such protection, he claims, but for 'lack of education and effort' to understand fully the rules of the game and use them to the utmost.[1]

This is the new religion. In *Turbo-Capitalism*, Edward Luttwak notes that the 'American elites do not merely approve of globalization, they treasure it as their only common ideology, almost a religion.' And in this Church, 'far from being condemned for greed, winners are held in the highest regard, and the greatest winners of all are almost in odor of sanctity.'[2] The economic and political elites throughout the world have embraced the ideology of globalization with the fervour of religious fundamentalists. It is thus easy to understand that, if globalization is becoming the official orthodoxy everywhere, it is not for want of realistic alternatives, but rather because the system's privileged castes have succeeded in convincing the masses that it is inevitable and inescapable. Those that oppose it are said to be unrealistic or idealistic.

If we examine civil society at the grassroots level or as it appears in global protests, we may find that a new paradigm is taking shape, which would be bound to replace the current neoliberal creed that has the world revolving around the market.

Idealists Vindicated by History

Throughout the history of civilizations, all those who struggled to broaden the scope of liberty and justice were, in their time, called idealists by the powers that be. And yet, thoroughly convinced that they could not live in a world where these values were not possible, these stubborn idealists succeeded in having their impossible dreams prevail. This was the case of the abolitionists who fought for decades to end slavery. This exemplary cause resembles in many ways that of the opponents to globalization.

In the eighteenth century, the trading and use of slaves were integral to a new international economic order dominated by Great Britain. Slave work was one of the system's most profitable components. Without slaves, cotton would not have been cheap cotton, and without that abundant white fibre from America, the British textile industry, the spearhead of its Industrial Revolution, could not have taken off and eliminated its Asian competitors. In this Age of Enlightenment, the elites gave their unqualified approval and praise to the established order. According to the conventional wisdom of the time, the businessmen who bought and sold Africans in the Liverpool and Bordeaux markets, as well as the Americans who repurchased and used them, were accomplishing good deeds by rescuing millions of blacks from their savagery to integrate them, albeit by force, into Christian civilization and modernity.

Thus, a practice today considered an infamy was, at the time, an integral part of a social and economic system believed to be unsurpassable and beneficial to all, including its victims. The abolitionists, long taxed as idealists and troublemakers, finally prevailed after over a century of relentless struggle. In addition to attacking the new industrial bourgeoisie's very lucrative production and trade system, they had to reverse a paradigm deeply rooted in the minds of their contemporaries by the preachers of the time.

The same can be said, *mutatis mutandis,* of the anti-colonialists. From Bolívar to Ho Chi Minh, they were all idealists who, as the South American Libertador liked to say, ploughed the ocean, the unfathomable ocean of colonial ideology, alienation and practices. In a few decades, their struggles against the current radically changed global geopolitics, given that at the start of the twentieth century barely 10 per cent of the world's population lived in an independent country.

Another, still unfinished, struggle is that of the feminist movement, launched by women driven by an ideal of justice that clashed head-on with a male chauvinism that has prevailed for thousands of years, and that all secular and religious powers have defended tooth and nail. The pioneers in this long march were treated not only as idealists but also as neurotics and perverts. In Canada, machismo was so deeply rooted in the political culture that women had to appeal to the Supreme Court of the British Empire to be recognized, in 1929, as human beings in the constitutional law of their own country.

The forerunners of modern ecology were also accused of unmitigated idealism, since they were challenging powerful interests. It was an honest biologist, Rachel Carson, who sounded the alarm in 1962. In the stinging *Silent Spring,*[3] she described the devastating effects of the first generation of agrochemical products, including the notorious DDT, and followed step by step the deleterious path of these poisons in the environment and the food chain. A massive counterattack was organized, led by

Monsanto, Cyanamid and the entire chemical industry, duly supported by the US Department of Agriculture and the American Medical Association. Mainstream media called her 'a hysterical woman', unqualified to write such a book. *Time* magazine maintained that her book was a collection of 'emotion-fanning words'.[4] Today, Rachel Carson is hailed throughout the world as an avant-garde, intelligent, shrewd and courageous environmentalist. Making amends thirty-seven years later in a special millennium issue, the very same *Time* magazine ranked her among the '100 most influential scientists and thinkers of the twentieth century'.[5]

All these pioneers bring us back to fundamental values, such as solidarity, sharing and co-operation, lost to an amazing degree in our civilization of self-interest and greed.

Two Pillars: Equity and Solidarity

The question is, who are the idealists? Used in the pejorative sense of impractical people who tend to daydream, neglect reality and believe in pipe dreams, this word perfectly fits the globalizers who senselessly dream of building a world based on their personal interests and the unlimited hoarding of wealth. A world ruled not by a democratically organized society, but by the market's blind mechanisms and, in the final analysis, by a handful of privileged beneficiaries of the system.

If, on the other hand, idealism means to be driven by convictions or a social ideal of solidarity, equity and respect for the biosphere, then the anti-globalizers will gladly claim to be idealists. If it is idealistic to propose another system of resource use and distribution, a less destructive and elitist system than that imposed by neoliberal capitalism, then the opponents of globalization will accept the compliment. They believe that promoting a fair social–economic order, based on democracy and respect for our earthly habitat is indeed a very realistic objective that takes into account all human and material realities. To deny the possibility of an alternative solution to globalization is to accept the inevitability of an antisocial, antidemocratic, anti-ecological and, in the final analysis, anti-economic system. It is to deny humanity's creative potential and power to shape its own destiny.

Granted, the challenge is formidable. It is nothing less than rethinking and refounding the world: rethinking humanity's place on Earth;

rethinking progress, the meaning of economic activity and the notion of sharing in solidarity; rethinking gender relations; rethinking relations between nations and international organizations. No doubt, this objective goes against globalization, which advocates individualism, competition, economic war, the extreme concentration of wealth and authoritarian management to the detriment of communities and ecosystems.

The pioneers' alternative proposal can be summed up in the following four points:

1. a community-based and civic-minded economy working in harmony with the entire biosphere and for the sake of all human beings;
2. a worldwide economic system based on equity and solidarity among all nations, and where there is no more Third World;
3. a political democracy in which all citizens can fully participate;
4. a radically new international system to ensure the sustainable and equitable use of the global commons and maintain peace among nations.

A Model to Be Invented from Below[6]

The gurus of ultraliberalism criticize their opponents for not having a general theory to oppose neoliberalism and globalization. In this respect, they are right. We do not have a complete set of dogmas to oppose the neoliberal creed. But this does not bother us; we know that all secular religions, including Marxism-Leninism and neoliberalism, have always been mystifications. They propose to the people an infallible interpretation of human motivations, socio-economic phenomena and the course of history. Such a compact construct made of false postulates, sophisms, 'scientific' laws and mathematical models cannot be required from the opponents to globalization.[7]

As David Korten, one of the most persistent activists of the alternative, wrote, 'no one has yet been where we must go'. We know in which direction we are going, but nobody can say exactly what the socio-economic order we need to build will be like. Although its general direction seems clear, no one can quite imagine what the final structure of the new system will be.[8]

The non-existence of a ready-made alternative model, as in the good old days of the Soviet Union, does not hinder action. New ways of practising economics and democracy are being invented through praxis – that is, through practice combined with a critical approach. Social thought and practice are gradually being renewed, in a proliferation of initiatives, actions, struggles and negotiations that are already taking place in villages, neighbourhoods and regions, both in the Third World and in our opulent societies.

Rethinking locally and globally the wide range of issues that globalization raises cannot be the exclusive matter of a book, of experts or of an intellectual elite, as some theoreticians like to think. As Michel Beaud writes, it can only be 'the fruit of a process taking place in different societies, through developments, awareness-raising, reflections, criticism, analysis, debates, rewrites and questionings'.[9] Conservationist, farmer, essayist and poet Wendell Berry shares this view: 'The real work of planet-saving will be small, humble and humbling. Its jobs will be too many to count, too many to report, too many to be publicly noticed or rewarded, too small to make anyone rich or famous.'[10]

CHAPTER 10

Who Will Do It?

No populist movement emerges full blown, knowing what it wants and how to get it. The values, goals, policies and strategy of this movement are still to be worked out, not from some authority on high, but on a day-to-day basis, by groups around the world with a diversity of passions and beliefs. But one thing is clear: civil society politics are the politics of the twenty-first century.

Maude Barlow

If we admit the possibility, and even the necessity, of creating a new world order, the questions at hand are who will do it and how. Since the state has given up on its responsibilities, what authority, what institution or what social group will have the vision, strength and courage to undertake the reconstruction of the world? Who will rise up to fight the pernicious effects of an intrinsically elitist system that is destroying the environment? Which historical actor will assume the leadership of this great transformation?

The Old Reformers

Albert Einstein warns us not to count on the current system's architects to change it: 'No problem can be solved with the mindset that created it.' The established powers, which approve and encourage globalization and profit from the resulting disorder, can only define the future on their own terms and according to their own interests.

Among the old reformers who formerly intervened to re-establish some balance between the forces of society, there was first of all the state, the official steward of the common good. In the twentieth century in particular, it often intervened to protect the destitute, enact legislation supporting workers and the middle class, and to curb the creation of monopolies and the appetite of big business. Today, the political class has no social project to offer the population, if not that of managing the decline of social, educational and cultural services. It never speaks out against the corporate class, which it considers to be the new sovereign constituency. Its sole project is to develop competitiveness – that is, the ability to compete in the global market, an all-purpose alibi it uses to free itself from its social responsibilities. Even parties claiming to be social-democratic have taken up the defence of the global market. The Greens, who have now entered several European parliaments, seem to have started on the wrong footing; still lacking an integrated alternative project, they seem to be in too much of a hurry to exercise power. Emasculated by its own leaders, the state is consequently no longer a tool for change. Activists working for a new social and economic order find that the state 'is no longer a prime framework for action', notes Immanuel Wallerstein; 'it has become a brake instead'.[1]

And the United Nations? It succeeded in lending its name to the sustainable-development project and became the standard-bearer of several major causes such as decolonization, development, peacekeeping, child protection and public health in the Third World. But, alas, we have seen how, after admitting that it is powerless, it is siding more and more with the new masters of the world to support the penetration of big corporate interests in underdeveloped countries. Obviously, the UN is drifting, thereby helping transnational lobbies convert states into their useful tools.

And the proletariat? Marxists thought that the historical actor for change would be the proletariat. Today, even the word itself has become obsolete. The life-size experiment carried out in the Soviet Union and elsewhere in the world has demonstrated that the working class cannot, on its own, resist the centralizing forces of the state bureaucracy. The flaw of the Communist regimes invented by Lenin and Stalin was to organize the strangling not only of the proletariat but also of civil society as a whole. In 1989, when the latter finally woke up, it brought down the totalitarian regimes of the former communist bloc in Eastern Europe, one after the other.

For a long time at the forefront of social rights struggles, trade unions are now too integrated into the system to challenge it. Globalization has weakened them even more and ended up disorienting them. Today, unionized workers represent only 17 per cent of the world's workforce. In 1960, one wage earner out of four was unionized, whereas in 2000, only one out of six was. Noting the danger of being overwhelmed by events, the labour movement has recently gone to great pains to rethink its strategy and even its policies. At its seventeenth congress held in Durban in May 2000, the International Confederation of Free Trade Unions (ICFTU) acknowledged its need to change the world labour movement in order to achieve real negotiating power vis-à-vis transnational corporations and international institutions. To this end, with 125 million members in 145 countries, the ICFTU intends to create new ties of solidarity between workers from the North and the South and carry out an in-depth review of its strategies and structures.

Reflecting on the vanguard struggles in Chile during the rise and fall of socialism, sociologist Tomás Moulian concludes: 'From now on, the struggles will take place simultaneously on multiple fronts and will be led by numerous protagonists. Diverse and dispersed, spontaneous or organized, they will encompass all kinds of organizations and networks.'[2] The events in Argentina since December 2001 have confirmed this viewpoint: it is not the unions that are leading the struggle against the IMF, the banks and corrupt leaders; it is rather the *piqueteros* (unemployed), the *caceroleras* (women from all classes banging pots and pans) and neighbourhood associations. Union activists simply rallied to this movement.

As for the traditional intellectual left, it has yet to get over the spectacular and sudden demise of the Communist regimes. For 150 years, it considered the conquest of state power as the means radically to transform society. This intelligentsia was left confused by the collapse or deviation of the Leninist and Stalinist regimes. Paralysed by the death of what it believed was the sole alternative to capitalism, it is going through 'a theoretical, programmatic and organizational crisis all at once', as Martha Harnacker, one of the most heeded voices of the old Chilean left, has written.[3]

The Associational Revolution

The rise of the civil society movement represents the most remarkable phenomenon of the late twentieth century. The Center for Civil Society at Johns Hopkins University is conducting a in-depth international study on this question. After completing the first phase of the project, the authors have confirmed that this is a 'veritable associational revolution'. 'So fast is this sector growing in size and importance that it will appear in retrospect as significant an historical development as the creation of the nation-state in the last part of the nineteenth century.'[4] Already in its 1993 annual report on human development, the UNDP noted 'the worldwide emergence of people's organizations – these are all part of a historic change, not just isolated events'.[5] The catalyst of this process, the document observed, is the outrage against rising inequalities and the wholesale aggression against the biosphere worsened by economic globalization.

Paradoxically, globalization's destruction of communities and production of disparities had an unexpected effect: the restructuring of the social movement. By ceaselessly excluding workers and casualizing labour, the globalization process has generated anti-establishment forces that are mobilizing against it. Everywhere consumers, rediscovering their status as citizens, are adopting new ways of practising politics that Maude Barlow, president of the Council of Canadians, calls 'civil society politics'. She observes that this is a global movement taking form in reaction to the globalizing forces: 'In the globalized world of state-less capital, people are searching for roots.'[6] This explains the return to local communities and associations, to ecological groups, to ad hoc committees to defend a territory, a forest, a region, the gene pool.

As early as the end of the 1960s, we witnessed the proliferation of so-called countercultural communities, in reaction to consumerism, that were rather isolated and separated from local populations. Then, citizens' associations gradually emerged in neighbourhoods, villages and peripheral regions.

At the same time, a new type of association appeared: non-governmental organizations (NGOs) working in the field of international development aid. Churches, universities, trade unions and students mobilized to help populations of underdeveloped countries, and to this effect created non-profit, 'non-governmental', organizations, as opposed

to official, governmental and multilateral, development assistance institutions. A few years later, the same phenomenon was echoed in the
Third World, where a flurry of NGOs were created.

In the last two decades, as the globalization of the world advanced,
the civil society movement has constantly grown in importance. Feeling
ridiculed and treated like disposable objects, previously docile consumers
are rediscovering their identity as citizens and challenging the arrogance
of multinational and transnational corporations that carry out their
activities with no respect for ecosystems, communities or social rights.
To this can be added a feeling of mistrust towards the political class that
not only admits its powerlessness but also co-operates wholeheartedly in
the dismantling of the social state. Citizens are increasingly aware that
local problems such as unemployment, the casualization of work, reductions in income, plant closures, the pollution of streams and rivers, the
overexploitation of forests and other abuses are generated by powerful
interests alien to the community and even the nation.

Consequently, people talk, meet and organize in thousands of associations, committees, base communities, co-operatives, pressure groups
and discussion groups. What are they searching for? Solutions to daily
and local problems such as housing, health, literacy, the environment,
women's rights and demilitarization. These groups are not created by
bureaucratic or centralized planning. They emerge from life itself, from
concrete needs and as a reaction to bank or mega-corporate arrogance
and government shortsightedness. They are both independent from established authorities and committed to reappropriating their environment, their quality of life, their social rights, and economic and political
processes. They oppose neoliberalism. In the Third World, the poor –
the old as well as the new poor – are uniting to organize daily struggles
to resist the global corporate assault on public goods and social rights.

The Association for Progressive Communications (APC) is one of
the most active and federative associations in the world. It is a global
alliance linking through the Internet over 50,000 civil society organizations and some thirty national and regional networks with the most
diverse objectives. The APC's goal is to help social organizations and
movements build strategies and initiatives based on principles of social
justice, participatory democracy and sustainable development.

There are many other regional or sector networks, such as the
Malaysia-based Third World Network, which brings together organ-

izations from the North and the South dedicated to civil society's reappropriation of development.

With its main headquarters in Honduras, Via Campesina, an international farmers' coalition founded in 1992, has become ten years later a global movement bringing together national and regional networks of associations of small and medium-size farm owners, farmworkers, landless peasants, as well as rural and native women. It has 70 million members representing more than seventy countries from every region of the world. It defends 'food sovereignty', biodiversity, the planet's gene pool and the environment. Promoting agrarian reform and human-sized farms, it fights against the agrochemical industry and agribusiness. This promising movement has the merit of understanding that in the age of globalization everything is interrelated: agriculture, a healthy diet, soil protection, the right of women to have their farmwork recognized, biodiversity, humanity's gene pool, water, forest management, the quality of the environment, sustainable development and the emancipation of the Third World.

The 1992 Rio Conference on Environment and Development was the first Earth Summit organized by the United Nations. The international civil society movement seized this opportunity to hold its own parallel summit with an agenda that was far broader than that of the official summit. About 850 federations of grassroots organizations representing thousands of associations and millions of members came from every corner of the world to participate in this meeting that took the form of a worldwide NGO forum. Marking the beginning of the search for an alternative to the globalization system, building networks, developing joint strategies, redefining human progress, this parallel summit gave birth to the global civil society.[7]

The Contours of Civil Society

Civil society is the generic term used today to designate the complex and changing universe of countless organizations, associations and groups of all kinds that are independent of public authorities and major economic interests, committed in many different ways to reappropriating economic, political, social and cultural processes at the local, regional, national and international levels. Civil society is open to all tendencies, all forms of organization – NGOs, unions, co-operatives, associations, clubs, and so forth – all movements, all social strata and all trades, so long as they oppose neoliberalism and support non-violent action. Non-exclusive, it rallies all dynamic and often dissimilar forces that are converging in their opposition to globalization policies. They are the civil society organizations (CSOs), a name that is broader than the more restrictive NGO.

Historian Joseph Ki-Zerbo, from Burkino Faso, summed up the essence of this new socio-political reality in a laconic formula: 'Civil society is the people in the face of power.'[8] This simple definition suggests that the fundamental source of all power lies in the people and its grassroots organizations. Only an organized people aware of its strength can defy the two other great powers: the oligopoly lobby and the state.

Civil society is today where public interest is being defined and promoted. Since civil society is made up of imperfect human beings, it is itself imperfect. All its projects can be hijacked by the global system, and sometimes they are, because the system is all-encompassing, if not totalitarian. Because it represents the last bastion of democracy, civil society must live with this paradox by constantly verifying the consistency of its positions and staying the course. It draws its strength from its social base.

Theoretically, the democratic state is a kind of general secretariat created by all the citizens of a given territory in order to defend and promote the public interest. Contemporary states are in fact disconnected from their social base and under the influence of major economic lobbies that are imposing their own agenda. Politicians boast that they are managing the state like a company. Indeed, they are striving to copy the absolute authoritarianism of large enterprises where the mass of employees and small shareholders have learned to rely completely on the board of directors and managers for the management of their interests. It is as if public authorities and bosses had succeeded in convincing citizens that it would be unwise for them to manage their own affairs when the established bureaucracies can take care of them far more efficiently. Bolstered by this illusion, politicians and the economy's super-managers act as if they were the owners of the public good.

The challenge is now for citizens to organize themselves and reverse the process: to reappropriate not only their environment and territory but also the political, economic, social and cultural spheres. This is the common cause uniting the numerous components of the civil society conglomeration.

Fascist, racist and criminal groups as well as other associations or institutions that are linked to state authorities or large economic interests, or both at the same time, are not included in this movement. This is particularly the case of many NGOs that have joined the jet set of the international development industry. International financial institutions (IFIs), such as the World Bank, provide these NGOs with generous contracts, rapidly converting them into their tools to renew their legitimacy in the eyes of the people they are impoverishing.

As for the concept of 'global civil society', it is worth noting, with the *Global Civil Society Yearbook*, that it is totally new:

> Neither the classical term *societas civilis* nor the state-centric concept of 'international society' is capable of grasping the latter-day emergence of a nongovernmental sphere that is called 'global civil society'. These words, 'global civil society', may well sound old-fashioned, but today they have an entirely new meaning and political significance.[9]

The Historical Role of Global Civil Society

Despite its limited experience as a worldwide dissenting force, global civil society already plays a significant role in developing a world conscience, formulating humanity's needs and aspirations and building a new world order. It is searching by trial and error the paths to a world democracy that may take up the major challenges humanity faces today. It is playing this role in three ways:

1. It is the world's moral conscience

Global civil society is challenging the new masters of the world, the money masters, the UN lords of poverty, the capitulating politicos and the blind and greedy bosses. Following the teachings of Amartya Sen, it reminds economists that economics is an ethical science.[10] It reaffirms the values of dignity, freedom and solidarity, rediscovers the place of humankind in nature and redefines the meaning of human progress. It vigorously defends the Earth, the shared homeland of today's and tomorrow's women and men. It stresses everyone's responsibilities towards present and future generations. In short, its function is to civilize human progress.

Is this not the role of religious institutions? This is what these institutions claim. Yet they disqualified themselves for centuries. As highly centralized and hierarchical institutions, they are usually subservient to existing political and economic power structures. The positive aspects of their message are today relayed by grassroots organizations, which do not exclude people of faith.

2. It expresses the needs and aspirations of humankind

Practically no current leader of the globalized world really thinks and talks about the public interest or defines popular needs and aspirations. Claiming to be the global elite, the new masters of the world are aware only of the financial solvency needs they create at will and manipulate to their advantage. Against this perverse policy, one or another component of world civil society rises up, at any time, in any place, to spell out the solvent and insolvent needs of the destitute, the excluded, subordinated women, working children, victims of war and other violence. Civil society defends the biosphere. It speaks in the name of endangered species, condemns transnational poachers and bemoans the distress of vegetation violently attacked by agribusiness and agrochemistry.

3. It leads the implementation of alternative practices

Civil society organizations are laboratories, where new forms of solidarity, production and trade are tried out every day. These experiments will henceforth be part of a general effort to rebuild the world. Through this praxis, citizens and communities are empowering themselves. This is also where the democrats who will work at renewing democracy are trained through social action and community economics. For democracy, it is often forgotten, cannot exist without democrats.

The Role of the State

Citizens concerned with the common good no longer trust politicians. The state is increasingly perceived as a system that cheats, spends lavishly, mismanages and wastes public funds, in addition to favouring friends, groups and companies close to power. There is a growing gulf separating the political class from the people. As soon as they are elected, politicians forget they are representatives of the people and become their party's servants. In many countries they have orchestrated a campaign, currently echoed by the media, promoting the idea that, to attract excellent candidates, politicians need to be better paid – as if integrity, conscience, imagination, political courage and concern for the public interest can be bought. Basically, a well-run democracy does not depend on the technical qualifications of its leaders or on the size of their pay cheques, but rather on the constant vigilance of its citizens.

The problems affecting our political system are more serious than generally believed. Beyond the mediocrity and submissiveness of politicians, the whole system can be felt to be rotting. As practised today, so-called representative democracy is based essentially on a worn and abused electoral process that elicits the people's punctual participation in a voting ritual once every four or five years. Mainstream parties entrust the planning and development of election campaigns to advertising agencies specializing in manipulating public opinion and creating the most favourable image possible of the main candidates. These agencies tell politicians what to say and above all what not to say. A party's real government programme is revealed only after it has been put into place. After casting a vote in the ballot box, the voter is left to accept the deeds and misdeeds of his or her elected representatives.

This being said, the fact remains that the state is responsible for promoting and defending the public interest and social rights. The state is not intrinsically bad or powerless. It tends to become impotent, irresponsible and corrupt in so far as civil society collapses and shows no further interest in its historical responsibilities and abandons them. The newly aware civil society does not seek to become an alternative to the state nor does it want it to disappear. It aims at building an anti-establishment force, a space where democracy can be healed, in order to make the state assume all its responsibilities. In this transition period, the political action of citizens has two simultaneous and complementary objectives:

- to monitor and criticize acting politicians and mandarins, in order to force them to accountability, to defend the environment and social rights, to promote the public interest, to broaden public debate, to stop the global economy's encroachment, and to ensure a fair re-distribution of the wealth produced by society as a whole;

• to develop an alternative political governance based on participatory democracy, an objective that can only be reached by practising a new kind of democracy at the grassroots level, allowing for the making of a new kind of democrat.

The choice is not between reinforcing the state as it is known today and eliminating it. The alternative lies in building a new democratic model where the state bows to civil society rather than to transnational economic interests or special interests. Participatory democracy today exists only at the planning stage.

Between civil society and the state lie local powers. According to the subsidiarity principle that has taken hold, at least in principle, in the European Union, the higher level of government should intervene only when the levels closer to the people cannot manage a particular area or situation. Consequently, the alternative model should promote local governments, the space where democracy really takes root. In fact, it is because democracy has a better chance of being efficient at the local level that governments are pushing municipal mergers so relentlessly, thus creating highly bureaucratized mega-cities that citizens will find hard to control. In the age of globalization, the ultimate objective of the merger promoters is to make ever bigger municipalities, and corporations, capable of competing – that is, ready to wage war against similar or smaller entities.

Is This a Revolution?

Since the alternative involves a radical transformation of the social, political, economic and ethical order, it is no doubt a revolution. However, because it is led not by a handful of charismatic leaders but rather by a conglomeration of social and community movements, because it does not call on violent means but rather on the genius of large numbers, this revolution will surely not be a sudden and violent up-heaval. Instead, it will take shape in a slow process involving mutations, empowerment and transformations. It may evolve for a long time at the grassroots level, sometimes in the form of informal or underground practices – behind the scenes – before appearing in broad daylight.

Alternative societies based on new values are already at work in the 'belly of the beast'. In *Nonviolent Revolution in India*, Geoffrey Ostergaard writes that 'the process [of a non-violent revolution] would be more like that of a biological organism renewing the cells of its body, or of a snake sloughing its old skin when its new skin has been formed.'[11]

One point must be stressed: to succeed, this revolution needs to do without professional revolutionaries, who, as social-change specialist Jean-François Kahn has observed, usually join ongoing social movements to radicalize and destroy them before vanishing into thin air.[12] Kahn goes on to explain that no revolution is successful without the convergence of numerous currents, many apparently antagonistic social strata, large sections of the middle classes, rebel intellectuals, the petty bourgeoisie and even part of the elites.[13] This is a new type of revolution, like no other century has ever seen. The task is all the more demanding, involving a complete transformation of the very concept of revolution.

Here is what a wise old man, philosopher and sociologist has to say on this issue. In *Introduction à une politique de l'homme*, Edgar Morin, who for several decades has been preparing our societies' entry into the twenty-first century, writes:

> In any case, we need to rethink and refine the idea of revolution, which has become reactionary and most of the time is a disguise for domination and oppression. The new concept of revolution needs to be tied to that of conservation, which also needs to be purified and developed. We must preserve nature, preserve cultures that want to live and preserve our past human heritage because it holds the seeds of our future. And at the same time, we must revolutionize this world in order to preserve it. We must preserve the idea of revolution by revolutionizing the idea of conservation.[14]

From Seattle to Porto Alegre

Since the 1992 Earth Summit, globalization has continued to make progress. And so has civil society. In Rio, the close to 850 delegates representing NGOs and other grassroots associations meeting on the beach of Guanabara Bay held their discussions without unduly worrying the 150 heads of state and government, who were generously making false promises to the peoples of the world in the city's top-class hotels. Since then, global civil society has pitched camp at all major UN conferences and G8 summits.

However, since the CSOs understand that, beyond the UN and parliaments, true power lies hidden in the transnational corporations and institutions, they also now demonstrate at each important meeting of the international financial institutions and the World Trade Organization. In November 1999, they converged on Seattle where the WTO had chosen to hold its extraordinary conference at the beginning of the third millennium. The Millennium Round was to kick off a new round of negotiations designed to complete, once and for all, the world's commodification. Proclaiming themselves as honorary hosts, Nike, Boeing and Microsoft graciously financed the event.

And this is how tens of thousands of angry citizens representing millions of CSOs showed up in Seattle. The large American unions and French farmers' organizations joined the protestors to say to the TNCs hidden behind the technocrats and politicians: *Basta!* Enough! The resistance initiated in Seattle marked the awakening of a civil society that has now become global. History will probably remember 30 November 1999 as the date marking the beginning of the twenty-first century, when world civil society succeeded for the first time in delivering a message of total rejection to the powerful economic interests that are coveting the control of the world. That day, the global market and globalization itself lost their innocence. This is what *Time* magazine acknowledged right after the events:

> In this moment of triumphant capitalism, of planetary cash flows and a priapic Dow, all the second thoughts and outright furies about the global economy collected on the streets of downtown Seattle and crashed through the windows of NikeTown. After two days of uproar scented with gas and pepper spray, the world may never again think the same way about free trade and what it costs.[15]

Indeed, since Seattle, global power elites are worried. The passion and stubbornness of their opponents puzzle them. They don't understand the protestors' demands, which seem contradictory to them. Immersed in the logic of profits and isolated from reality by a wall of wealth, globalization crusaders cannot imagine that the resistors to globalization could go to so much trouble and take so many risks without being paid. 'They do not understand doing something because it is right', notes Steve Emmott, a member of the European Parliament's Green Group.[16]

In any case, leaders now pay very close attention to civil society movements. Not because they are now more willing to meet the demands of 'those idealists', but rather because they are seeking to control or coax them. At its July 2000 meeting in Okinawa, the G8 mentioned civil society several times in its enticing final communiqué, inviting it to join a 'new partnership'.

The moral to this story is suggested by an old Ethiopian proverb: 'When spiders unite, they can tie up a lion.' The transnational corporation lobby is far from tied up, but the CSOs have shown that one day they will succeed in doing it by uniting worldwide and setting themselves better defined and increasingly realistic and feasible objectives.

Participating in the first World Social Forum (WSF) in January 2001, French farmer unionist José Bové, who challenged McDonald's, stated: 'Today is a great day! If the twenty-first century started in Seattle, the third millennium starts in Porto Alegre.' Indeed, Porto Alegre, Brazil, a symbolic city because of its participatory budget, was the first meeting place of this genuine global civil society assembly, aware of its historical responsibility as the main actor called upon to refound the world. Timed to coincide with the World Economic Forum, the event attracted more than 10,000 activists from all over the world.

And in January 2003, coming from all continents and in far greater numbers, they were all present in Porto Alegre for the third WSF: ecologists, pacifists, feminists, co-operative members, unionists, landless peasants, artists, natives, grassroots community members, members of southern and northern NGOs, and dissident intellectuals. Over 100,000 participants, 5,710 associations and federations from 156 countries met in 1,300 workshops and seminars to share their alternative experiences, develop strategies, create networks, listen to Third World activists and, in this way, participate in the emergence of a global collective consciousness capable of crying out: ANOTHER WORLD IS POSSIBLE!

Renowned dissident intellectuals, such as Noam Chomsky, Samir Amin and Adolfo Pérez Esquivel, came to add their voices to this multifaceted meeting and enhance its credibility. Many wish future meetings to give more time and space to grassroots organizations, field experience, local self-development and self-financing initiatives in the Third World and elsewhere. What should not be forgotten is that Porto Alegre is both a process and a movement. A movement that knows where it is going – towards a society based on solidarity, fairness and respect for the commons – but that is taking a road that no one has ever taken before, a road that it is building as it goes.

We have the chance of witnessing and participating in the emergence of a citizens' force that is all at once old and new, local and global, humble and superbly proud, patient and impetuous: global civil society. Maude Barlow is not exaggerating when she observes that civil society represents the emerging force of the new millennium.[17]

CHAPTER 11

Reclaiming the Economy

Without a prosperous local economy, the people have no power, and the land no voice.

Wendell Berry

As the globalitarian system primarily involves the authoritarian appropriation of economic processes by a transnational oligarchy, the key to an alternative lies in civil society's democratic reclaiming of the economy. True to its mercantile ethos, the global market structures and orients each society in accordance with the products supplied by it. The alternative logic would see society structuring and orienting the economy in accordance with people's aspirations, fundamental rights and needs.

Resistance is arising throughout the world in every sphere of activity, but the struggle for equality and for preserving and sharing the commons fairly must first be carried out in the realm of economics. One effect of such a movement will be the reuniting of the economy with society as a whole.

All Economics is Social by Definition, but...

The term 'social economics' is a pleonasm of sorts because economics is intrinsically social – that is, the economy is completely immersed and rooted in society, and is dependent on common goods and humanity's technological legacy. Neo-capitalist economics has obliterated the social sphere from its field of vision (and accounting) by engineering an unnatural separation. Hence, the aberrant 'externalization' of the costs of damages wreaked upon the environment and communities. Like it or not, even the most ultraliberal capitalist company is a social institution. In effect, it is in society's debt regarding the material, human and technological resources and infrastructures it needs to operate. This fact notwithstanding, neither business leaders nor conventional economics are willing to acknowledge any genuine social responsibilities. Milton Friedman's (in)famous maxim only confirms what the global elite practises and thinks: 'The social responsibility of business is to increase its profits.'[1] The very concept of corporate social responsibility is an oxymoron; as billionaire philosopher George Soros so pithily put it: 'You can't ask them to jump out of their skin.' At best, large corporations are willing to contribute to certain community projects through philanthropic foundations, either to avoid taxes or to improve their corporate image.

To put it bluntly, capitalist companies will acknowledge their social responsibilities only if the state forces them to do so, and the state will recognize its responsibilities only if it is forced to do so by civil society or in the event of a serious systemic breakdown. This is what happened during the Depression of the 1930s, when governments were prompted to introduce social security. However, the state's absorption of the social sphere had unintended side effects. The welfare state rapidly became paternalistic. Civil society became complacent, allowing public administrations to monopolize and overgovern the social sphere. People came to see the state as an ally, when in reality it was simply encouraging consumption to shoulder capital accumulation and profit generation. Demobilized by the system's paternalism and contaminated by its individualistic ideology, civil society became apathetic.

In the early 1980s, encouraged by its growing influence over the state, the powerful transnational corporation lobby began pressuring governments to revise their social policies. The new masters of the world complained that when social assistance and unemployment insurance programmes are too generous, they harm labour flexibility and, by the same token, competitiveness. Using the crisis in public finances as a pretext, politicians complied, stealthily at first, and later increasingly overtly. Social rights won through hard-fought battles during the last century became simple needs to be satisfied by the private sector, provided that the beneficiaries could afford them. As for the unprofitable needs, families and charities remain to assume those responsibilities. This is the historical setting into which the new social economics emerged.

The New Social Economics

A number of alternative economic practices have evolved since the middle of the nineteenth century. Grouped under what is called social economics, these practices have pretty much melded into the landscape of classical capitalism. In 1844, a group of weavers, disciples of British reformer Robert Owen, founded the first co-operatives: the Rochdale Society of Equitable Pioneers. This innovative company would become a model for the co-operative movement that would soon spread throughout Europe. In the wake of this movement, seen as an answer to cutthroat competition and the social inequalities inherent to capitalism, the first financial co-operation experiments appeared in Germany. Based on a visionary concept advanced by Friedrich Wilhelm Raiffeisen, they aimed at empowering people to gain control over their own destiny through economic and social solidarity.

Since the beginning of the 1990s, the attraction of the globalitarian economy has been undermining this vision. If, today, Raiffeisen were to visit institutions claiming to follow his principles, such as the powerful Rabobank (Coöperatieve Centrale Raiffeisen-Boerenleenbank), the largest financial institution of the Netherlands, or the Desjardins Movement in Quebec, he would likely be quite astonished and disappointed. Rather than fulfilling their own potential and *raison d'être*, co-operative credit and savings institutions, as well as so-called popular and co-operative banks, have been seized by a frantic rush to expand massively in the belief that their security and future now hinges on the size of their assets and their competitiveness with conventional banks. Lacking the courage and daring required to apply the principles of co-operative solidarity in tune with the social environment, they look for models among the heroes of high finance.

Combating this aberration are numerous forms of solidarity economics developed over the last two decades, in the wake of the retreat of the welfare state. These new experiments are trying to revive the intrinsically social dimension of economic activity. Grouped under the generic heading of social economics, these initiatives bear many names:

solidarity economics, the parallel economy, the third sector, community development initiatives, the plural economy, the non-market economy, the people's economy, participatory economics, the informal economy, and so on. The driving force behind them is a very diverse range of social movements – such as the community-based, women's, environmental, labour and co-operative movements. Each one defines in its own way the rules for implementing solidarity and the social dimension of economic activity.

All economic systems are social, but only social economics recognizes this. This is, or should be, translated in the assertion of solidarity values and the establishment of democratic structures in economic projects designed to be social. Whatever their form, size or activities, these institutions all claim to follow five fundamental principles:

1. independence from the state and big capital interests;
2. voluntary membership;
3. democratic governance and management structure;
4. primacy of community, people and labour over capital;
5. fair distribution of income and surpluses.

Some theorists tend to pigeonhole the social economy in the community services sector (home-care services, daycare, the reinsertion of the unemployed into the labour market, and so on), as well as culture, sports and the environment. The new practitioners of social and solidarity economics give it a far larger role, seeing it as a space 'for the democratization of the economy, where the economic and social spheres are reconciled and where alternatives can be built within a social project that is more supportive of and fairer to all.'[2] Legally, a social economics project may take the form of a co-operative, a membership organization, a non-profit organization, or even a joint-stock company, as long as the shareholders institute by-laws that accord with the objectives of social economics.

Is State Recognition a Good Thing?

Throughout the world, the powerful emergence of diverse social economics initiatives has caught the eye of governments grappling with huge budget deficits, high unemployment rates and an upsurge in undeclared work. Instead of fighting this movement, public authorities have chosen to channel and, indeed, make use of it. Whence a change in public discourse which marked a shift in public policy towards the social economy. Even the OECD has kind things to say about it. This transformation occurred in the USA and several EU countries at the beginning of the 1980s. Agents of social economics were invited to work in partnership with the state, which had opened up for them a niche in the provision of social-utility goods and services. These include personal home services, the transportation of persons with impaired mobility, daycare services, literacy, humanitarian relief and support for sports and cultural activities. There was enthusiastic talk of a new 'pool of jobs' for the unemployed and others excluded from the neoliberal economy.

In France, the creation in June 2000 of a Ministry of Social Economics and Solidarity gave national exposure to this 'third sector', which encompasses not only community services but also the vast field of some 1,400 co-operative production companies, or SCOPs, and mutual financial companies. Official recognition of the social economics and solidarity sector by the French authorities has not been without numerous paradoxes. While the champions of social economics readily talk of new economic practices, they don't go so far as proposing social economics as an alternative to the neoliberal model.

Hailed as a victory by such proponents, this state intervention into the field of social economics has created ambiguities that divide the concerned social movements and give rise to criticism. Does state involvement represent a genuine recognition of the contribution of social economics to the transformation of neoliberalism or are we witnessing an attempt on the part of governments to use this movement to their own advantage? This is a thorny question. Politicians insist that there is a 'new partnership'. Beware this fashionable buzzword! The partnerships proposed by governments are seldom equal, for they are not based on shared values and objectives. In such alliances, the stronger party, the state in this case, inevitably and subtly tries to take advantage of the weaker party to impose its own views.

Beyond its stated intentions, what is the government's real perspective? What are its objectives? Finance ministers and state bureaucracies certainly see social economics as a means of providing jobs to people who would otherwise swell the welfare and unemployment lines, but they also see it as a means of providing essential services that have already been, or are on the verge of being, abandoned by the government. It is worth noting that in this partnership, the government finances a certain percentage of the costs, but forces community organizations to find the rest in the pockets of beneficiaries or in the guise of volunteer work.

Should one, then, conclude that it's a lost cause, that social economy organizations will inevitably be co-opted? It depends. Such an outcome is by no means certain and many organizations have succeeded in avoiding it. As indicated earlier, all civil society projects can potentially be co-opted by the powers that be. Even if community economics projects do not always produce the results hoped for at the outset, they often help raise awareness and develop distinct local patterns of endeavour, derived from self-organization.

In short, in a world where nothing is perfect, all forms of social economics, whatever their ambiguities, belong to a space where alternative development models can be tested; out of these experiments, tools are forged that may serve to initiate processes of change. It should never be forgotten that social economics is a school for workers and citizens, the main virtue of which is to prefigure the coming of a new type of economy.

Tell Me Who Pays the Piper...

The key challenge of social economics is, of course, the raising of consciousness among its participants, a process that requires time and practice. Immediately after comes the financing problem. Any number of social economics experiments carried out throughout the world have shown that when it comes to community development, local development or social development, the rub is in the financing. Underfinancing is certainly the key obstacle encountered by the popular and community movement in fulfilling its mission. Because of the weak direct and recurring financing they receive, the vast majority of groups are forced to resort to government job creation or employability programmes in order to survive. Yet, as we saw earlier, it is dangerous for alternative economics projects to be too dependent on government grants since such grants, which more often than not are uncertain and involve conditionalities, tend to divert the action of the beneficiary organizations.

It bears noting that it is entirely normal and desirable that the state help finance community development and access to employment. After all, it is responsible, *ex officio*, for the redistribution of wealth in society. It is only fair and equitable that communities and the different social justice and anti-poverty movements demand their fair share of the public purse. Consequently, public financing of social enterprises is welcome, as long as the latter also remain relatively independent so far as financing is concerned – that is, able to resist government-bureaucracy pressure and negotiate on an equal footing. Otherwise, sooner or later, the state will impose its views. For that is in the nature of things. Civil society can gain some control over government policies only by creating a power relationship which hinges on a certain degree of financial independence. Popular movements which are to some extent financially independent must maintain their cohesion if they are to make governments think again and possibly bend.

As for traditional banks, in these times of global competition, they are no longer interested in financing small clients, or willing to take risks to help launch social companies, much less very small companies, which they deem high risk and not very profitable. They would rather give up this part of their mission, even though it is essential, to concentrate on far more profitable activities such as asset management and myriad speculative ventures. They are taken aback by the attitude of social economy entrepreneurs who are ready to sacrifice some financial profitability in favour of social profitability. Indeed, the very logic of social economics escapes them. Consequently, their clever rhetoric notwithstanding, banks and even large financial co-operatives are willing to invest only a very small share of their assets in social economics projects. If, from time to time, they offer some support to such projects, it is out of humanitarian concerns rather than a willingness to take part in an alternative model.

This behaviour on the part of governments and conventional financial institutions forces alternative social enterprises intent on preserving their mission to create new 'social financing' sources in the interests of maintaining their independence. Without some freedom of thought and action, these enterprises cannot participate in a genuine reappropriation process. It is no secret that the freedom of communities, as well as of individuals, requires a certain degree of financial independence.

This raises an issue seldom addressed by social economics theorists: the importance of mobilizing local savings to finance social enterprises and community-centred development. Surprisingly little attention is paid to this essential factor in the creation of material, social and human capital. Yet, sooner or later, one way or another, the need to save catches up with us all. Both for communities and individuals, savings are the price of autonomy, freedom and development. Moreover, it has been observed that the educational effect of savings, at the different stages of its mobilization and management, often plays a greater role in community development than the investment itself.

The reasoning behind the traditional neglect of local savings is straightforward: how can a community finance itself if it is poor and destitute to start with? Since the community does not have any money, it depends on grants. This is a rather weak argument. A closer look reveals that if the communities lack funds to finance their development projects it's because their local resources are funnelled to the large centres. Banks, insurance companies, lotteries and, alas, traditional financial co-operatives relentlessly siphon off the potential savings of neighbourhoods, villages and regions and redirect them to the centres of power, which serve themselves generously and don't hesitate to invest the rest abroad.

Three axioms may be derived from the preceding points:

1. A social economics project can ensure its independence and survival only if it enjoys a sufficient degree of self-financing.
2. The precariousness of a social economics project is in direct relation to its dependence on external financing over which it does not exercise control.
3. The state will lend its disinterested support to the development of social economics only when forced to do so; otherwise, it will try to co-opt the process to favour its own political ends through tied contributions.

The New Financial Instruments of Social Economics[3]

Since the resurgence of neoliberalism, we are witnessing the emergence of a new form of 'social finance', the apparent seed of a financial counterculture. Like social economics, social finance is the daughter of necessity, the necessity of creating an alternative to the bankrupt traditional banking system which has demonstrated its inability to meet the financial needs of the least well-off. This is no doubt why the first contemporary micro-credit experiments were developed in the poorest countries of the world: Bangladesh, Bolivia and several countries in sub-Saharan Africa.

In Europe, starting in 1989, the new financial instruments of social economics have formed a Brussels-based network called the International Association of Investors in the Social Economy (INAISE). This network has some fifty members, characterized by highly varied legal structures, sizes and financial tools. INAISE includes popular banks, financial mutual associations, investment trusts, associations and guarantee funds. However, these institutions all share common features:

- they are closely tied to social movements;
- they work almost exclusively with small and very small companies that create jobs;
- they are young (most of them are less than 10 years old) and therefore small; most of them have only just completed their first full financial-investment cycle (mobilization of savings, loans, investments, recovery of funds, loans); and
- they are profitable, capital recovery being a requirement for making capital available again to the community; that said, profitability is not seen in exclusively financial terms, as social profitability counts too.

Here are a few examples:

- ART (Aston Reinvestment Trust) of Birmingham, Great Britain, aims at overcoming the chronic shortage of investment and, consequently, jobs, in Birmingham's underprivileged neighbourhoods. In operation since 1996, this social economics institution works with very small companies, particularly in the field of energy conservation, by providing support services together with its partners.
- CRÉDAL (Crédit alternatif), based in Louvain-la-Neuve in Belgium, was created in 1984 by small investors challenging the way traditional financial institutions used their savings. Its customer base includes mainly associations and co-operatives that adhere to the principles of social economics and solidarity and that are involved in developing job-creating projects.

• La Société financière de la NEF (Nouvelle économie fraternelle), created in France in 1987, is a co-operative financial organization active throughout France. It collects activist savings and makes loans to social enterprises that are ignored by the traditional banking system.

Before ending this brief overview of the social economy's financial instruments, it is worth mentioning the rapid expansion of a local monetary system called LETS, for Local Exchange Trading System. Members of an association or community applying this system define a unit of account for measuring the value of their transactions. On this basis, they locally exchange a wide range of goods and services outside official monetary circuits. 'The first community-currency system was born in Canada in 1983. Since then, the concept has spread to more than 2,000 communities across North America, South and Central America, Europe, Africa and Asia.'[4] As tools for relearning democracy, the various types of LETS are designed to return money to its true purpose, that of fostering trade between human beings as opposed to effortless personal enrichment through speculation on the wealth produced by others. The emergence of LETS is demystifying money. People come to realize that they can create their own currency and needn't wait for banks or governments to create local trade networks.

The Hidden Side of the Third World Economy[5]

In the other, underdeveloped and maldeveloped, world, globalization has prompted a spectacular upsurge in the informal sector of the economy, a sector which until recently had been deemed archaic in light of the development of modern industry. The informal economy, more appropriately called the people's economy, is the hidden face of the Third World. The casualization of labour and generalized impoverishment, caused by the IMF's and World Bank's structural adjustment programmes, have forced people to invent new ways of surviving. As a result, in the face of impotent governmental bureaucrats, a genuine popular economy is developing beyond any regulations, public accounting, tax collection and conventional notions of the GNP. If necessary and when possible, this sector uses the official financial system, which generally refuses to provide regular banking services to women and the poor. It gladly feeds on the official sector by recycling the was rich. The people's economy dispenses with permits and licens_ whelmed by this incredible dynamism, the state simply cannot keep count of and register all these organizations and their numerous activities: there's too much going on! This may mean these organizations are in some sense illegal, but this is not necessarily so, because governments are forced to tolerate them, and even grant them some legitimacy in order to ensure their own survival.

Long ignored and disparaged by international development experts, the informal economy is now recognized as the people's spontaneous and legitimate answer to the state's inability to fulfil the vital needs of the impoverished masses, who have been left on the sidelines of the global economy. In most underdeveloped countries, the informal economy represents over half of the official GNP. In India, the informal manufacturing sector creates twice as many jobs as the official one. In Latin America, studies have found that in major cities, 65 per cent of jobs depend on the informal sector. When Vicente Fox, the president of Mexico, took office in December 2000, he publicly recognized that in his country, a member of NAFTA since 1994, 50 per cent of the population depends on the informal sector. In less advanced countries, this percentage is higher still. The World Bank has estimated that 'in Western Africa, the informal sector provides a livelihood to most of the active population. According to estimates, it employs 90 per cent of the labour force in Senegal, 85 per cent in Mali, and 62 per cent in Guinea.[6]

Formal and informal micro-financing and self-financing institutions have also mushroomed since the early 1980s, with local savings as their main source of funds. The Third World's voluntary savings capacity is now well documented. Marguerite S. Robinson, a long-time specialist of local empowerment, estimates that 'rural undersaving is a myth'. Her work has shown that what has been lacking up to now are institutions capable of tapping into and mobilizing small savings.[7] More and more institutions of this kind are being created.

In Bolivia, BancoSol (Banco Solidario), an unorthodox bank founded in 1992 to foster popular savings, micro-credit and the development of very small enterprises, manages a portfolio of over $50 million and serves tens of thousands of small investors and businesspeople, 70 per cent of whom are women. BancoSol has innovated by lending to the poor without any guarantee other than the co-responsibility of borrowers: groups of five or six borrowers are jointly responsible for the loans. Created in 1976 in Bangladesh by economics professor Muhammad Yunus, the Grameen Bank (village bank) is the pioneer of solidarity micro-credit. In 2002, it had 2.4 million members, 95 per cent of whom were women. Since its creation, it has always followed the principles of solidarity micro-credit, lending the incredible sum of US$3.5 billion and receiving $150 million in deposits.[8] This shows how short the turnaround period is in this kind of popular financial intermediation institution.

In 1995, intrigued by the unprecedented proliferation of microfinancing institutions in the Third World, the World Bank ordered a wide-ranging study to inventory these formal and informal financial entities. The researchers found tens of thousands of institutions managing 46 million accounts worth $19 billion.[9]

Is the informal economy now spreading in the expanses of the Third World an embryonic alternative to the official economy? No small matter given that the latter has failed to free even one country from underdevelopment or maldevelopment since the advent of international aid. Nobody knows for sure, but we can only note with Bruno Lautier, a renowned specialist on the informal economy, that it already is 'a social alternative, fostering the renewal of democracy at the grassroots level, with general meetings taking decisions on everything from community kitchens to the creation of community jobs'.[10] Lautier adds:

> It involves not only individual but also collective self-organization (e.g. the emergence of new commercial networks and spreading of innovations). This popular economy is defined as counter-capitalist and as the only means for the poor to change their situation – that is, through economic rather than political mobilization as in the 1960s and 1970s.[11]

How does this economy of the poor and destitute concern us? Why should it interest an industrialized world sailing in a sea of prosperity? Lautier's conclusion is food for thought:

> The informal economy in the developing countries holds up a mirror to us, in the industrialized countries. It reflects an image of us or, perhaps, a caricature, we may wonder. What can it teach us? How can what is happening there be considered not simply as backwardness, but also in part as a possible foreshadowing of our future?[12]

The answer to these questions lies in three observations:

1. Whether it is seen as a problem or a solution, the development of the informal sector of the economy arises from situations also found throughout the industrialized world.
2. Casual work, underemployment and the impoverishment of the masses are no longer realities observed exclusively in the far reaches of the Third World.
3. The spreading of undeclared work in industrialized countries is similar, in both its causes and its effects, to the informal economy; here and there, the underground economy is the tax haven of the people.

These Third World self-help initiatives also provide us with another lesson, summed up in a saying from Andean America:

> No hay desarrollo
> Sino a partir de su propio rollo

Development is possible only if it is based on self-generated means: development is possible only through self-development. That is the lesson of fifty years of foreign aid and indebtedness. Moreover, NGOs with several decades of experience in implementing savings and loan co-operatives in the Third World have drawn the following lesson: development projects failed every time an ill-considered contribution of external capital disturbed the internal dynamics of community co-operation and development. In contrast to 'warm money' generated by local savings and 'heated' by local people's work, 'cold money' from outside has a negative impact on the development of co-operatives.

What has proved to be damaging for Third World economies will also be damaging for a social economy too dependent on grants and the influx of external funds beyond its control.

Reference Points for the Alternative Economy

Although there is no ready-made alternative economy model, successful experiments and novel forms of solidarity do exist. These have been invented by people everywhere and may serve as an inspiration for action. These breakouts against the dominant trends of globalization and the neoliberal faith represent beacons shedding light on and marking out the path to an increasingly popular alternative order. Without constituting a theory per se, they appear as main themes out of which coherent ideas may be extracted for the rebuilding of our communities and the world.

Solidarity, keystone of the alternative economy

Solidarity is the keystone of the alternative economy. As a basic individual and collective value predicated on sharing common resources fairly, it links humanity and nature, women and men, young and old, the North and the South, today's generation and future generations, the Earth and the universe. Without solidarity there is no equality, and without equality no freedom.

The first challenge facing the artisans of the alternative economy is to replace the individualism at the heart of the neoliberal order with solidarity-based values. Globalization dislocates communities, cities and villages; the alternative economy defies this trend by rebuilding ties and networks. This is the fundamental feature of alternative order projects. Community kitchens in Peru, village banks in Africa and Asia, peasant demands in Europe – all these initiatives are based on a central value: solidarity. And it is for good reason that these diverse economic activities, which all tend to reunite the economic and social realms, all fall under the umbrella of social economics.

The champions of neoliberalism view this solidarity ideal as utopian. Didn't the ancestor of all neoliberal preachers insist that the sum of all perfectly selfish individual interests represents the basic framework of social organization? Throughout history, haven't domination and exploitation prevailed over mutual aid and solidarity? The builders of the alternative would no doubt answer yes... but is that a reason to continue such barbaric practices? After all, hasn't human destiny been a long enterprise in the civilizing of our own species?

The primacy of ecological rationality

In the alternative economy, *Homo ecologicus* takes precedence over *Homo economicus*. Today, any planning, and any economic and social activity, require a green perspective. In turn, this presupposes a global view of humanity and its destiny, its place in the universe and history, its link to all other living beings and its radical dependence on the limited resources

Box 11.1   Peru's community kitchens

The community kitchen movement, which is experiencing rapid
expansion in Quebec, emerged in Peru in the 1980s. In a country
already ravaged by underdevelopment and the corruption of its political elites, the IMF's imposition of structural adjustment programmes
further deepened the health, housing and nutrition problems in the
slums. Everywhere in the world, when it comes to subsistence and
survival, women take the initiative by first tackling the most urgent
problem, hunger. In Peru, they decided to address this problem with
solidarity and dignity, by joining forces and sharing their limited
resources to provide their families with a balanced and affordable diet.

This is how the *comedores populares* (community kitchens) were
created, as genuine popular restaurants or cafeterias serving each day's
main meal to members. Several of the kitchens also provide breakfast,
an afternoon snack and special diets for pregnant women suffering
from vitamin deficiencies. They also give vocational training to their
participants. Today, there are over 10,000 community kitchens throughout Peru bringing together 250,000 women and feeding 1.3 million
people every day. They are bona fide mutual enterprises that are
sufficiently self-financed to not depend on the government or charities. Several of them have extended their activities to the production,
supply and retail sectors (bakeries, butcher shops, etc.). United in
regional organizations and a national federation, the *comedores populares*
represent today an economic and political force that politicians only
ignore at their peril.

Source: Lucie Fréchette, *Entraide et services de proximités. L'expérience des cuisines
collectives*, Sainte-Foy. Presses de l'Université du Québec, 2000.

of our nurturing mother, the Earth. This perspective throws light on all
the other points of reference. It necessarily generates a culture based on
sharing and, consequently, on the frugal enjoyment of nature's fruits. It
is a guiding light shining brightly on rebuilding projects everywhere.

Ecological reconstruction requires that economic rationality be subordinated to ecosocial rationality. Such subordination is incompatible
with the deregulated competition plaguing the world markets. In that
regard, nature itself sometimes gives object lessons to economic and
political leaders.

When in the mid-1980s, following the precepts of pure economic rationality, Exxon decided to eliminate the pilot boats escorting its supertankers in the waters of Prince William Sound near Valdez, in southern Alaska, it saved several million dollars. However, when one of its tankers ran aground in the Sound, the petroleum giant lost billions of dollars in the clean-up, in legal fees and in damages paid out to the area's residents and 34,000 fishermen. And this does not include the incalculable damages caused to the environment and society in general.

In the United Kingdom, every government since Mrs Thatcher's rise to power has applied neoliberal deregulation policies to agriculture in order to implement a laissez-faire regime. This is why, over the years, the Department of Agriculture closed half of its sanitation centres responsible for monitoring the health and food quality of farm animals. Government laboratory budgets were cut in half, dozens of veterinary positions were eliminated, and the number of slaughterhouses was reduced by two-thirds. Almost half of all family farms disappeared while an oligopoly cornered downstream activities: five groups now control distribution. This allows them to impose their views, standards and prices on producers. All this produced an impressive success story in one sense: since 1990, retail prices have dropped by 10 per cent. And yet Great Britain imports ever more agricultural products. Despite their extra efforts constantly to increase productivity, most farmers are working at a loss and only survive thanks to the millions of euros of aid they receive every year from the European Union. Constantly destabilized by market fluctuations, the sector remains in thrall to insecurity. All the preceding facts were as so many warning signals, blinking for several years. However, cut off from reality, politicians refused to see them – until the animals themselves rebelled against this system in violation of the laws of nature. Trembling sheep, swine with foot-and-mouth disease and cattle with BSE… all of them are condemning, in their own way, the productivity race and the madness of deregulation. The happy consumers that were saving 10 per cent on their food bills have now been forced to put on their taxpayer hats and asked to foot the bill for cleaning up this huge mess, a bill totalling several billion pounds.

In Ontario, when the most neoliberal government in Canada took office in 1995, it gave concise instructions to its civil servants: business first, environment second. As a result, it saved several million dollars by slashing 45 per cent the budget of the Department of the Environment, which was seen as an obstacle to economic growth. This was called the 'common sense revolution' – until the summer of 2000, when catastrophe struck in the small agricultural municipality of Walkerton, northwest of Toronto. The water system there became contaminated with *E. coli* bacteria: 2,300 people fell ill, many seriously, and at least seven people died. The government was forced to confront a crisis that in the end would cost over $1 billion in hospital fees, tax and tourism losses, works to restore the water-supply system, and lawsuits. In a sad way, Walkerton helped bring home to opportunistic politicians the real meaning of 'common sense': a healthy environment is a necessary condition for a healthy economy.[13]

The co-operative system, backbone of the alternative economy

Designed from the outset as an alternative solution to the antisocial nature of capitalism, the co-operative system is by definition inextricably economic and social, as well as profitable and democratic. The genuine co-operative refuses to choose between economic profitability and social utility, embracing both at the same time. The fact that the principles of co-operativism coincide in all respects with those of social economics has probably not been sufficiently stressed. These principles are:

- *democratic management*, which fosters the burgeoning of solidarity, equality and dignity;
- *autonomy*, which places value on independence from centres of power, on self-help – that is, taking over one's own affairs, on proper administration of the co-operative and on its integration into a pro-active community;
- *equity*, which means the fair distribution of income and surpluses;
- *voluntary membership*, which recognizes the values of liberty and personal accomplishment.

Those are the principles. In practice, today's co-operative movement is not exempt from contradictions. For example, imbued with hubris driving from the gigantic size of their assets, some financial and agri-cultural co-operatives have heeded the siren calls demanding that they pit themselves against the global economy's mega-institutions. They

Box 11.2   Mondragón Corporación Cooperativa: a
co-operative island in a capitalist sea

Created in 1956 in Spain by foundry workers wishing to manufacture
kerosene stoves, the Mondragón co-operative group gradually diversified
its activities and is present today in practically all economic sectors,
from heavy industry to the manufacture of silicon chips. The group
comprises eighty production entities, two distribution co-operatives, a
dozen service co-operatives (including insurance, design, consulting,
social security, etc.), fifteen agricultural co-operatives and a network
of savings and credit co-operatives controlled by a self-managed bank,
the Caja Laboral Popular, or workers' credit union. In addition, the
group manages three research centres and numerous education centres,
including four university-level schools and a secondary-level vocational
school.

Mondragón Corporación Cooperativa has annual sales of US$5
billion. It employs 30,000 worker–owners. Its salaries are slightly higher
than the average paid in this part of the Basque country. The ratio
between the lowest-paid employees and highest-paid managers varies
from 1:3 to 1:7, depending on the type of company. Ecology is an
integral part of the decision process. During the 1975–85 recession, at
a time when the Basque country (2.1 million inhabitants) was losing
100,000 jobs, the Mondragón group continued to hire.

Mondragón is, of course, subject to regional and international
economic realities. Since the early 1990s, as globalization has progressed,
it has been confronted by new challenges. As a result, the co-operative's
administrators are sorely tempted to short-circuit some of the principles
of co-operation by invoking the imperatives of competition. Some of
the co-operative's entities wish to hire non-member workers under
conditions inferior to those enjoyed by member workers. Solidarity-
based values are maintained only through the permanent action of
counter-powers organized at the base. Co-operative members are
offering proof day-in day-out that co-operativism is based on solid
principles and can represent a realistic alternative to the neoliberal
economy.

Sources: Roy Morrison, *We Build the Road as We Travel*, Philadelphia and Gabriola
Island, BC: New Society Publishers, 1991; and www.mondragon.mcc.es.

desperately seek integration into the system of exploitation which they were originally mandated to civilize – this, at the risk of co-optation.

When such institutions experience bureaucratization stemming from expansion, their original values can only be maintained through the ceaseless work of counter-powers forcing renewal upon them. Happily, these counter-powers exist and are already at work in rebuilding co-operativism, which, due to its long experience, should assume a role as a flagship of social and solidarity economy.[14] In the Basque country, in Spain, an entire region (200,000 inhabitants) lives by the co-operative creed. For forty years, the Mondragón co-operative group has demonstrated that true co-operativism can be the backbone of a profitable and democratic socio-ecological economy, capable of responding to the needs and aspirations of modern society (see Box 11.2).

The democratically controlled and regulated market

The social and solidarity economy is fighting not against the market but rather against neoliberalism, which has perverted the market's mechanisms. As progressive economist Karl Polanyi has noted, the market has existed since the first human communities settled and created cities. It has existed in all civilizations, since humanity first learned to trade its surplus production, some 10,000 years ago. But, Polanyi adds, 'never before our time were markets more than accessories of economic life. As a rule, the economic system was absorbed in the social system.'[15]

Unless one assumes that humans are angelic by nature, it is impossible to see how a democratic social economy could do without the market as a mechanism for trading goods and services. However, contrary to neoliberal capitalism, the alternative economy does not subscribe to the view that the market can on its own determine the public interest. It is a useful tool for realizing economic and social objectives set by local communities and, ultimately, the nation as a whole. The social control of investments and trade will always be an essential counterweight to the monopolistic and anarchistic trends of the market.

Those who might be tempted by the centralized planning of production and distribution as an alternative to the market need only examine the still-fresh experience of Soviet-style Communism, which demonstrated its propensity for inefficiency and the authoritarian concentration of power. Properly controlled by the community and the democratic state, the market remains a vital space for economic trade and dialogue and the most efficient mechanism to indicate to producers and even planners what needs to be produced, and in what quantities and varieties.

Internationally, the wholesale liberalization of trade has paved the way for the complete perversion of market mechanisms. The world fair-trade movement was created as an alternative solidarity market to nibble away at the coyotes' monopolistic market and open up a path for world solidarity.

Capital without capitalism

Local and community development, as well as all the other forms of the new social economy, show that financing plays an essential role in the start-up, operation and durability of businesses. Obviously, the alternative economy needs capital. Does this mean that the alternative economy will be capitalist? While the social economy cannot work without capital, it can and should use capital without lapsing into the faults of capitalism, much less those of neoliberal capitalism. What is capital, if not accumulated work, put aside to manufacture or buy tools that increase productivity?

Let us not be scared of words. In addition to good will, the social economy needs capital to operate in a harmonious, independent and progressive fashion. It must also be profitable in order to ensure its continuity and independence. Social economics differs from asocial and amoral capitalism in that communities and company members exercise control over their investments and profits. That makes all the difference. In a mutual or social company, capital is put in its place: it becomes a means instead of an end.

The alternative economy will need a new Adam Smith to explain the role and place of capital, the market, labour and co-operation in a system based on the public interest and ecological rationality, as opposed to the pursuit of special interests and unlimited enrichment.

The people's right to feed themselves

Liberalism, followed by globalizing ultraliberalism, has created a world where food dependence, malnutrition and hunger coexist on a permanent basis with the overabundance of food. Industrialized countries, in harvesting huge agricultural surpluses, claim that they are acting out of compassion, that they want to feed the starving populations of the Third World. The reality is more mundane: their primary motive is to dispose of surpluses by dumping them in Third World markets. In the name of 'comparative advantage' and with the help of the World Bank and IMF, they encourage underdeveloped countries to specialize in export crops (coffee, cocoa, peanuts, tropical fruits, and so on) to the detriment of subsistence farming. This binds poor countries to the worst of all submissions: food dependence.

In the past few years, disenchanted with the broken promises of globalization, many Third World peasants have returned to subsistence farming. Experience has taught them that the foundation of development lies in this vital activity.

In Europe, episodes such as the BSE and dioxin-contaminated chicken crises, as well as the WTO decision forcing Europe to import hormone-fed beef from the United States, has sparked the wrath of peasants, aroused the suspicions of the public and raised awareness of the abuses occasioned by the globalization of food and agriculture. The builders of the alternative world order understand that food and agriculture have more than just a commercial and financial dimension. The relationship between human beings and their 'daily bread' is so vital that food self-sufficiency is the first and most essential sovereignty. Without this type of minimal autonomy, no world order based on fairness and solidarity will ever see the light of day.

Necessary Trials and Errors

The reclaiming of the economy and the construction of an alternative model represent an adventure into the unknown. Replacing a model over two centuries old will undoubtedly prove a long process; one which starts with the rebuilding of the social fabric and economic power at the grassroots level. Having only a few years of experience, the various forms of the alternative economy are in effect the alternative order's first drafts. As such, they need to be critically assessed but not scorned. Like all major socio-economic transformations, they require a long nurturing period.

Such is the meaning of this new economy that is developing within associations, co-operatives and communities. Just as capitalism matured within feudalism over several centuries before asserting itself as the dominant system, the alternative economy will likewise need to develop slowly within capitalism before gradually asserting itself in a community, a region, a country and finally throughout the world.

In the final analysis, the reclaiming of the economy is based on the firm belief that women and men should be trusted to achieve, by trial and error, and no doubt after many failures, the creation of fairer economic relations between all human beings. These relations will be based on the unavoidable need to share the limited resources of our finite world.

CHAPTER 12

The Four Forms of Reappropriation

Perhaps we have been so busy searching the distant horizon for exotic
answers to our deepening crisis that we have failed to notice the obvious
answers that are right in front of us.

David C. Korten

The reappropriation of economic, social, political and cultural processes
can take on four essential and complementary forms: understanding,
criticizing, resisting and building. Each of us is called upon to play the
role or roles that suits us best, where we can be the most efficient and
useful. In all cases, the objective is the same: to win back from the
globalization mega-machine life spaces that are compatible, in the mid-
and long term, with the fulfilment of individuals and communities and
the integrity of ecosystems.

Understanding Our Globalized World

To oppose the system efficiently, it is first necessary to understand it, to
become aware of its workings. This preliminary stage can lead to indig-
nation, and then to criticism and resistance. It is only by enhancing our
analytical skills that we will find the tools required to raise the veil of
neoliberal ideology and uncover the hidden side of globalization.

Contrary to what the holders of ideological power would like to
have everyone believe, anybody can learn how the economy works.
What is required is diligence and a little time. No degree in economics

is required, just as it is not necessary to have a degree in ecology to be an ecologist. As J.K. Galbraith has noted, the economy concerns all of us in a very practical way: 'To have a working understanding of economics is to understand the largest part of life.'[1]

Economics is the art of managing one's household and personal business, as well as the business of one's community, of one's country and of the entire world. In addition to being a practice, economics is also an academic discipline claiming to be a science imbued with considerable authority. Conventional economists pompously lecture on the fact that economics is complex and impenetrable for mere mortals. Several economists have broken ranks to show that conventional economics is largely based on a set of beliefs and false postulates and that, far from being natural, the real laws of economics are in fact created and controlled by people in the flesh. It is well known that the American Business Forum convinced negotiators to include in the NAFTA accord clauses such as those found in Chapter 11, which place foreign investors above national laws and tribunals. It is well known that major lobbies such as the Business Roundtable put pressure on the US Congress to pass the laws on the implementation of NAFTA. Consequently, it is easy to see that in reality so-called natural market laws are designed, promoted, introduced and manipulated by major economic interests with the help of willing political allies, the bottom line being that these market laws operate to their advantage.

In fact, the first part of this book is designed as a tool to understand the ins and outs of globalization. Everyone can pursue and complete this study by closely following the events occurring in the globalized world – mergers, massive lay-offs, fabulous bank profits, daily recantations of politicians, and subsidies to the corporate bums so they can exploit our resources and run off with the profits. All this can be observed, judged and criticized as one learns to distinguish between the masters of the globalized world and their overseers, their ideological discourse and actual practice, words and facts, democracy and electoral games, the plundering of resources and sustainable development. It goes without saying that such an exercise requires reading, the exchange of views, discussion and participation in alternative movements. Much information is available online.

What needs to be understood above all, when we look at our brave new globalized world, is that a very serious ethical problem lies behind the economic stakes. This does not concern superficial ethics of compassion and tolerance but rather the fundamental principle that we all belong to the same human species and the same Earth, that the destinies of the peoples of the South and the North are intertwined, and that greed, the motor of the global economy, must make way for a spirit of sharing.

Criticizing the System at the Root

Awareness is followed by criticism – that is, questioning the current practices and underlying values of the system. This involves exposing and denouncing the embellishing and often misleading language of company and government advertising and public relations. If activists don't assiduously question the system, an activity that can require a great deal of effort, they stand at any moment to be baffled by simplistic and apparently serious arguments. This task is formidable because our society is suffering from a huge deficit of critical thought.

Criticizing the globalization system cannot be left to a handful of experts, no matter how intelligent and shrewd they may be. This is a collective task in which each of us can shed some complementary light, according to our specific experience. The ideology distilled by the conservative think-tanks – which are firms of TNC-appointed experts – must be opposed with the widespread social criticism simmering within social networks. The criticism of non-experts is often far more realistic, insightful and bold than that emanating from academic circles.

As we have seen, neoliberalism represents an airtight ideology, a credo, a complete set of postulates, laws and deductions articulated into a global whole, with an apparently irrefutable logic. Market logic justifies everything and has an answer to everything. To be efficient, the criticism of neoliberalism must be radical. This means taking neoliberalism by its roots, by demonstrating: the absurdity of infinite growth and hoarding; the contradictions of unfettered competition that self-destructs and results in monopolies; the inconsistencies of a self-regulating and monopolizing market; the incompatibility between unlimited concentration of wealth and poverty reduction; the market's 'invisible hand' sham; and the myth of the consumer-king.

Criticism of contemporary neoliberalism can only be radical – that is, it must identify this ideology and question its very foundations. To try to mend the system's course by applying cosmetic changes will only reinforce it and allow it to go further. To try to give it a 'human face', by containing its excesses, is to play into its hands and contribute to its depoliticizing and brainwashing enterprise. To think within the framework of neoliberal economics inevitably leads to thinking like it. To want to come to terms with the globalitarian system without questioning its foundations is to condemn oneself to condoning it and submitting to its complete application.

Good criticism is always constructive. One should never underestimate its importance. As the author of *Voltaire's Bastards* asserts, 'Nothing frightens those in power so much as criticism.'[2]

Resisting McWorld

To know how to say 'Basta! Enough!' is essential for deconstructing the globalitarian order. Resistance is an expression of free citizens that refuse to be impressed by a destructive system they have not chosen. Resisting with all their strength the savage appropriation of the world by a handful of oligopolies, the privatization of the human genome, the tinkering with our food, the commodification of our air and the poisoning of our water is today becoming an imperative for every free woman and man.

But beware: this form of reappropriation must not be aimed at converting the billionaires or their overseers. In general, power and money have irremediably corrupted their ethics. Although some individuals might have a sudden burst of conscience, it is almost a foregone conclusion that the major bureaucratic and economic institutions cannot be reformed. Consequently, resistance is basically aimed at slowing the progress of money totalitarianism and limiting the scope of damage caused to the biosphere, communities and globalization's losers, at stopping the destruction and plundering while an alternative is being prepared at the grassroots level.

Chinese journalist Dai Qing, who has shown exemplary stubbornness in her opposition to the construction of the Three Gorges Dam – a project which, by the time it is completed, will have displaced over one million people and flooded 100,000 hectares of arable land – believes that in some circumstances, 'the highest expression of dignity can be

Box 12.1   Millions of resisters in India

Rural India is home to one of the largest, most dynamic and vocal environmental movements in the world.

Subsistence farmers, traditional fisherfolk, tribal peoples (Adivasi), and untouchables (Dalit), sweatshop workers, women's groups, and villagers displaced by dams are all vociferously opposing what new coalitions of environmental and social movements are calling the 'recolonization' of India by global corporations and the economic policies of international institutions such as the World Trade Organization (WTO), the International Monetary Fund (IMF) and the World Bank....

For all India's rapid modernization and growing middle classes, 60–70 per cent of the population, or more than 600 million people, are desperately poor and depend directly on the environment for survival. Environmentalism, they say, is not so much a luxury, as it is often portrayed in the West, but a necessity.

'It is the life resource for the two-thirds majority of our population whose subsistence directly depends on the water, the forests and the land. It is about justice', says Thomas Kocherry, a leader of the National Fish-workers' Forum. The new coalitions have mostly emerged since 1992, when India launched its economic liberalization regime in the name of 'development' and 'globalization'.

From the peasant farmers who gathered in huge numbers outside the Karnataka state government offices and laughed all day at their policies, to villagers who swore to drown if their river was dammed, to the fishing unions' strike that involved mass fasting and harbour blockades against industrial overfishing, the protest tactics are as diverse as the broad movement itself.

Among the largest of the coalitions are the National Alliance of Peoples' Movements (NAPM), formed from 200 grassroots organizations in 1993, and the Joint Forum of Indian People Against Globalization (Jafip), formed in May 1998 by 55 member groups of farm and labourers' unions. Their constituencies number millions and come from a whole range of backgrounds. Mostly inspired by Gandhi, they are dedicated to non-violent civil disobedience and call for a development based on self-reliance and village-level democracy.

As a result of the movement, illiterate peasant farmers in some regions are more likely to have heard of the WTO than the average Briton. Hundreds of thousands of farmers, labourers, tribal people and industrial workers from all over India gathered last year at a Jafip conference in Hyderabad, demanding India's withdrawal from the WTO. The protest was sparked partly by 450 suicides of peasant farmers in the states of Andra Pradesh and Karnataka, which Jafip says were the result of WTO policies such as the removal of tariffs on edible oils.

Source: Katherine Inez Ainger, *The Guardian*, 17 January 1999.

summed up in a single word: No!' This No can be expressed in many ways. It can be organized or improvised; collective or individual; centralized or spontaneous; local, regional or planetary; physical, spoken, written or electronic.

Throughout their experience, opponents to globalization have converted resistance into a science and an art based on three principles:

* *transparency*, in order for actions always to remain democratic and open to the public;
* *non-violence*, to avoid having their message overshadowed by physical attacks against people and not to provide a pretext for repression;
* *training*, so participants may act with full knowledge of the risks and assume the consequences of their actions.

Since Seattle, the resistance movement has grown so much that the masters of the global village fear it might threaten the triumphant march of globalization. This apprehension explains their eagerness to take advantage of the trauma created by the 11 September 2001 attacks. They stoke fear among their populations to keep them in the grip of a terror frenzy: the enemy is everywhere and can strike anytime! Frightened citizens tend to give up their individual and collective rights more easily. All the new laws hastily voted by parliaments throughout the world undermine rights and freedoms. Having fallen prey to the security fury unleashed by Washington, governments now give precedence to security over individual and collective rights. Using a very subtle technique, they have succeeded in criminalizing resistance by putting terrorists and opponents of the established order in the same bag. Civil liberties and everything that has sustained democracy since the first human-rights declarations are being rolled back. Repression is becoming militarized and more violent in the major anti-globalization demonstrations.

Future G8 and IFI meetings will show the effects of the repressive policies passed by the lords of globalization. The deployment of a new repression apparatus only reveals the system's anti-democratic nature. And, contrary to what many had expected, instead of breaking the resistance, the 9/11 backlash has actually strengthened it.

In his essay *Farmageddon*, Brewster Kneen gives numerous examples of resistance. One case shows how the poorest of the poor, because they are the hardest hit by the ill effects of globalization, often demonstrate the greatest determination in resisting the infringements of the TNCs. While people in Canada and the United States are only just starting to react to genetically modified crops and foods, in India stiff resistance has been organized for several years now. In November 1998, peasants from Sindhanoor in southern India destroyed Monsanto's experimental transgenic cotton crops. In a press release, they explained to the general public the nature of and grounds for their action and announced that the owner of the fields would be compensated for any loss incurred:

> The direct campaign of Indian farmers, Operation 'Cremate Monsanto', started today in the village of Maladagudda, about 400 km north of Bangalore. M. Basanna, owner of a field where an illegal genetic experiment was being conducted without his knowledge and Professor Nanjundaswamy, president of KRRS [a Gandhian movement of 10 million farmers in the Southern Indian State of Karnataka], uprooted together the first plant of genetically modified cotton, inviting the rest of the local peasants to do the same. Within a few minutes, all the plants in the field were piled up and ready to be set on fire...
>
> We are calling ONLY for nonviolent direct actions. Nonviolence in this context means that we should respect all (non-genetically modified) living beings, including policemen and the people who work for these TNCs.[3]

Building Alternatives

In addition to saying No to globalization, we must also know how to say Yes to an alternative order – a Yes embodied in new ways of doing things, new solidarities, and new economic practices at the grassroots level. Consequently, while some resistors are asserting their rights by saying No, others are saying Yes by implementing, in their part of the world, projects based on sharing, solidarity and equity. These concrete experiences are where future organizational structures are being created. From these actions, new ways of thinking economics, community action and the organization of the world are emerging. Pure and perfect achievements are not of this world. It is only when a host of alternative projects have seen the light of day that true democracy will emerge at the local level first, then at the regional and national levels, and finally everywhere. We must insist: it is at the grassroots level that the future is gradually taking shape, in countless places around the world.

Where to start? Right where we are, each with our skills, talents, means and preferences. Any action going in the right direction, no matter how small and humble it may be, will contribute to refounding the world. Above all, *Take it Personally*, as suggested by Anita Roddick in her excellent reader, a guide 'to making conscious choices to change the world'.[4] Furthermore, students and young people in general will find in Tony Clarke and Sarah Dopp's *Challenging McWorld* a genuine workbook, full of practical references 'designed to provide some tools to enable youth to develop skills required for challenging McWorld in their daily lives on several fronts'.[5] Remote areas suffering from chronic unemployment, which in the past have always relied on multinationals for their development, today can choose between continuing to beg for subsidies and large investments from the outside and empowering themselves, creating local industries and transforming their resources on their own. The first step, of course, consists in equipping themselves to tap, retain and invest local and regional savings. Then they will need a good dose of imagination and daring. There is no more Messiah. Let's do it ourselves!

CHAPTER 13

A Cause for the Twenty-first Century

It is now our time to accept responsibility for our freedom or perish as a species that failed to find its place of service in the web of life.

David C. Korten

Rebuilding the world. Building a worldwide democracy. Never before has humanity faced such a formidable challenge, a cause worthy of our collective capabilities and hopes. There is, however, an implicit existential question: is the game worth the candle? Is it worthwhile to expend so much effort to make the Earth more humane? We are at a crossroad. Will greed, violence, unthinking stupidity and selfishness overcome solidarity and the heightening awareness that the Earth is finite?

The Misdeeds of *Homo sapiens demens*

In humanity's short history, from the founding of the first cities and the setting off of the caravan of civilizations, the human spirit has proven surprisingly creative – and equally destructive. Since the invention of gunpowder, humanity has been unceasing in the development of ever more devastating tools of destruction. History books are an endless chronicle of battles, wars, conquests, massacres, pillaging, destruction, enslavement, inquisitions and torture. Adding to the millennial subjugation of women, mankind invented slavery and colonization. In the twentieth century alone, two world wars and hundreds of regional conflicts sowed ruin and killed tens of millions. Nazism barbarized, for a time, one of the most civilized nations in the world. Contemporary dictators, from Pinochet to Suharto and Kabila, killed, eliminated, tortured, imprisoned and displaced millions of people.

Today, before our very eyes, the lords of globalization are driving tens of thousands of species into extinction, vandalizing the human gene pool, polluting the air we breathe, contaminating the water we drink, and laying waste to the soil that nourishes us and upon which we tread. In so doing, they inflict often horrible hardships and unspeakable suffering on entire populations. This has prompted philosopher Edgar Morin to wonder if our species might be more aptly named *Homo sapiens demens* rather than *Homo sapiens sapiens*:

> What can be expected from *Homo sapiens demens*? How can we ignore the gigantic and terrifying problems of human deficiencies? Always and everywhere, domination and exploitation have prevailed over mutual assistance and fellowship: everywhere, hatred and contempt have prevailed over friendship and understanding. Until now, religions of love and ideologies of brotherhood have brought more hatred and disagreement than love and fellowship.[1]

Is humanity a hopeless case beyond redemption? Should we abandon the project of a more humane world, of a duly respected and protected terrestrial habitat, of a peaceful and democratically organized worldwide community?

The Inconceivability Principle

Yes, humanity often finds itself under the sway of the ambitions, blindness and selfishness of a handful of despots. However, it never fails to resume its constant quest for freedom, equality, knowledge and technical progress. At the heart of this adventure lies 'the attraction of an inexhaustible future'. Without that hope, notes Teilhard de Chardin, without a fundamental love of life and the drive to build a better and more meaningful tomorrow for itself and future generations, humanity would rapidly cease to invent and create: 'And, stricken at the very source of the impetus which sustains it, it would disintegrate from nausea or revolt and crumble into dust.'[2] This, of course, is exactly what happens to an individual when confronted with closed and inescapable horizons.

Among the reasons for hope, Edgar Morin posits what he calls the 'hope within hopelessness principle'. 'All the great transformations or creations', he writes, 'have been unthinkable until they actually came to pass.'[3] Every age has its Cassandras who predict the withering of history. Prophets, forecasters and futurologists have uttered an endless litany of unbelievable howlers – they forgot that the unthinkable is always possible and, moreover, that it often happens:

- In 1899, Charles Duell, head of the US Patent Office, solemnly declared: 'Everything that can be invented has been invented.'[4]
- Lee DeForest, inventor of the Audion tube, wrote in 1926: 'While theoretically and technically television may be feasible, commercially and financially I consider it an impossibility.'[5]
- When Richard van der Riet Wooley assumed his position as official astronomer of the British Crown, in January 1956, he declared that 'space travel is utter bilge'.[6]
- In 1958, Thomas Watson, then president of IBM, predicted that 'there is a world market for about five computers'.[7]
- In 1977, Kenneth Olsen, president of Digital Equipment maintained that 'there is no reason for any individual to have a computer in their home'.[8]

Let Humanity Take Its Time

It took several tens of thousands of years for the human species to scatter to every corner of the globe. Large numbers of human communities developed in isolation, becoming strangers to each other, separated by language, beliefs, mores and distance. Then, as the need to trade goods and ideas emerged, contact between these dispersed societies started to grow – whether the motive was trade, plunder or the basic desire to see and discover one another. At the end of the fifteenth century, advances in the means of transportation shrank distances on a planetary scale and signalled the adventure of an emerging world civilization.

Today, we are still in the stone-age phase of a worldwide organization of human relations. Only 10,000 years have passed since the dawn of the first civilizations, barely five centuries since the definitive bridging of the continents, a century since the still incomplete recognition of the obvious equality between the two genders making up humanity and only a scant few decades since we realized that the Earth is, in fact, finite. After expending such great, if brief, efforts, are we already losing hope and giving up? Wouldn't that betray a serious lack of perspective? The far-reaching transformations in gestation today must be measured in accordance with the long and patient evolution of our thinking species. As a bemused Teilhard de Chardin has noted: 'After all, half a million years, perhaps, or even a million, were required for life to pass from the prehominids to modern man', and yet we grow impatient when the Earth fails 'to transform itself under our eyes in the space of a generation'. 'Each dimension has its proper rhythm. Planetary movement involves planetary majesty' in sync with the languor and hesitations of human action.[9] Great historical movements are characterized by their duration and the patient efforts they require. New models of social organization and world governance can neither emerge spontaneously nor arise in the short term. They first need to take root, develop and become organized at the grassroots level, in millions of villages, neighbourhoods and communities. It is there, in the social fabric of communities, that solidarity is being rebuilt.

This will certainly take time. But confronted as we are with worldwide and global problems threatening our spaceship Earth and the very destiny of humanity, why shouldn't we devote a few decades, or even several generations or centuries, to the task of bringing sense and meaning to our world?

In this icy age of globalization, if the Earth seems to be regressing, it is because it knows how to wait and make haste slowly. It is waiting for humanity to pull itself together, for dynamic forces to emerge from within to propel it forward once again. As with all human development, individual and collective self-realization takes time. In the manner of mountains, which appear so unchanging and yet undergo incredible transformations over time, humankind advances and changes imperceptibly. Such changes can only be observed over time, by setting one's gaze across the depths of centuries.

How can we know whether we are going in the right direction? By observing over time the fruits borne by the Earth. Ever since it acquired a conscious layer, it is in the Earth's nature to develop greater consciousness, freedom, dignity and solidarity. Should it instead produce more unthinking stupidity, subservience and inequality, as it appears to be doing under the influence of globalization, then it is going backwards. The role of global civil society is crucial in pushing it in the right direction. To every generation falls the task of helping civilize and reunify humanity.

Women Hold Up Half the Sky

In theory, the emancipatory legislation of the twentieth century has established the equality of women and men; in practice machismo survives. The history of exploited, raped, veiled, battered, excluded, underpaid and underrepresented women remains one of the great outrages of our time. Globalization has integrated and justified chauvinist ideology. According to a UN report on the implementation of the Platform for Action of the Beijing World Conference on Women (1995), policies linked to globalization lead to a growing feminization of poverty and, 'by the same token, undermine the efforts to ensure greater gender equality'.[10]

The time for resignation has passed. Establishing a new order based on equality and solidarity is impossible without redressing this age-old injustice. The project for an alternative society challenges macho ideology. More than an emotional plea for justice, the World March of Women 2000, which united over 5,300 organizations from 159 countries, seemed to herald the birth of a worldwide phenomenon: throughout the world, women form the vanguard of a movement to reclaim social-economic and political processes. A new feminism is leading an exciting new global struggle for global democracy.

The Third World offers proof of this trend in that it is women who basically control self-financed and self-managed development there. As the IMF's structural adjustment policies extend their influence, while a banking elite holds the reins of international finance, women are experimenting with new ways of financing and managing local development. To a great extent, they are taking their place in the Third World's emerging community-based and co-operative movement. All of which is further proof that the emancipation of underdeveloped countries will not be achieved without the equal participation of both genders.

Likewise, in the industrialized countries, women are playing a prominent role in the resistance to globalization and in the building of a new social order. It's as if the extreme scale of globalization's impoverishing policies had converted their infinite patience into active wrath. Through concrete actions, they are telling the macho elite 'enough is enough!' Could it be that the greatest force for renewal on Earth today is the deep anger smouldering in the hearts of millions of women?

The world is in labour, and only with the equal and complementary participation of both halves of humankind will it give birth to a new Earth.

The Necessary Emancipation of the Third World

Development – that is, self-development – is not doomed to failure. The emancipation of the Third World figures prominently on the agenda for an alternative order, since its problems cannot be separated from those of the rest of the world.

NGOs, whether from the North or the South, understand that solidarity is a universal value that cannot be confined to a community, a country or even several regions of the world. It must necessarily spread to all of the world's inhabitants. We cannot envision the world as the signatories of the Bretton Woods accords did, in terms of developed regions versus underdeveloped regions. The world system cannot be based on the economic exploitation of four-fifths of humanity.

The current global economic system benefits a small group of countries, a small group of institutions and a predatory plutocracy. Not only is this model an appalling aberration, it is also leading humanity into a dead-end. Even if the Third World could miraculously develop within the framework of the model proposed and imposed by globalization, it would be too much for the planet to bear. As it is, the Earth cannot bear the stress to which it is subjected by the development model currently practised by just a fifth of humanity. According to the Worldwatch Institute, the city of London needs fifty-eight times its area to supply its inhabitants with food and wood. If all the citizens of the world consumed as much, more than three planets the size of the Earth would be needed to accommodate them.

The objective is clear and realistic: to allow countries now condemned to performing subsidiary functions in the world economic system to reclaim their own development. Is it too ambitious an objective to propose that the peoples of the Third World be left to govern themselves, feed themselves and shape their own destinies as they see fit? Such a project cannot be carried out under the auspices of the current system. What are the main impediments to realizing such a project? In a word: globalization – that is, unfair trade, deregulated markets, unfair competition and the geopolitics of an infectious corruption.

If it is realistic to envisage the emancipation of the Third World, it is no less realistic to believe that the present masters of the world will not assist in making it happen. Despite their speeches on the liberating virtues of the market, they do not believe in the only development that can be: self-development. Nevertheless, just as industrialized countries did in the past, Third World countries will have to do it on their own and follow the path of independent development. One can observe that the new North–South solidarity currently taking shape at the grassroots level is gradually finding ways to overcome the impasse.

A Formidable Challenge

The scope and scale of globalization are so monumental that this un-precedented situation poses a formidable challenge to humanity. The destruction of ecosystems, the widening of disparities, the deterioration of democracy and the commodification of life are forcing a global response and global participation. The reclaiming of social-economic processes by civil society requires the equal participation of both genders on every level: economic, political, social and environmental. It includes the emancipation of the Third World. In other words, it needs the participation of all peoples throughout the world. It requires the end of the terrible destruction occasioned by the recourse to war to resolve – or, more frequently, to fail to resolve – conflicts.

Fortunately, the new generation includes a bold, socially and envi-ronmentally conscious contingent that knows how to make the best of frugal comfort. In the vanguard of a civil society that is resisting and building, the young, women and men alike, are well represented and determined to reorganize the world in line with values other than greed and self-interest.

All generations are invited to participate in this refounding. It falls on us to live through not only an era of change but also a changing of eras. No, the Earth is not boringly flat. Nor is it immutable and subject to a species of mercantile fatalism. On the contrary, the world is on the move. It only needs to be nudged in the direction of life and solidarity.

Notes

Chapter 1

1. Christopher Columbus did not discover America and was not the first European to reach its shores, but he was the first to establish a colony ruled and financed by a European monarch.
2. The mercantilist system, which characterized this period, typically based national prosperity on the accumulation of monetizable precious metals and exotic goods. Under the guidance of governmental authorities, it encouraged the rapid enrichment of the merchant class and reinforced the state, which provided vigorous support to its sea-going merchants. It eventually fostered a degree of industrial development and, to that end, advocated the protection of domestic markets. Great Britain was a case in point.
3. Bartolomé Bennassar, 'Trente ans après Colomb, l'économie mondiale existe déjà', *Historia*, special issue, March–April 1998.
4. The essence of capitalism lies precisely in the permanent and limitless transformation of income into capital, capital into production, and production into capital. It feeds on technological innovation and profits made from the sale of its products. It draws its vitality from the rational division of labour and the ever changing combination of labour, technology and capital. At the beginning of the twentieth century, the insensitivity of American big business made capitalism so odious that the word itself became synonymous with trusts, and trusts synonymous with social exploitation and the destruction of small business. This is when capitalism was renamed 'the market economy', as opposed to the socialist system's planned economy. Having restored capitalism's reputation by defeating communism and in the wake of the global economy's triumphant rise, big capitalists are now proud to flaunt themselves as such. The author of this book has always preferred to call a spade a spade, and to call the economic system based on the unlimited accumulation of private capital by its name, capitalism. Moreover, as we

shall see in Chapter 2, capitalism did not invent the market; instead, it has used and overexploited this old institution to the point of destroying its social mechanisms.

5. See André Philip, *L'Inde moderne*, Paris: Alcan, 1930.

6. Daniel Cohen, *Richesse du monde, pauvretés des nations*, Paris: Flammarion, 1997, p. 54.

7. Emmanuel Todd, *L'illusion économique. Essai sur la stagnation des sociétés développées*, Paris: Gallimard, 1998, p. 83.

8. Fernand Braudel, *La dynamique du capitalisme*, Paris: Flammarion, 1985, pp. 56–7.

9. It was only in 1911, following a Supreme Court decision and a four-year epic trial that the Standard Oil Trust was finally dismantled, thus creating thirty-eight companies which continued to control the market. All these companies remained the property of the same group of persons, led by Rockefeller, who still held a quarter of all the shares. Ten major corporations would finally emerge after the original trust was dismantled: Exxon, Mobil, Chevron, Amoco, Arco, Continental, Marathon Oil, BP USA, Ashland and Pennzoil. With the advent of today's globalization process, Rockefeller's former monopoly is being built up again before our very eyes: Exxon has merged with Mobil, British Petroleum has bought out Amoco and Arco...

10. Quoted by Anthony Sampson, *The Seven Sisters: The Great Oil Companies and the World They Made*, New York: Viking, 1975, p. 25.

11. Takeovers are said to be friendly when they are carried out with the consent of those who control the 'target'; otherwise, they are hostile or unfriendly.

12. With a fortune of $900 million in 1913, J.D. Rockefeller remains the richest man of all times; in constant 1999 dollars (189.6 billion), his fortune still exceeds, and by far, Bill Gates's approximately $60 billion. However, Mr Gates is still in short pants...

13. This is the case of Volkswagen, Siemens, Krupp and some one hundred German multinationals. The case of General Motors and Ford is even more outrageous. These two American multinationals that 'controlled 70% of the German automobile market when the war broke out, in 1939, rapidly became suppliers of war materiel to the German army ... GM and Ford agreed to convert their German factories for the production of military equipment' (*Courrier international*, 10–16 December 1998, reproducing an article published in the *Washington Post*).

14. The legality of the Social Security Act was challenged and the case brought before the Supreme Court. In its epic confrontation with the highest court of the land, the Roosevelt administration criticized it for not abiding by the legislative branch's decisions. To break the impasse, Roosevelt tabled a bill changing the Supreme Court's make-up. In the meantime, the latter changed its mind and recognized the legality of the Social Security Act.

15. 1 May 1886 is a date worth recalling. On that day, over 200,000 workers participated in the first attempted general strike in the United States. The goal: the eight-hour work day. The focal point of the struggle was Chicago

where, following a bloodbath, the movement's main leaders were hanged.

16. See Paul Kennedy, *The Rise and Fall of the Great Powers: Economic Change and Military Conflict from 1500 to 2000*, London: Fontana, 1989.

17. To learn more about the CFR's role in the planning of the new world order during the war, see Laurence H. Shoup and William Minter, 'Shaping a New World Order: the Council on Foreign Relations' Blueprint for World Hegemony', in Holly Sklar, ed., *Trilateralism: The Trilateral Commission and Elite Planning for World Management*, Montreal: Black Rose Books, 1980.

18. Slogan introduced by President Warren Harding (1921–23), who established strict protectionism and supported the large trusts during his brief presidency.

19. It is under these circumstances that, in a CFR memorandum dated July 1941, the terms *underdeveloped areas* and *underdevelopment* appeared for the first time. Truman would officialize these terms in 1949 when, in point IV of a famous speech, he inaugurated the system of public aid to 'underdeveloped areas'.

20. According to the CNUCED *World Investment Report 1999*, in 1998, there were 60,000 multinationals with 500,000 foreign subsidiaries.

21. Quoted in *Le Devoir*, Montreal, 30 November 1999.

22. *Business Week*, 6 November 2000.

23. Jonathan Coe, *What a Carve Up!*, Harmondsworth: Penguin, 1994, p. 493.

24. George Soros, 'The Capitalist Threat', *The Atlantic Monthly*, February 1997.

25. Majid Rahnema, 'Poverty', in Wolfgang Sachs, *The Development Dictionary*, London: Zed Books, 1995, p. 168.

26. Theodore Levitt, 'The Globalization of Markets', *Harvard Business Review*, May–June 1983, pp. 92–103.

27. 'Challenges of the New Millennium', in *Finance & Development*, December 1999.

Chapter 2

1. See Fernand Braudel, *La dynamique du capitalisme*, Paris: Flammarion, 1985, pp. 32 ff.

2. A close relative of the jackal, this infamous carnivore mercilessly hunts the poorly protected herds of small peasants.

3. See Laure Waridel, *Coffee with Pleasure: Just Java and World Trade*, Montreal: Black Rose Books, 2002, pp. 42–50.

4. There are some 80,000 public markets in Europe. In Canada and the United States, this institution practically fell into disuse due to the activism of large grocery chains, which do not hesitate to clog surface and air routes to ship foodstuffs over long distances, to the detriment of freshness and the environment. However, in the United States, citizens are rediscovering the virtues of the local market, whose numbers rose from 2,000 in 1996 to 3,000 in 1999.

5. The City, the largest financial centre in the world, is a district of London

where the head offices of large national and international financial institutions are located.

6. *Business Week*, 1 April 2002.
7. Quoted in a *Business Week* editorial, 26 June 2000.
8. *Business Week*, 13 November 2001.
9. *Business Week*, 31 January 2000.
10. John Kenneth Galbraith and Nicole Salinger, *Almost Everyone's Guide to Economics*, Boston: Houghton Mifflin, 1978, p. 34.
11. Quoted by Patrick Sabatier, 'Le nouveau maître du cybermonde', *Le Devoir*, 12 January 2000.
12. *Business Week*, 10 July 2000.
13. 'Could It Happen Again?', *The Economist*, 20 February 1999.
14. What distinguishes investment banks – also called merchant banks – from commercial banks and other credit institutions is that they specialize in major financial deals: share and bond issues, budget monitoring of issued shares, government and municipal loans, company mergers and acquisitions. They are not interested in offering cash or savings accounts, nor mortgage or personal loans.
15. *Business Week*, 11 January 1999.
16. *The Economist*, 4 April 1998.
17. 'America's Most Admired Companies', *Fortune*, 2 March 1998. See also 'Un capitalisme de copinage', *Courrier international*, 29 April to 15 May 1998.
18. Robert Boyer, 'State and Market: A New Engagement for the Twenty-first Century', in R. Boyer and D. Drache, eds, *States against Markets: The Limits of Globalization*, London and New York, Routledge, 1997, p. 103.
19. This observation is from Calouste Gulbenkian, an intrepid Armenian oil exploration pioneer in the Middle East who, between the First and Second World Wars, was caught by the oil multinationals when they entered the region, messing up local entrepreneurs.
20. *The Economist*, 7 October 1995.
21. Bank of International Settlements, *Three-year Studies*, Basel, 2002.
22. Quoted by Hans-Peter Martin and Harald Schumann, *The Global Trap: Globalization and the Assault on Democracy and Prosperity*, London: Zed Books, 1997, p. 45.
23. *The Economist*, 13 October 1999.
24. Nicholas D. Kristof, 'Asian Crisis, a Disaster for Women', *International Herald Tribune*, 12 June 1998.
25. Michael Richardson, 'West Snaps Up Asian Businesses', *International Herald Tribune*, 20–21 June 1998.
26. See *The Collected Writings of John Maynard Keynes*, London: Macmillan, 1980, vols 25–27.
27. Structural adjustment programmes are far-reaching economic reform plans designed by the IMF and the World Bank and applied, since the early 1980s, to Third World countries in order to carry out deep changes to their economic structure. SAPs are articulated around five policies designed to foster integration into the global market: liberalization, privatization, deregulation, exports, and public-spending cuts. This last dimension is aimed

at compressible expenditures such as education, health, housing, and public service.

28. Sandrine Trouvelot, 'L'OMC, un arbitre sous influence', *Alternatives économiques*, May 1998.

29. The Lomé Convention concerned the economic co-operation between the European Union and 69 poor countries of Africa, the Caribbean and the Pacific. Signed in Lomé, the capital of Togo, in 1975, it created a 'one-way preferential' system in favour of the ACPs, which resulted in preferential prices and an agricultural exports income stabilization system for the ACPs. The Lomé Convention converted the European Union into the most important donor in the world, by adjusting market laws in favour of poor countries. The WTO's relentlessness led to the replacement of the Lomé Convention with the Cotonou Agreement, signed in February 2000, designed to ensure that trade between the European Union and the ACPs fully complies with WTO rules (see *Social Watch Report 2001*, The Third World Institute, Montevideo).

30. Mike Moore, interview in *El Financiero*, Mexico, 12 June 2000.

31. In 2002, the WTO had 142 members.

Chapter 3

1. Jeffrey E. Garten, 'Megamergers Are a Clear and Present Danger', *Business Week*, 25 January 1999.

2. With a circulation over 985,000 copies, *Business Week* is the most widely read and highly respected weekly magazine among American and Canadian businesspeople.

3. Donald Barlett and James Steele, 'The Corporate Welfare System', *Time*, 9 November 1998.

4. 'Federal Handouts to Business: 14.9 Billion since 1994', *The CCPA Monitor*, September 1999.

5. Seagram was sold in June 2000 to Vivendi Universal, a French multiservice group.

6. *La Presse*, 8 May 1998; *Le Soleil*, 2 January 1999.

7. Quoted by *Jeune Afrique* magazine, 26 February 1997.

8. Quoted by Hans-Peter Martin and Harald Schumann, *The Global Trap: Globalization and the Assault on Democracy and Prosperity*, London: Zed Books, 1997, p. 84.

9. With a circulation of 685,000 copies, the British weekly *The Economist* is the most influential business magazine in the world; 83 per cent of its readers live outside the United Kingdom.

10. 'The Central Bankers as Gods', *The Economist*, 14 November 1998.

11. Philip Stevens, 'The Money Masters', *Financial Times*, 27 March 1998.

12. Jean Beaumier, *Ces banquiers qui nous gouvernent*, Paris: Plon, 1983, p. 263.

13. Ibid., p. 265.

14. Adam Smith, *An Inquiry into the Nature and Causes of the Wealth of Nations*,

Vol. I, Book I, ch. VIII, Homewood, IL: Richard D. Irwin, 1963, p. 54.

15. It was US president Ulysses Grant (in office from 1868 to 1872) who coined the term 'lobby', in the sense of pressure group. When the White House was being repaired, Grant stayed at a hotel where businessmen would beset him. Hoping to have greater access to the statesman, given the circumstances, they would crowd the hotel lobby to present him their requests. Partly flattered and partly astounded, Grant called them 'lobbyists'. Since then, Washington has never ceased to be a lobbying paradise. It is said that some 20,000 lobbyists of all kinds are regularly active around Congress and the White House.

16. 'The Global Billionnaires', Forbes, 5 July 1999.

17. See Holly Sklar, ed., Trilateralism: The Trilateral Commission and Elite Planning for World Management, Montreal: Black Rose Books, 1980.

18. David C. Korten, When Corporations Rule the World, West Hartford: Kumarian Press, 1995, pp. 144 et seq.

19. John MacArthur, The Selling of 'Free Trade': NAFTA, Washington, and the Subversion of American Democracy, New York: Hill & Wang, 2000.

20. See Tony Clarke, Silent Coup: Confronting the Big Business Takeover of Canada, Toronto: CCPA/Lorimer, 1997, pp. 249 et seq.

21. Taken from an information brochure of the Bretton Woods Committee.

22. 'In Praise of the Davos Man', The Economist, 1 February 1997.

23. Quoted by Susan George in 'À l'OMC, trois ans pour achever la mondialisation', Le Monde diplomatique, July 1999.

24. Jean Ziegler, Les seigneurs du crime. Les nouvelles mafias contre la démocratie, Paris: Seuil, 1998.

25. Jean de Maillard, Un monde sans loi. La criminalité financière en images, Paris: Stock, 1998, p. 44.

26. Christian Chavagneux, 'L'avenir radieux du blanchiment', Alternatives économiques, March 2000.

27. United Nations Office for Drug Control and Crime Prevention, Financial Havens: Banking Secrecy and Money-Laundering, Vienna, June 1998, p. 20.

28. 'Money Laundering on Wall Street?', Business Week, 10 August 1988.

29. Business Week, 26 June 2000.

30. Offshore centres are so named by analogy with Prohibition-era boats, sailing offshore − that is, outside of American territorial waters − on which the rich would drink and gamble unhindered.

31. Forbes, 12 November 2001.

32. Andrew Golding, 'Are You or Your Clients Truly Offshore?', Offshore Finances Canada, July−August 1998.

33. See Claude Dauphin, Le guide vraiment pratique des paradis fiscaux, Paris: Éditions First, 1998.

34. The European Union, considering this use of tax havens by US multinationals a form of unfair competition, filed a complaint to the WTO in 1998. Finally, after numerous appeal submissions, on 14 January 2002, the WTO's Dispute Settlement Body finally reached a decision favouring the European Union. Recognizing that the FSCs were an illegal export subsidy, the tribunal authorized the EU to impose sanctions that could exceed

$4 billion. US Trade Representative Robert Zoellick first described this verdict as a 'potential nuclear bomb', meaning that the United States would blow up the house before complying with the decision. He later indicated his willingness to negotiate a compromise with the Europeans. In other words, to obtain the status quo...

35. Michel Chossudovsky, 'Comment les mafias gangrènent l'économie mondiale', *Le Monde diplomatique*, December 1996.

36. *Offshore Finance Canada*, July–August 1998, p. 12.

37. *Atlas économique mondial 2000*, Paris: Atlaseco, 2000, p. 37.

38. *L'Actualité*, Montreal: 1 June 1998.

39. *Canadian Press*, *Le Soleil*, 16 November 1996.

40. Paolo Mauro, IMF economist, 'Corruption: Causes, Consequences and Agenda for Further Research', *Finance and Development*, March 1998.

41. John Bahn, former Moody's CEO, quoted by *Le Monde*, 4 May 1998.

42. *New York Times*, 27 February 1995.

43. *Business Week*, 18 January 2000.

44. 'The Global 1000, The World's Most Valuable Companies', *Business Week*, 9 July 2001.

45. Here is another enlightening comparison: for the same 2002–2003 period, the US foreign aid budget reached a paltry $10 billion.

46. Created in 1949 to defend its member countries (there are 19 of them today) against possible attacks from the USSR and its satellites, NATO was forced, after the collapse of Communism in 1991, to find itself a new mission. In April 1999, in Washington, on the treaty's fiftieth anniversary, a conference of member countries adopted a 'new strategic concept' that leaves the door open to unilateral action by NATO, without any clear or specific mandate from the United Nations Security Council. The Yugoslav war was an opportunity to put this new concept to the test. See Noam Chomsky, *The New Military Humanism: Lessons from Kosovo*, Monroe, ME: Common Courage Press, 1999.

47. Interview to *La Presse*, 27 September 1999. Also, all the major dailies carried in their 26 and 27 September issues the details surrounding the G20's creation. On 27 September, *La Presse* headlined: 'The first board of directors of the global economy.'

48. See Chapter 4 for a description of the political G8's subordinate role. The G8 is made up of Canada, France, Germany, Italy, Japan, Russia, the United Kingdom and the United States.

Chapter 4

1. George Draffan, *Report on Corporations*, quoted by *New Internationalist*, July 2002.

2. Reported by Jim Stanford, 'Pity Those Who Don't Understand Why Bankers Get Paid So Much', *The CCPA Monitor*, April 2000.

3. *Time*, 5 August 2002.

4. John Saul, *Voltaire's Bastard: The Dictatorship of Reason in the West*, Toronto: Penguin Books, 1993, pp. 22 and 23.

5. See the excellent *Fortune* report on this topic, 'Why CEOs Fail', 21 June 1999.

6. *Business Week*, 'Covering Your Behind at Tyco', 24 June 2002.

7. *Business Week*, 11 September 2000.

8. *Business Week*, 15 April 2002, in a special report entitled 'Executive Pay'.

9. John A. Byrne, 'How Executive Greed Cost Shareholders $675 Million', *Business Week*, 10 August 1998 and 17 April 2000.

10. Report by Miville Tremblay, 'Comment payer les administrateurs de sociétés ouvertes?', *La Presse*, 29 October 1998.

11. *Business Week*, 1 July 2002.

12. American corporation headquartered in Danbury, Connecticut. In 1999, by merging with Dow Chemical, it became a world giant of the chemical industry. The new transnational is called Dow Chemical, eclipsing the Union Carbide name.

13. This case is described by Jerry Mander, 'The Rules of Corporate Behaviour', in Jerry Mander and Edward Goldsmith, eds, *The Case against the Global Economy and for a Turn Toward the Local*, San Francisco: Sierra Club Books, 1996, p. 315.

14. *Mandarins*: these senior civil servants of the Middle Kingdom empire exercised a sizeable share of Chinese imperial power by controlling the flow of bureaucratic information and the organization of the administrative apparatus.

15. *Time*, 13 April 1998.

16. 'India Urged to Adopt UK Sell-off Model', *Financial Times*, 27 March 1998.

17. Manuel Guitián, 'The Challenge of Managing Global Capital Flows', *Finance & Development*, June 1998.

18. Donald Savoie, *Governing from the Centre: The Concentration of Power in Canadian Politics*, Toronto: University of Toronto Press, 1999, p. 273.

19. For an account of this event, see Ralph Nader and Lori Wallach, 'GATT, NAFTA, and the Subversion of the Democratic Process', in Mander and Goldsmith, eds, *The Case against the Global Economy*, pp. 92–3.

20. John B. Judis, *The Paradox of American Democracy: Elites, Special Interests, and the Betrayal of Public Trust*, New York: 2000, Pantheon Books, p. xii.

21. Quoted by *Courrier international*, from 27 June to 3 July 1996.

22. *New Internationalist*, July 2002.

23. Robert B. Reich, *The Work of Nations*, New York: Vintage, 1992, pp. 282 et seq.

Chapter 5

1. From the Greek *phusis*, nature; and *krate*, supremacy, force: supremacy of nature. The physiocrats were the first economics theorists to call themselves *economists*.

2. This essay is not marginal, as some commentators give to understand, nor without any relation to Smith's 'more serious works' on economy. On the contrary, it is at the heart of his thought. It was reprinted five times during his lifetime, including twice after the publication of *The Wealth of Nations*. Smith continued working on it until his death.

3. Adam Smith, *An Inquiry into the Nature and Causes of the Wealth of Nations*, Homewood, IL: Richard D. Irwin, 1963, Vol. I, Book I, ch. II, p. 12.

4. Ibid., Vol. II, Book IV, ch. II, pp. 22-3.

5. Ibid., Vol. II, Book IV, ch. VII, section 3, p. 154.

6. The debate over the lifting of these protectionist laws lasted three decades. The industrialists achieved the abolition of the Corn Laws in 1846, once Great Britain's industrial and commercial supremacy had been established on all continents.

7. Dimitri Uzunidis, 'Firme mondiale et État national. Le libéralisme en cause', in Jean-Pierre Michiels and Dimitri Uzunidis, eds, *Mondialisation et citoyenneté*, Paris: L'Harmattan, 1999, p. 161.

8. Robert L. Heilbroner, *The Worldly Philosophers: The Lives, Times and Ideas of the Great Economic Thinkers*, 7th edn, New York: Simon & Schuster, 1999, p. 168.

9. Léon Walras, *Elements of Pure Economics or the Theory of Social Wealth*, New York: Augustus M. Kelley, 1969, p. 71.

10. Named after a Swiss village near Montreux, where Hayek brought together, in April 1947, about forty American and European personalities for a ten-day private retreat, to reflect on 'private property and the free market'.

11. Milton Friedman, *Capitalism and Freedom*, Chicago: University of Chicago Press, 1962.

12. Ibid., p. 23.

13. Ibid., pp. 23-4.

14. Ibid., p. 24.

15. Quoted in *The CCPA Monitor*, June 1998, p. 18.

16. *Capitalism and Freedom*, p. 174.

17. Milton Friedman, 'The Social Responsibility of Business Is to Increase its Profits', in W. Michael Hoffman and Jennifer Mills Moore, eds, *Business Ethics: Readings and Cases in Corporate Morality*, New York: McGraw Hill, 1984.

18. *Capitalism and Freedom*, p. 200.

19. See William Breit and Roger W. Spencer, eds, *Lives of the Laureates: Thirteen Nobel Economists*, Cambridge, MA: MIT Press, 1999.

20. This giant bankruptcy mobilized the upper crust of American finance, since it threatened dozens of large investors and prestigious banks such as Merrill Lynch. Instead of letting these intrepid managers and tireless opponents of state intervention go bankrupt, the president of the American Federal Reserve came running to their rescue. At his request, fourteen American and European financial institutions invested $3.6 billion to save this group of swindlers in trouble.

21. Peter Coy, 'The Mother Teresa of Economics', *Business Week*, 26 October 1998.

22. See T. Morgan, 'Theory versus Empiricism in Academic Economics', *Journal of Economic Perspective*, vol. 2, no. 4, 1988, p. 163.
23. Georges Corm, *Le nouveau désordre économique mondial*, Paris: La Découverte, 1993, p. 17.
24. *Alternatives économiques*, July–August 2000 and December 2000.
25. Bernard Maris, *Des économistes au-dessus de tout soupçon, ou la grande mascarade des prédictions*, Paris: Albin Michel, 1990, p. 89.
26. See Jean Stefanic and Richard Delgado, *No Mercy: How Conservative Think-Tanks and Foundations Changed America's Social Agenda*, Philadelphia: Temple University Press, 1996. See also David Callaban, '$1 Billion for Conservative Ideas', *The Nation*, 26 April 1999.
27. Reported by *Courrier international*, 20–27 May 1998.
28. Quoted by Paul Browe, 'Advice from the Fraser Institute', *The CCCP Monitor*, June 1998.
29. *Le Devoir*, 19 April 1996.
30. Quoted by Edgar Roskis, from a review by Alain Accardo, *Journalistes précaires*, Bordeaux: Le Mascaret, 1998, in *Le Monde diplomatique*, January 1999.
31. Richard Swift, in a *New Internationalist* editorial, July 1999 (special issue on the rise of corporate propaganda).
32. See the UNDP's *Human Development Report 1998*, New York: UNDP, 1998.
33. Philippe Breton, *La parole manipulée*, Paris and Montreal: La Découverte/Boréal, 1997, p. 61.
34. *La Presse*, Montreal, 8 February 1997.
35. Donald J. Johnston, 'Globalize or Fossilize', *The Observer*, OECD, December 1999.
36. 'L'OCDE en un coup d'œil', *Les publications de l'OCDE*, Paris: OECD, 1998.

Chapter 6

1. Created after the First World War on the basis of an American project and President Wilson's '14 points', the Geneva-based League of Nations proved to be ineffective throughout its short existence. The main cause of this failure was the conservative and isolationist US Congress, which refused to join it. While the League of Nations never really worked, the need for such a universal political organization, guarantor of peace and freedom, nevertheless became firmly rooted in everyone's mind.
2. In 1941, when Roosevelt and Churchill agreed on the broad outline of a future universal organization, the British prime minister suggested that it be called the 'Associated Powers Organization'. Roosevelt corrected him: 'United Nations Organization'. The name was used for the first time on 1 January 1942, when the representatives of twenty-six Allied countries signed the Declaration on the United Nations, in which they pledged to fight to the end the war against the Axis powers (Germany, Italy and Japan).
3. Chiang Kai-shek's China added its name to the three powers' invitation.

Displeased for having been excluded from the earlier negotiations and the Yalta conference, De Gaulle refused to sign the invitation on behalf of France. Moreover, he would never think highly of 'that thing', as he liked to call the United Nations.

4. Entrusted to shed light on the crimes of apartheid, the South African Truth and Reconciliation Commission has given credence to the suspicions surrounding this accident. By searching through the past of South Africa's former leaders, it unearthed documents involving the United States, the United Kingdom and South Africa in a conspiracy to eliminate Hammarskjöld, whose 'activism' threatened powerful interests in one of the world's regions richest in natural resources (according to *Associated Press* and *Agence France Presse*, Cape Town, 20 August 1998).

5. Quoted by Ian Williams, *The U.N. for Beginners*, New York: Writers and Readers, 1995, p. 105.

6. 'The Five Virtues of Kofi Annan', *Time*, 4 September 2000, p. 14.

7. In 2000, the United States was the most important arms exporter in the world with total sales of 19 billion dollars. It was followed by Russia with 8 billion dollars; France, 4 billion; the United Kingdom, 1 billion; and China, 1 billion. Foreign arms sales totalled 37 billion dollars, of which 68 per cent went to the Third World.

8. Williams, *The U.N. for Beginners*, p. 36.

9. Quoted by the *New Internationalist*, December 1994.

10. Quoted by Pierre-Édouard Deldique, *Le mythe des Nations Unies. L'ONU après la guerre froide*, Paris: Hachette, 1994, p. 86.

11. Quoted in *Au courant*, a publication of the Canadian Council for International Co-operation, October 2000.

12. Journalist and essayist David Korten, who was present, made a detailed report of this meeting. See *The CCPA Monitor*, October 1997.

13. Reported in *The CCPA Monitor*, September 1998.

14. *The CCPA Monitor*, September 1998.

15. Reported by Katherine Ainger, 'Earth Summit for Sale', *New Internationalist*, July 2002.

16. *Le Devoir*, Montreal, 29 June 2000.

17. Maurice Bertrand, *L'ONU*, Paris, La Découverte, 1994, pp. 88–9.

18. Boutros Boutros Ghali, *Unvanquished: A U.S.–U.N. Saga*, New York: Random House, 1999, p. 337.

19. Bertrand, *L'ONU*, p. 89.

Chapter 7

1. This title refers to the tragedy of the enclosure or privatization of the *commons* or *common fields* in England in the seventeenth and eighteenth centuries. The Enclosure Acts put an end to the commons system, benefiting the large farmers at the expense of the peasants, who, to survive, were forced to move to the cities where they swelled the ranks of the proletariat and the

unemployed. In referring to Garrett Hardin's article 'The Tragedy of the Commons' (*Science* 162, 1968), several economists recently tried, yet again, to cite the enclosures case to argue in favour of the effectiveness of privatization for developing public goods.

2. See Paul Ehrlich, *The Population Bomb*, New York: Ballantine Books, 1968.

3. Neologism coined by palaeontologist and cosmic philosopher Teilhard de Chardin. See his main work *The Phenomenon of Man*, New York: Harper & Row, 1995 (first published in 1965).

4. See Rudolph Kaiser, 'Chief Seattle's Speech(es)' in Brian Swann and Arnold Krupat, *Recovering the Word: Essays on Native American Literature*, Berkeley: University of California Press, 1987, pp. 497–536.

5. James E. Lovelock, *Gaia: A New Look at Life on Earth*, Oxford: Oxford University Press, 1987.

6. Eugene Linden, 'A World Awakens', *Time*, special issue, November 1997.

7. To study the future of the Earth's atmosphere, the UN commissioned a group of several thousand experts from many countries. The IPCC is undoubtedly the largest scientific group ever to tackle such a complex task. Its latest report is based on about 3,000 new studies.

8. Lester R. Brown, 'The Future of Growth', in Lester R. Brown et al., *State of the World 1998*, New York: W.W. Norton/Worldwatch Institute, 1998, p. 10.

9. Michael Wigan, 'Out of Our Depth', *Financial Times*, 9–10 May 1998.

10. See Maude Barlow and Jeremy Rifkin, 'The Treaty Initiative: To Share and Protect the Global Water Common', in Robin Broad, ed., *Global Backlash: Citizen Initiatives for a Just World Economy*, Boulder: Rowman & Littlefield, 2002, p. 274.

11. Commission on Sustainable Development, *Comprehensive Assessment of the World's Freshwater Resources*, 5th session of the CDD, April 1997.

12. *Le Devoir*, Montreal, 17 March 1999.

13. Rodolphe de Koninck, *The Shrinking Forests of Vietnam*, Ottawa: IDRC, 1997.

14. Brown et al., *State of the World 1998*, p. xviii.

15. Susan George, 'Une terre en perdition', *Le Monde diplomatique*, November 1995.

16. For the entire issue of transgenic foods, see Brewster Kneen's very well documented book *Farmageddon: Food and the Culture of Biotechnology*, Gabriola Island, BC: New Society, 1999.

17. *Time*, 20 May 2002, p. 55.

18. See Louise Nepveu, 'Qui veut manger des OGM?', *Le Devoir*, 5 May 2000.

19. The protocol enabling the connection of all the networks developed since 1970 became operative in 1974. This is the Internet Protocol (IP), whose creation is considered the birth certificate of this network of networks. The IP established Internet's operating parameters and, at the same time, gave it its name.

20. Forests are believed to be areas capable of capturing carbon dioxide that help reduce the greenhouse effect. Canada and the United States insist that these 'carbon sinks' should be taken into account when measuring the efforts

of a country in reducing greenhouse gases. An idea that the European Union finds rather unconvincing.

21. *National Post*, 1 May 2001.
22. Reported by AFP and AP, 27 March 2002.
23. According to the Worldwatch Institute, the Global Climate Coalition collapsed in the summer of 2000, when several of its senior leaders left because of its image problems.
24. *Le Devoir*, Montreal, 4 December 1997.
25. *Time*, 3 November 1997.
26. Quoted by Yves Brunswick and André Danzin, *Naissance d'une civilisation. Le choc de la mondialisation*, Montreal: VLB Éditeur/UNESCO, 1998, p. 50.

Chapter 8

1. *Atlas économique mondial 2000*, Paris: Atlaséco, p. 69.
2. UNDP, *Human Development Report 1999*, New York: Oxford University Press, 1999, p. 36.
3. Sources: the World Bank's *World Development Indicators*, the UNDP's *Human Development Report* and UNICEF's *Annual Report*.
4. Joseph E. Stiglitz, *Globalization and Its Discontents*, New York, London: W.W. Norton, 2002, p. 214.
5. UNDP, *Human Development Report 1999*, p. 37.
6. Source: *United for a Fair Economy*, Economic Apartheid Data Center, Boston: October 2001.
7. James Gustave Speth, Foreword to the *Human Development Report 1996*, New York: Oxford University Press, 1995, p. iii.
8. UNDP, *Human Development Report 1997*, New York: Oxford University Press, 1996, p. 87.
9. Isabelle Bensidoun and Laurence Boone, 'La notion de convergence', in CEPII, *L'économie mondiale 1999*, Paris: La Découverte, pp. 97–8.
10. Data quoted by *Business Week*, 7 August 2000.
11. See Kevin Phillips, *Wealth and Democracy: A Political History of the American Rich*, New York: Broadway Books, 2002.
12. Michel Beaud, 'Richesse et pauvreté dans la mondialisation', *Alternatives économiques*, Occasional Paper, 1st Quarter, 1998.
13. German essayist Hans-Peter Martin was one of the few journalists present at this meeting. He described it in Hans-Peter Martin and Harald Schumann, *The Global Trap: Globalization and the Assault on Democracy and Prosperity*, London: Zed Books, 1997, pp. 1–5.

Chapter 9

1. Mike Moore, interview given to *El Financiero*, Mexico, 12 June 2000.
2. Edward Luttwak, *Turbo Capitalism: Winners and Losers in the Global Economy*, New York: HarperCollins, 1999, p. 18.
3. Rachel Carson, *Silent Spring* (1962), Boston and New York: Houghton

Mifflin, 1994.

4. See Al Gore in his introduction to the re-issue of *Silent Spring*, ibid.

5. *Time*, 29 March 1999.

6. See Jeremy Brecher, Tim Costello, and Brendan Smith, *Globalization from Below: The Power of Solidarity*, Cambridge, MA: South End Press, 2000.

7. This paragraph is drawn directly from a text by French sociologist Raymond Aron, who, in 1948, going against the general acceptance of the French intelligentsia, spoke out against the Soviet Communist system's dogmatism. He wrote: 'We do not have a doctrine or a creed to oppose the Communist doctrine or creed, but this does not daunt us, because secular religions are always mystifications.' R. Aron, *Le grand schisme*, Paris: Gallimard, 1948, p. 302. A striking parallel can be drawn between today's neoliberal crusaders and yesterday's Communist believers. Despite their differences regarding the means to be used, the two camps share a blind faith in the liberating power of their respective theories, supposedly endowed with unequalled and incomparable historical efficiency. Both are fundamentally materialistic and claim to be scientific. The two systems ruin and impoverish the vast majority, but consider these disasters as evils necessary to one day reaching prosperity for all.

8. David C. Korten, *When Corporations Rule the World*, San Francisco and West Hartford: Berrett-Koehler/Kumarian Press, 1995, pp. 10 et seq. See also Korten's *The Post-Corporate World: Life after Capitalism*, San Francisco and West Hartford: Berrett-Koehler Publishers/Kumarian Press, 1999.

9. Michel Beaud, *Le basculement du monde*, Paris: La Découverte/Syros, 2000, p. 263.

10. Quoted by Michael Shuman, 'The End of Globalization? Multinational Corporations Are More Vulnerable than You Think', *Utne Reader*, July/August 2002, p. 53.

Chapter 10

1. Immanuel Wallerstein, *L'après-libéralisme. Essai sur un système-monde à réinventer*, Paris: L'Aube, 1999, p. 19.

2. Tomás Moulian, *Socialismo del siglo XXI. La quinta vía*, Santiago: Editorial LOM, 2000, p. 174.

3. Martha Harnecker, *La izquierda en el umbral del siglo XXI. Haciendo posible lo imposible*, Madrid: Siglo XXI de España, 2000, p. xv.

4. Quoted by Maude Barlow and Tony Clarke, *The Global Showdown: How Activists Are Fighting Global Corporate Rule*, Toronto: Stoddart, 2002, p. 3.

5. UNDP, *Human Development Report 1993*, New York and Oxford: Oxford University Press, 1993, p. 1.

6. Interview for *Le Devoir*, Montreal, 8 June 1998.

7. See Mario Pianta, 'Parallel Summits of Global Civil Society', in Helmut Anheier, Marlies Glasius and Mary Kaldor, eds, *Global Civil Society 2001*, Oxford: Oxford University Press, 2001, p. 174.

8. Quoted in *Alternatives*, July–August 1996.
9. John Keane, 'Global Civil Society?', in Anheier, et al., *Global Civil Society 2001*, p. 26.
10. Amartya Sen, *L'économie est une science morale*, Paris: La Découverte, 1999.
11. Geoffrey Ostergaard, *Nonviolent Revolution in India*, New Delhi: J.P. Amrit Kosh, Sevagram and Gandhi Peace Foundation, 1985, p. 13.
12. Jean-François Kahn, *De la révolution*, Paris: Flammarion, 1999, pp. 93 et seq.
13. Ibid.
14. Edgar Morin, *Introduction à une politique de l'homme*, Paris: Seuil, 1999, pp. 174–5.
15. Richard Lacayo, 'The Rage against the Machine', *Time*, 13 December 1999.
16. Quoted by Brewster Kneen, *Farmageddon: Food and the Culture of Biotechnology*, Gabriola Island, BC: New Society, 1999, p. 183.
17. Interview for *Le Devoir*, Montreal, 8 June 1998.

Chapter 11

1. Milton Friedman, 'The Social Responsibility of Business Is to Increase Its Profits', in W. Michael Hoffman and Jennifer Mills Moore, eds, *Business Ethics: Readings and Cases in Corporate Morality*, New York: McGraw Hill, 1984.
2. Nancy Neamtam, 'Le chantier de l'économie sociale poursuivra le travail entrepris', *Économie et solidarité* (Quebec) 1, 1999, p. 18.
3. See INAISE and Benoît Granger, *Banquiers du futur. Les nouveaux instruments de l'économie sociale en Europe*, Paris: Éditions Charles L. Mayer, 1998.
4. Jeff Powell, 'Printing Our Own Money', *New Internationalist*, November 2000.
5. See Jacques B. Gélinas, *Freedom from Debt: The Reappropriation of Development through Financial Self-reliance*, London: Zed Books, 1998, pp. 95 et seq.
6. *The CGAP Newsletter*, Consultative Group to Assist the Poorest, World Bank, 2 September 1996.
7. Marguerite S. Robinson, 'Savings Mobilization and Microenterprise Finance: The Indonesian Experience', in Maria Otero and Elizabeth Rhyne, eds, *The New World of Microenterprise Finance: Building Healthy Financial Institutions for the Poor*, West Hartford: Kumarian Press, 1994, p. 47.
8. According to *Grameen Dialogue* (newsletter published by the Grameen Trust, Bangladesh), January 2002.
9. See Julia Paxton et al., *Sustainable Banking with the Poor: World-wide Inventory of Microfinance Institutions*, Washington, DC: World Bank, 1996.
10. Bruno Lautier, *L'économie informelle dans le tiers monde*, Paris: La Découverte, 1994, p. 35.
11. Ibid.
12. Ibid., p. 113.
13. See *The CCPA Monitor*, September 2000.
14. See Greg MacLeod, 'The Co-operative Corporation as Counterweight to

Globalism', *Économie et solidarités*, vol. 33, no. 1, 2002.
15. Karl Polanyi, *The Great Transformation* (1944), New York: Reinhart, 1957, p.68.

Chapter 12

1. John Kenneth Galbraith and Nicole Salinger, *Almost Everyone's Guide to Economics*, Boston: Houghton Mifflin, 1978, p. 2.
2. John Saul, *Voltaire's Bastard: The Dictatorship of Reason in the West*, Toronto: Penguin Books, 1993, p. 8.
3. Brewster Kneen, *Farmageddon: Food and the Culture of Biotechnology*, Gabriola Island, BC: New Society, 1999, pp. 188–9.
4. Anita Roddick, ed., *Take it Personally: How to Make Conscious Choices to Change the World*, Berkeley: Conari Press, 2001.
5. Tony Clarke and Sarah Dopp, *Challenging McWorld*, Ottawa: Canadian Centre for Policy Alternatives, 2001.

Chapter 13

1. Edgar Morin and Anne Brigitte Kern, *Homeland Earth: A Manifesto for the New Millennium*, Cresskill, NJ: Hampton Press, 1999, p. 147.
2. Teilhard de Chardin, *The Phenomenon of Man*, New York: Harper & Row, 1995, p. 232.
3. Edgar Morin, *Introduction à une politique de l'homme*, Paris: Seuil, 1999, p. 148.
4. Quoted in *Time*, 29 March 1999.
5. Ibid.
6. Ibid.
7. *Business Week*, quoted in the editorial, 27 December 1999.
8. Ibid.
9. Teilhard de Chardin, *The Phenomenon of Man*, p. 255.
10. Quoted by Agnès Gallamard, 'Les femmes à l'assaut du ciel', *Le Monde diplomatique*, June 2000.

Bibliography

Albert, Michael, *The Trajectory of Change: Activist Strategies for Social Transformation* (Cambridge, MA: South End Press, 2002).

Amin, Samir, *Capitalism in the Age of Globalization* (London and New Jersey: Zed Books, 1997).

Anheier, Helmut, Marlies Glasius and Mary Kaldor (eds), *Global Civil Society* (Oxford and New York: Oxford University Press, 2001).

Barlow, Maude and Tony Clarke, *Global Showdown: How the New Activists Are Fighting Global Corporate Rule* (Toronto: Stoddart, 2002).

Barndt, Deborah (ed.), *Women Working the NAFTA Food Chain: Women, Food and Globalization* (Toronto: Second Story Press, 1999).

Bauman, Zygmunt, *Globalization: The Human Consequences* (Cambridge: Polity Press, 1998).

Baumier, Jean, *Ces banquiers qui nous gouvernent* (Paris: Plon, 1983).

Beaud, Michel, *Le basculement du monde* (Paris: La Découverte/Syros, 2000).

Bertrand, Maurice, *L'ONU* (Paris: La Découverte, 1994).

Boutros Ghali, Boutros, *Unvanquished: A U.S.–U.N. Saga* (New York: Random House, 1999).

Boyer, Robert and Daniel Drache (eds), *States against Markets* (London and New York: Routledge, 1997).

Braudel, Fernand, *La dynamique du capitalisme* (Paris: Flammarion, 1985).

Brecher, Jeremy and Tim Costello, *Global Village or Global Pillage: Economic Reconstruction from the Bottom Up* (Boston: South End Press, 1994).

Brecher, Jeremy, Tim Costello and Brendan Smith, *Globalization from Below: The Power of Solidarity* (Cambridge, MA: South End Press, 2000).

Breton, Philippe, *La parole manipulée* (Paris and Montreal: La Découverte/Boréal, 1997).

Broad, Robin (ed.), *Global Backlash: Citizen Initiatives for a Just World Economy* (Lanham and New York: Rowman & Littlefield, 2002).

Carson, Rachel L., *Silent Spring* (1962) (Boston and New York: Houghton Mifflin, 1994).

Cavanagh, John, Daphne Wysham and Marcos Arruda, *Beyond Bretton Woods: Alternatives to the Global Economic Order* (London and Boulder: Pluto Press, 1994).

Chossudovsky, Michel, *The Globalization of Poverty* (London and New Jersey: Zed Books, 1997).

Clarke, Tony and Maude Barlow, *MAI: The Multilateral Agreement on Investment and the Threat to Canadian Sovereignty* (Toronto: Stoddart, 1997).

Clarke, Tony, *Silent Coup: Confronting the Big Business Takeover of Canada* (Ottawa and Toronto: CCPA/Lorimer, 1997).

Clarke, Tony and Sarah Dopp, *Challenging McWorld* (Ottawa: Canadian Centre for Policy Alternatives, 2001).

Coe, Jonathan, *What a Carve Up!* (London: Penguin Books, 1994).

Cohen, Daniel, *Richesse du monde, pauvretés des nations* (Paris: Flammarion, 1997).

Coote, Belinda, *The Trade Trap: Poverty and the Global Commodity Markets* (Oxford: Oxfam UK and Ireland, 1996).

Corm, Georges, *Le nouveau désordre économique mondial* (Paris: La Découverte, 1993).

Daly, Herman E. and John B. Cobb Jr., *For the Common Good: Redirecting the Economy toward Community, the Environment, and a Sustainable Future* (Boston: Boston Press, 1994).

Dauphin, Claude, *Le guide vraiment pratique des paradis fiscaux* (Paris: Éditions First, 1998).

Dobbin, Murray, *The Myth of the Good Corporate Citizen: Democracy under the Rule of Big Business* (Toronto: Stoddart, 1998).

Ehrlich, Paul, *The Population Bomb* (New York: Ballantine Books, 1968).

Estay, Jaime, Alicia Girón and Osvaldo Martinez (eds), *La globalización de la economía mundial* (Mexico: Editorial Miguel Angel Porria, 1999).

Estefania, Joaquin, *La nueva economía. La globalización* (Madrid: Debate, 1997).

Flores Olea, Victor and Abelardo Marina Flores, *Crítica de la globalidad* (Mexico: Fondo de Cultura Económica, 1999).

Friedman, Milton, *Capitalism and Freedom* (Chicago: University of Chicago Press, 1962).

Galbraith, John Kenneth and Nicole Salinger, *Almost Everyone's Guide to Economics* (Boston: Houghton Mifflin, 1978).

Galbraith, John Kenneth, *A Journey through Economic Time* (Boston: Houghton Mifflin, 1994).

Gélinas, Jacques B., *Freedom from Debt: The Reappropriation of Development through Financial Self-reliance* (London and New York: Zed Books, 1998).

Gordon, Terrence W., *Marshall McLuhan: Escape into Understanding* (Toronto: Stoddart, 1997).

Granger, Benoît and INAISE, *Banquiers du futur. Les nouveaux instruments financiers de l'économie sociale en Europe* (Paris: Éd. Charles Léopold Mayer, 1998).

Greider, William, *One World, Ready or Not: The Manic Logic of Global Capitalism* (New York: Simon & Schuster, 1997).

Guillén Romo, Hector, *La contrarrevolución neoliberal* (Mexico: Era, 1997).

Harnecker, Martha, *La izquierda en el umbral del siglo XXI. Haciendo posible lo imposible* (Madrid: Siglo XXI de España, 2000).

Heilbroner, Robert L., *Worldly Philosophers: Lives, Times, and Ideas of the Great Economic Thinkers* (7th edn) (New York: Simon & Schuster, 1999).

Heilbroner, Robert and William Milberg, *The Crisis of Vision in Modern Economic Thought* (New York: Cambridge University Press, 1995).

Heilbroner, Robert and Lester Thurow, *Economics Explained: Everything You Need to Know About How the Economy Works and Where It's Going* (New York: Simon & Schuster, 1996).

Hines, Colin, *Localization: A Global Manifesto* (London and Sterling: Earthscan Publications, 2000).

Hopkins, Terence K., Immanuel Wallerstein et al., *The Age of Transition: Trajectory of the World-System* (London: Zed Books, 1996).

Ianni, Octavio, *Teorías de la globalización* (Mexico: Siglo XXI, 1996).

Ianni, Octavio, *La sociedad global* (Mexico: Siglo XXI, 1998).

Jackson, Andrew and Matthew Sanger, *Dismantling Democracy: The Multilateral Agreement on Investment (MAI) and its Impact* (Ottawa and Toronto: CCPA/Lorimer, 1998).

Jacoud, Gilles and Éric Tournier, *Les grands auteurs de l'économie* (Paris: Hatier, 1998).

Judis, John B., *The Paradox of American Democracy: Elites, Special Interests, and the Betrayal of Public Trust* (New York: Pantheon Books, 2000).

Kahn, Jean-François, *De la révolution* (Paris: Flammarion, 1999).

Kennedy, Paul, *The Rise and Fall of the Great Powers: Economic Change and Military Conflicts from 1500 to 2000* (New York: Random House, 1989).

Kennedy, Paul, *Preparing for the Twenty-first Century* (New York: Harper Perennial, 1994).

Keynes, John Maynard, *The General Theory of Employment, Interest, and Money* (1936) (San Diego, New York and London: Harcourt Brace, 1991).

Kneen, Brewster, *Farmageddon: Food and the Culture of Biotechnology* (Gabriola Island, BC: New Society, 1999).

Knor, Martin, *Rethinking Globalization: Critical Issues and Policy Choices* (London: Zed Books, 2001).

Koninck, Rodolphe de, *The Shrinking Forests of Viêt Nam* (Ottawa: IDRC, 1997).

Korten, David C., *When Corporations Rule the World* (West Hartford: Kumarian Press, 1995).

Korten, David C., *The Post-corporate World: Life after Capitalism* (West Hartford and San Francisco: Kumarian Press/Berrett-Koekler, 1999).

Lautier, Bruno, *L'économie informelle dans le tiers monde* (Paris: La Découverte, 1994).

Levitt, Theodore, 'The Globalization of Markets', *Harvard Business Review*, May–June 1983.

Lovelock, James E., *Gaia: A New Look at Life on Earth* (Oxford University Press, Oxford, 1987).

Luttwak, Edward, *Turbo Capitalism: Winner and Losers in the Global Economy* (New York: HarperCollins, 1999).

MacArthur, John, *The Selling of 'Free Trade': NAFTA, Washington, and the Subversion of American Democracy* (New York: Hill & Wang, 2000).

McLuhan, Marshall, *Global War and Peace in the Global Village* (New York: Bantam, 1968).

Madeley, John, *Hungry for Trade: How the Poor Pay for Free Trade* (London and New York: Zed Books, 2000).

Maillard, Jean de, *Un monde sans loi. La criminalité financière en images* (Paris: Stock, 1998).

Mander, Jerry and Edward Goldsmith (eds), *The Case against the Global Economy and for a Turn Toward the Local* (San Francisco: Sierra Club Books, 1996).

Maris, Bernard, *Des économistes au-dessus de tout soupçon, ou la grande mascarade des prédictions* (Paris: Albin Michel, 1990).

Martin, Hans-Peter and Harald Schumann, *The Global Trap: Globalization and the Assault on Democracy and Prosperity* (Zed Books: London, 1997).

Mokhider, Russel and Robert Weissman, *Corporate Predators: The Hunt for Mega-Profit and the Attack on Democracy* (Monroe, ME: Common Courage Press, 1999).

Morin, Edgar, *Introduction à une politique de l'homme* (Paris: Seuil, 1999).

Morin, Edgar and Brigitte Kern, *Homeland Earth: A Manifesto for the New Millennium* (Cresskill, NJ: Hampton Press, 1999).

Moulián, Tomás, *Socialismo del Siglo XXI: La Quinta Vía* (Santiago de Chile: Editorial LOM, 2002).

Murphy, Brian, *Transforming Ourselves, Transforming the World: An Open Conspiracy for Social Change* (London and New York: Zed Books, 1999).

Otero, Maria and Elizabeth Rhyne (eds), *The New World of Microenterprise Finance* (West Hartford: Kumarian Press, 1994).

Pauly, Louis W., *Who Elected the Bankers?* (Ithaca and New York: Cornell University Press, 1997).

Paxton, Julia (ed.), *Sustainable Banking with the Poor: World-wide Inventory of Microfinance Institutions* (Washington, DC: World Bank, 1996).

Philip, André, *L'Inde moderne* (Paris: Alcan, 1930).

Phillips, Kevin, *Wealth and Democracy: A Political History of the American Rich* (New York: Broadway Books, 2002).

Polanyi, Karl, *The Great Transformation* (1944) (New York: Rinehart, 1994).

Rahnema, Majid and Victoria Bawtree (eds), *The Post-Development Reader* (London: Zed Books, 1997).

Reich, Robert B., *The Work of Nations* (New York: Vintage Books, 1992).

Rist, Gilbert, *The History of Development: From Western Origins to Global Faith* (London: Zed Books, 1997).

Roddick, Anita, *Take It Personally: How to Make Conscious Choices to Change the World* (Berkeley: Conari Press, 2001).

Sampson, Anthony, *The Seven Sisters: the Great Oil Companies and the World They Made* (New York: Viking Press, 1975).

Saul, John Ralston, *Voltaire's Bastards: The Dictatorship of Reason in the West* (Toronto: Penguin Books, 1992).

Savoie, Donald, *Governing from the Centre: The Concentration of Power in Canadian Politics* (Toronto: University of Toronto Press, 1999).

Saxe-Fernandez, John (ed.), *Globalización: crítica a un paradigma* (Barcelona: Plaza & Janés, 1999).

Sen, Amartya, *Development as Freedom* (New York: Anchor Books, 1999).

Sen, Amartya, *L'économie est une science morale* (Paris: La Découverte, 1999).

Shrybman, Steven, *The World Trade Organization: A Citizen's Guide* (Ottawa and Toronto: CCPA and James Lorimer, 2001).

Shuman, Michael, *Towards a Global Village: International Community Development Initiatives* (London and Boulder: Pluto Press, 1994).

Shutt, Harry, *A New Democracy: Alternatives to Bankrupt World Order* (London: Zed Books, 2001).

Singer, Daniel, *Whose Millennium? Theirs or Ours?* (New York: Monthly Review Press, 1999).

Sklar, Holly (ed.), *Trilateralism: The Trilateral Commission and Elite Planning for World Management* (Montreal: Black Rose Books, 1980).

Smith, Adam, *An Inquiry into the Nature and Causes of the Wealth of Nations* (1776) (Homewood, IL: Richard D. Irwin, 1963).

Soto, Hernando de, *The Mystery of Capital: Why Capitalism Triumphs in the West and Fails Everywhere Else* (New York: Basic Books, 2000).

Stiglitz, Joseph E., *Globalization and Its Discontents* (New York and London: W.W. Norton, 2002).

Strange, Susan, *Mad Money: When Markets Outgrow Governments* (Manchester: Manchester University Press, 1998).

Swift, Jaime, *Civil Society in Question* (Toronto: Between the Lines, 1999).

Teilhard de Chardin, Pierre, *The Phenomenon of Man* (1965) (New York: Harper & Row, 1995).

Todd, Emmanuel, *L'illusion économique. Essai sur la stagnation des sociétés développées* (Paris: Gallimard, 1998).

Ugarteche, Oscar, *The False Dilemma − Globalization: Opportunity or Threat?* (London and New York: Zed Books, 2000).

Wallerstein, Immanuel, *L'après-libéralisme. Essai sur un système-monde à réinventer* (Paris: L'Aube, 1999).

Waridel, Laure, *Coffee with Pleasure: Just Java and World Trade* (Montreal: Black Rose Books, 2002).

Went, Robert, *Globalization: Neoliberal Challenge, Radical Responses* (London and Sterling: Pluto Press, 2000).

Yergin, Daniel and Joseph Stanislaw, *The Commanding Heights: The Battle Between Government and the Marketplace that Is Remaking the Modern World* (New York: Simon & Schuster, 1998).

Ziegler, Jean, *Les seigneurs du crime. Les nouvelles mafias contre la démocratie* (Paris: Seuil, 1998).

Index

dollar, 14; as world currency, 75–6; convertibility of, 15
Drake, Francis, 5
drought, 166
drug trafficking, 68
Duell, Charles, 235
Dulles, John Foster, 123
Dumbarton Oaks plan, 127
DuPont, 155

Earth: as living organism, 146; five spheres of, 143–6; limited resources of, 236, 238; old paradigm of, 181–2; ten traumas of, 146–57
Earth Summit (Rio de Janeiro, 1992), 139, 157–8, 193, 199; Rio+5, 158
ecological rationality, primacy of, 216–19
ecology, 143, 184, 220
economics, as science, 112
economy, reclaiming of, 203–24
Eigen, Peter, 72, 114
Einstein, Albert, 188
Elf Aquitaine, slush fund, 72
elites, global, secession of, 96–7
Elizabeth I, 5
Emmott, Steve, 200
Energy Information Agency (EIA), 159–60
Enron, collapse of, 79–80, 84, 86
environmental costs: accounting for, 163; externalizing of, 162–3
environmental laws, 91
environmentalism, necessity of, 229
equity, 185–6, 219 see also gender equality
Ernst & Young, 87
Esquivel, Adolfo Pérez, 201
ethical problems behind globalization, 226–7
Ethyl Corp., 32–3
European Central Bank (ECB), 60, 62
European Commission, 66
European Council, 68
European Roundtable of Industrialists (ERI), 66
European Union (EU), 68, 198, 207, 218
externalities, 204; costs of, 162
Exxon Valdez disaster, 218
Exxon Mobil, 17, 58, 65; merger, 38–9

factory production system, 105
Fairmount Hotel meeting, 175–7
famine, 135, 165; reasons for, 112
feminism, 184, 237
Fiat, 66
financial markets, 76; supremacy of, 41–4
fish stocks, decline of, 150–51
flexibility of labour, 16, 95, 121–2, 176, 204
flooding, 153, 166
Fogel, Robert William, 111
Forbes 400, 57
Forbes magazine, 64
Forbes Platinum 100, 57
Ford, 37, 58
Ford, Henry, 10
Fordism, 176
foreign sales corporations (FSCs), 71
forests: access to, 142; deterioration of, 150; management of, 193; sustainability of, 149
Fortune 500, 57
fossil fuels, consumption of, 158–9, 162
Fox, Vicente, 213
France, 8, 127, 212; economics in, 113; economy of, 100; Ministry of Social Economics and Solidarity, 207
Fraser Institute, 115
fraud, in large corporations, 87
free trade, 14, 48; ideology of, 103–5
Free Trade Area of the Americas (FTAA), 32, 34, 35–6, 65
Friedman, Milton, 108–10, 111, 115, 204
futures market, in grain, 42–3

G8, 68, 94–6, 201, 231; as world government, 95; financial, 77
Gage, John, 175
Gaia hypothesis, 146
Galbraith, John Kenneth, 25, 37, 42, 114, 226
da Gama, Vasco, 4
Gandhi, Mahatma, 141, 229
Gates, Bill, 34–6, 38, 67
gender equality, 236, 237–8
gene pool, transnationals' takeover of, 154–6
General Agreement on Tariffs and Trade (GATT), 14, 32, 50, 56, 126, 132;

Titles of Related Interest
from Zed Books

Obsolescent Capitalism: Contemporary Politics and Global Disorder
Samir Amin

'Globalization is just another word for US dominance' – Henry Kissinger
Capitalism is going senile. Its ambition is now restricted to maintaining the wealth of the wealthy in the world, while the poor, condemned to remain out of the loop, are increasingly demonized as the enemy.

Hb ISBN 1 84277 320 8   £45.00 $69.95
Pb ISBN 1 84277 321 6   £14.95 $22.50

Killing Hope: US Military and CIA Interventions Since World War II
William Blum

'Far and away the best book on the topic.' – Noam Chomsky

Hb ISBN 1 84277 368 2   £50.00
Pb ISBN 1 84277 369 0   £12.99

Another World Is Possible: Popular Alternatives to Globalization at the World Social Forum
Edited by William F. Fisher and Thomas Ponniah

We are constantly misinformed that globalization is irresistible. But of course there are alternatives. And nothing has become more important for the development of these alternatives than the global justice movement and its annual meeting at the World Social Forum in Porto Alegre, Brazil.

Hb ISBN 1 84277 328 3   £39.95 $59.95
Pb ISBN 1 84277 329 1   £12.99 $19.95

Behind the Scenes at the WTO: The Real World of International Trade Negotiations
Fatoumata Jawara and Aileen Kwa

Based on interviews with people actually participating in the negotiations, this remarkable book lifts the shroud of secrecy surrounding these ostensibly democratic negotiations.

Hb ISBN 1 84277 310 0   £36.95 $59.95
Pb ISBN 1 84277 311 9   £12.99 $19.95